MY NAME IS
MAHTOB

MY NAME IS
MAHTOB

MAHTOB MAHMOODY

NELSON
BOOKS

An Imprint of Thomas Nelson

Published in Nashville, Tennessee, by Nelson Books, an imprint of Thomas Nelson. Nelson Books and Thomas Nelson are registered trademarks of HarperCollins Christian Publishing, Inc.

Thomas Nelson titles may be purchased in bulk for educational, business, fundraising, or sales promotional use. For information, please email SpecialMarkets@ ThomasNelson.com.

Scripture quotations marked NIV are taken from the Holy Bible, New International Version°, NIV°. Copyright © 1973, 1978, 1984, 2011 by Biblica, Inc.™ Used by permission of Zondervan. All rights reserved worldwide. www.zondervan.com.

Scripture quotation from Proverbs in chapter 21 is taken from the Holy Bible, New International Version°, NIV°. Copyright © 1973, 1978, 1984 by Biblica, Inc.™ Used by permission of Zondervan. All rights reserved worldwide. www.zondervan.com.

Library of Congress Cataloging-in-Publication Data

Mahmoody, Mahtob.
  My name is Mahtob : a daring escape, a life of fear, and the forgiveness that set me free / Mahtob Mahmoody.
    pages cm
  ISBN 978-0-7180-2210-5
1. Mahmoody, Mahtob. 2. Mahmoody, Betty. 3. Parental kidnapping--Iran.
4. Children of abused wives--Iran. 5. Mothers and daughters--United States.
6. Christian life--United States. I. Title.
HV6604.I7M34 2015
362.88--dc23
[B]

2015010665

Printed in the United States of America

15 16 17 18 19 RRD 5 4 3 2 1

To my mom,
who never stopped fighting for me
and
to Anja, my guardian angel,
whose dream for me is now a reality

THE WEAVER

My life is but a weaving
Between my Lord and me.
I cannot choose the colors
He weaves so skillfully.

Sometimes He weaveth sorrow
And I in foolish pride
Forget He sees the upper
And I the underside.

Not 'til the loom is silent
And the shuttles cease to fly
Will God unroll the canvas
And explain the reasons why

The dark threads are as needful,
In The Weaver's skillful hands
As the threads of gold and silver
In the pattern He has planned.

B.M. FRANKLIN (1882–1965)

PROLOGUE

Darkness surrounded me, deep in the heart of the forest, as I ran for my life. The scraggy earthen path beneath my feet was serpentine and uneven. Even the trees conspired against me, their limbs assaulting my body as I aimed for the sanctuary of the cave that was just beyond sight. All the while the phantom, pursuing me from the shadows, was gaining ground . . . its gallop, its panting signaling that it was closing in on its prey.

My lungs ached and my legs burned from exertion. Looking over my shoulder, I glimpsed the moon glaring in his feral eyes. I would have recognized those eyes anywhere. I was being hunted by a fox.

I looked ahead just in time to spot a crooked root that had grown into the path, as if the tree were ever so slyly sticking its foot out to trip me. Stumbling, I lost precious fractions of a second. I could almost feel the sticky, hot breath of the fox on my neck. Regaining my footing, I charged for the cave. I could see it now. The safety it promised was almost within my reach.

Heart pounding, sprinting faster than my legs could carry me, I glanced back once more, giving an opportunistic tree just the break it needed. I didn't even see it coming—the root that triggered my demise. It ensnared my foot and I crashed to the ground, landing on my back just as the fox lunged for me.

Suddenly everything moved in slow motion. I lay helplessly mere steps from the unreachable cave. Unable to flee, I shielded my face with my arms. The fox was in midair, paws outstretched, on the verge of tearing my body to shreds. Drool dripped from its fangs.

I awoke with a gasp, trembling, eyes open wide. My heart was racing. My forehead was dewy with perspiration. *It's just a dream. It's just a dream*, I assured myself, yet I fought with all my might against the heaviness of my eyelids, knowing that as soon as they closed the fox would continue his hunt. For now, at least, I had escaped.

I took a deep breath, drinking in the smell of home—the wonderful aroma of caramelized onions, basmati rice, and freshly chopped mint mingled with Earl Grey tea, cinnamon, and the fruit of the season.

Most nights were the same. Sleep would beckon me. I knew it was inevitable. No matter how desperately I willed my eyes to stay open, eventually they would close, and the ever-prowling fox would be lurking in the darkness, eager to devour me.

Predawn light filtered through the curtains, casting shadows that danced on the walls. I hugged my Cabbage Patch doll close to my chest. How I wished we hadn't had to leave Mr. Bunny in Iran with my dad. I missed my bunny.

Sluggishly my eyes blinked closed. I could feel myself drifting in that heavy space between sleep and waking. I forced them open and took a breath. *Stay awake. Stay awake. Stay awake!*

I turned my attention to my memory work. I was six years old, a first grader at a Lutheran elementary school where each week we learned Bible passages and hymns about God's love for us, his children. Mrs. Hatzung, my teacher, said if we committed something to memory, no one could ever take it away from us. Even if my dad found me and took me back to Iran, I could carry God's Word with me invisibly. My dad wouldn't even know.

"Jesus loves me, this I know," I hummed, touching the fingers of my right hand to my left palm and vice versa, then crossing my arms over my heart before pointing at my chest. "For the Bible tells me so." I held my hands flat in front of me like a book. "Little ones to him belong," I continued, swinging my cradled arms at my waist. "They are weak but he is strong." This was my favorite part. I raised my bent arms to shoulder level and flexed, showing off muscles I didn't have.

It was working. I was staying awake.

Done with the song, I moved on to a prayer we were learning, the one about bread. How did that go? It was something about being given bread every day, like when God gave the Israelites manna to eat while they traveled in the desert. My eyelids sagged. I blinked in a futile attempt to wake them. "Daily bread"—that was it. What was the rest? My eyes yearned for sleep. *Stay awake. Stay awake. Stay aw—*

It was dark. I was running. There were trees and roots, and my path was dotted with pebbles that rolled my ankles, threatening my balance. The fox snarled as he hurtled toward me. The wind rustled ominously through the dense leaves. The cave—where was the cave? I had to find it. Alone and frightened, I ran in the only direction I could—away from the fox. Frantic, I looked over my shoulder, only to discover that the fox was getting closer. I hurdled a root and pushed on. There, at last, I caught a glimpse of the black opening that was ready to transport me beyond the fox's grasp. I looked back, tripped over the root, and landed on my back. In slow motion the fox flew through the air, baring its jagged teeth, and I shielded my face with my arms in anticipation of being crushed.

I awoke in a cold sweat, trembling and choking for air. I was in my bedroom. *I'm safe. It's just a dream.* This time, instead of the familiar smells of home, I was struck by the stench of urine. I had wet the bed.

Furtively I peeled back the covers and sat on the edge of my bed, hugging my knees to my chin. I knew the fox wasn't in the room, and yet I was afraid to put my feet on the floor. I had visions of him crouching beneath my bed, ready to sink his teeth into my ankle the instant my toes touched the carpet. Garnering my courage, I bounded as far from my bed as I could and tiptoed toward the door, my damp Care Bear nighty chilly against my thighs. Silently I opened the door and examined the hallway for any sign of the fox. Convincing myself the coast was clear, I inched my way along the corridor toward Mom's room. The reassuring rhythm of her snoring met me as I burst into her room. I jumped onto her bed and buried myself in the warmth of the covers. Only there, safe in my cave, could I at last give myself over to sleep.

Mom and I had escaped.

But we were not free.

CHAPTER 1

Thirty-two moves in as many years. This last transition has been perhaps my most joyful. For the first time I am a homeowner. I have put down roots and resolved to stay put a little longer than usual—I hope. I sit in my sunroom basking in the rays of light that stream in through the windows. A mug of my favorite Berres Brothers coffee, creamy with milk, warms my hands and I think, *How is it that I should be so blessed?*

Outside the birds sing their thanks for newly hung feeders brimming with seeds. Spring in Michigan is magnificent. The snow has receded, laying bare a blanket of matted brown earth tinged with wisps of yellowish-green. Beside me stands an end table resplendent with the illustrative trinkets of *No-ruz*, the Persian New Year celebration. Known as the *haft sin*—literally the "seven *s*'s,"—this symbolic table setting serves as a map of ancient wisdom intended to guide the transition from one year to the next. Chief among the tasks of *No-ruz* is cleansing: cleansing one's mind of negativity, cleansing one's body, and even cleansing one's home.

I sip my coffee and feel a surge of ambition. I don't know if it's all the chatter of spring cleaning or the sight of my haft sin, but today, I decide, will be the day I tackle the last few boxes thrown in the basement marked "misc." Three months is long enough to ignore them.

I make my way down to the basement, feeling more than a little delighted that these softly carpeted steps actually belong to me. Lingering at the sliding glass door in the empty room that will one day be a den, I inspect the nearly vacant strip of dirt along the perimeter of my patio. Just the first hints of tulips and daffodils poke through the semifrozen soil. The lilac bushes are still bare. I look forward to filling this space with flowers and herbs, maybe even some tomato plants. That however, is a task for another day.

At the back end of the basement is an unfinished section, a perfect hiding place for clutter. Even before I open the door, a sigh escapes. *There aren't that many boxes to unpack*, I tell myself walking in. *I'll feel better once this is done.*

My workstation is ready for me. There's even a box waiting at the end of the folding table begging to be opened. Digging in, I find letters, newspaper clippings, photos, ticket stubs, the red keychain I won at my high school talent competition—random items of little or no worth other than their sentimental value. That is why these boxes are so difficult to unpack. They're filled with relics of my past that don't quite fit into my present, yet I can't let them go.

I sift through the layers, spotting memories that span the length of my life, and realize this is not going to be a quick task. It will require a comfortable chair and another cup of coffee. Balancing the box on my hip, I turn off the light, close the door, and head upstairs to the sunroom.

The first thing that captures my attention there is a photo album. Its cover is dark blue with a smattering of stars and a yellow crescent moon, because "Mahtob means moonlight." I smile as I think of my friends teasing me with that movie line. As I lift the book from the box, an envelope slips out, and my mind wanders back several years earlier to the last time I tried to finish filling it.

I was working then as the community relations liaison for a mental health organization in Michigan. I loved my job, my coworkers, my town, my quirky and eclectic group of friends. Life was good but just incredibly busy. When the opportunity came to get away for a long weekend, I jumped at it, and on a whim, as I packed, I threw in this album and the envelope of photographs. As the plane took off, I started loading the stack of pictures into the album and contemplated why I just couldn't find time for these little chores at home. *Does life really need to be so busy,* I wondered amid the roar of the plane's engine.

As soon as I had a place of my own, my sentimental mother had begun filling my house with carloads of treasures from all aspects of my heritage, including boxes filled with a lifetime of loose photographs. Brazenly bounding across the backs of the photos that marked the first months of my life was the stamp of a fox—the same fox that haunted my dreams in the years following our escape. It was just his outline printed in red ink, but the likeness was unmistakable. He lunged through the air with paws outstretched, ears back, tail extended behind him. Beneath him in block letters were the words *Fox Photo.*

The pictures I had with me on the plane were more recent. They hadn't been developed at Fox Photo. I knew there would be no predator on their backs and yet, without giving it a thought, I checked anyway. It was an unconscious habit born of a lifetime of hypervigilance. It is no coincidence this was the image my mind captured in childhood as a symbol of my father. He was, after all, the photographer of the family, and I was his favorite subject. My life very easily could have turned out differently. I wonder who I would have become if things had gone according to my father's plan.

I was lost in my memories when the glamorous woman seated beside me began to chat. I had noticed her immediately as she boarded the plane. She had a striking presence, dressed all in black except for her leopard-print stilettos. She carried an oversized satchel and a trendy straw hat. Her short blonde hair was held back with a pair of giant designer sunglasses. As often happens with me, the conversation quickly turned to literature, and before long I was scribbling her reading recommendations into the margin of the book of *New York Times* crossword puzzles I had brought with me for the trip: *The Guernsey Literary and Potato Peel Pie Society, The Help, The No. 1 Ladies' Detective Agency.*

It didn't take me long to give up on finishing my album. I slipped the rest of the photos back into the envelope and tucked them inside the back cover.

Complete strangers have a habit of pouring their hearts out to me. It's been a part of who I am at least as far back as second grade. My classmates would wait in line for their turn to swing beside me and, as we say in the mental health world, "process their feelings." If I didn't know better, I'd think there was a thought bubble floating above my head that read, "Psychiatric Help 5¢" or a placard hanging from my neck that proclaimed, "The Doctor Is In," in the style of Lucy in the *Peanuts* cartoon.

My seatmate and I talked nonstop for the rest of the flight and by the time we landed, we had covered *The Glass Castle*, *Water for Elephants*, and *The Secret Life of Bees* like long-lost friends.

"So how long's your layover?" she asked as we waited our turn to join the stampede toward the exit.

"About two hours."

"Then you have time for lunch." It wasn't a question.

I protested, but she was insistent. We made our way to a restaurant, where our conversation continued over wine and seafood. One topic led to the next, and soon this beautiful woman found herself telling me about a heartrending experience from her past. For years she had carried the emotional burden of her experience in silence, not sharing her pain with even her closest friends.

As her eyes filled with tears, I couldn't help but think of the tattered black picture frame that sat on the corner of my desk at work. On a sheet of ivory linen stationary, I had printed the words of "The Weaver's Poem." They were inscribed exactly as my friend Hannah taught them to me on the day of our high school graduation. I had been eighteen then, and it had been one of the saddest days of my life.

These certainly were dark threads that my new friend described. And like all threads, I was convinced, there was a blessing in them somewhere, whether we could see it or not.

"I can't believe I'm telling you these things," she sniffled. "I feel like I've known you for years, and I just realized I don't even know your name."

"My name is Mahtob," I said with a smile, reaching across the table to shake her hand with feigned formality.

"Mahtob. What a beautiful name. What's its origin?"

"It's Persian."

"Persian, like Iranian?"

"M-hm," I answered, sipping my Riesling. "My dad was from Iran."

"I read an interesting book several years ago," she began, dabbing her eyes with her cloth napkin. I knew instantly where this was heading. "It was about a woman from Michigan actually. She married a man from Iran. He took her and their young daughter back to visit his family and held them hostage. There was a war going on, and there were bombings. This really happened. Can you even imagine? The mother and daughter finally escaped. It was an amazing story—they even made a movie. What was it called?"

"Not Without My Daughter."

"Yes, *Not Without My Daughter*. That's it. Have you read it?"

"No." I chuckled. "I lived it!"

CHAPTER 2

The tapestry of my life began in Texas in 1979, on the cusp of the Iranian Revolution and in the midst of a hurricane. On the day I was born, September 4, the front page of the *Houston Chronicle* announced, "David Smashes Central Fla. Coast." The barometric pressure drop from a tropical storm that made landfall more than a thousand miles away was enough to bring me into the world a month ahead of schedule.

Hurricane David was minor compared to the storm brewing even farther away in my father's homeland. A good part of the *Chronicle's* seventh page that day was dedicated to Iran's ongoing military skirmish—"Iranian Troops Breach Kurdish Defense Lines." From the article it was clear the secular democrats were crumbling under the lethal force of the rising Islamic regime of the Ayatollah Khomeini. The eye of the revolution's storm may have hit seventy-five hundred miles away, but it dealt a catastrophic blow in my family's home.

My dad, Sayyed Bozorg Mahmoody, had left his country at the age of eighteen to study English in London. From there he moved to the United States to attend university. Enjoying the world of academia, he became a university math professor, then an engineer. He worked for NASA in the 1960s. Then he went to medical school. Apparently still thirsting for knowledge, he went on to complete his residency in anesthesia.

My parents met in Michigan in 1974 while he was doing an internship at Carson City Hospital. Mom worked nearby in the administrative side of the automotive industry that at that time was thriving in the state. They married and moved to Texas in the summer of 1977.

At the time of the Iranian Revolution, my dad changed. His mild-mannered, charismatic charm was instantly replaced with a violent shade of political extremism. Once a lover of "the West" and the opportunities it offered, he now vehemently condemned the United States and everything for which it stood.

Mom had known him only as a nonpracticing Muslim. That, too, changed with the revolution. She was shocked when he came home one day and threw out all the alcohol in the house. He was the one who was accustomed to imbibing it, yet she was the one he castigated because of the evils of these spirits. From that day on he insisted she buy only kosher food, as it was as close to halal (food sanctioned by Islamic law) as was available, and his fervent anti-American rants became commonplace.

There's a picture of me as an infant—one of the many images bearing the mark of the fox. I'm cradled in the arms of a young man whose head is wrapped in a white gauze bandage. He was one of the dozens of Iranian men who brought the Iranian Revolution to the streets of Texas. My dad was their leader.

While taking full advantage of the US Constitution's assurance of the freedom of speech, my father helped organize demonstrations that lambasted the United States, which he saw as having a Westernizing and immoralizing influence on his country. The irony is confounding. The man holding me in the picture had been stabbed in the head while marching in an anti-American protest my father had helped facilitate.

My parents and I moved to Michigan when I was six months old. My mother, fed up with my father's fanaticism, had threatened divorce. In an effort to salvage the marriage, he promised to leave the cause of revolution behind and to make a fresh start in Mom's home state. That would prove to be just another promise he neglected to keep.

Michigan looks like a mitten. Ask anyone from Michigan where they live and, as if compelled by an innate reflex, they'll lift their hand and point to the precise freckle or knuckle or hangnail that represents their location. I've lived all over the mitten, but from the time I was six months old until I was four, I lived near the uppermost joint of the pointer finger, in Alpena.

The east side of my state is fondly referred to as the sunrise side. It is practical, spartan, and built on industry, as opposed to the sunset side of the state, where the coastline has been commercialized and the economy built on tourism. It would be many years before I would learn that what smelled like home to me as a child was really the saccharine odor of pollution escaping the massive smokestacks of the Abitibi-Price mill, which manufactured wall paneling.

My family's house was on Thunder Bay River. The water that flowed through our backyard wound its way along the banks of my favorite park, past Alpena General Hospital, where my dad worked as an anesthesiologist, through town, and over the Ninth Street Dam before emptying into Thunder Bay. From the pier at the marina, you could gaze out over the open water and watch the giant freighters inch their way toward the horizon, loaded down with the stuff of industry. Somewhere out there on the water was an invisible border where Thunder Bay washed into Lake Huron. And beyond the line where the sky and the water met was Canada.

The park at the bend of the river was one of my favorite spots. Mom took me there to feed the birds, and it was through such experiences that she passed on her love of ornithology. Whereas some parents would draw a young child's attention to "the pretty birdie," my parents, both eager to impart their wisdom, taught me the proper names of each species. We saw Canada geese, swans, herons, and all kinds of ducks. When the weather warmed, we watched robins pull worms from the soil to eat. The spotting of the first robin of the year was pure joy, signaling the close of northern Michigan's seemingly endless winter and the birth of spring, which would give way to an all-too-brief summer.

The first babysitter I remember was Patty, a teenager who lived across the street. She was one of a host of family friends who liked to polish my fingernails. I loved having my nails painted. Though young, I happily sat still and soaked up their pampering. There are photos where I'm barely big enough to stand beside the coffee table, yet I have glittery red fingernails and gold stud earrings. My parents had pierced my ears when I was just six weeks old. Mom marked my earlobes and Dad pulled the trigger on the piercing gun. Mom cried more than I did.

Besides painting my nails, Patty took me to a ceramics studio to paint pottery. She chose a bud vase for me to decorate. She worked in shimmery pastels appropriate for the decade, while I went for one of my two favorite colors, grape purple. My other favorite, of course, was ballerina pink.

The kitchen is the heart of the home, and that truth has been one of the few constants in my life. Many of my earliest recollections revolve around the kitchen. At two or three, I sat on the linoleum floor with a wooden spoon, stirring orange juice in an avocado green Rubbermaid pitcher, chasing the frozen chunk of concentrate around until it dissolved. All the while, Mom fluttered to and fro flipping eggs, frying hash browns, buttering toast as it popped out of the toaster, and not minding one bit that I had sloshed juice on the floor. Making messes is how children learn to cook, and it was important to her that I felt at home in the kitchen.

Another time I remember giggling with Mom over my dad and his silly, self-imposed misery. He loved spicy food, the kind that cleans out your sinuses and makes you sweat. On this particular occasion he sat at our kitchen table crunching raw hot peppers until his mouth was afire and his face flushed. He mopped the perspiration off the top of his bald head with a handkerchief, huffing and puffing, yet clearly exhilarated by the experience. He wore a pale blue Lacoste shirt with the signature green alligator appliqué on the chest.

Both of my parents were talented epicureans and masters of the art of hospitality. They made a dynamic pair in that regard. Our home was frequently filled with friends, and when there were friends, there was sure to be an abundance of food. They taught me that it is over food that friends adopt each other as family.

And so it was that there came to be an Armenian branch on my family tree. I'm not sure how our families first met. Maybe it was through John, who was my parents' eye doctor, or through his sister-in-law, Annie, who was our seamstress. But from my infancy to the day shortly before my fifth birthday when my dad put his evil plan into action, our families happily fell into the habit of feasting with one another. We didn't need a special occasion to gather together around a table.

Sometimes John and his wife, Vergine, hosted. On such occasions Vergine, along with her sister, Annie, and their mom, affectionately known as Nana, would spend hours preparing mouthwatering Armenian delicacies. Other times my parents hosted, and they would work side by side to whip up the most delectable Persian fare.

My dad, especially, took pride in making the food look beautiful. Sometimes he would set up an extravagant display of fruit, every morsel of which he had painstakingly arranged. With the precision of a surgeon, he would carve a watermelon lengthwise into a basket, leaving a handle of rind in the middle. He would let me help scoop out its flesh with a melon baller. But we couldn't just put the watermelon balls back into the rind and serve it. That wouldn't be nearly colorful enough. We had to add matching orbs of cantaloupe along with red and green grapes and Alpena strawberries or blueberries depending on the season. Only then would the fruit be ladled back into the watermelon-rind basket. The table would be filled with cascading mountains of fresh fruit. My dad didn't know the meaning of moderation.

Regardless of where we gathered or what we ate, grown-ups and children alike sat together and enjoyed each other's company. The varied personalities, ages, interests, and cultures all added to the charm of the interaction. Those meals were loud and boisterous, and they lasted for hours. When I think of my childhood, those are the sounds, smells, tastes, and images that flood my mind.

Food was not about necessity. It was a means to nurture, to teach, to care for—to love. The process of making the meal was as important, if not more important, than the actual eating of the meal. I learned this not only from my parents, but from Nana and Annie, who passed on to me their tradition of rolling *kibbe*.

I sat atop the table. One of them reached into the mixing bowl filled with a dough of ground beef and bulgur. Pinching off just the right amount, they plopped the mixture into my hand. Nana, who didn't speak English, motioned for me to follow her lead. Giving the dough a couple of squeezes to make it stick together, she began to roll it around the tip of her index finger, twisting her finger with each roll.

Deftly she dipped her hand into the dish of cold water that sat between us. "Just a little," she instructed in Armenian. Once the precise shape had been achieved and a sufficient cavity had been formed, it was stuffed with a concoction of spiced meat and pine nuts. Another tiny dip in the water bowl, and it was time to pinch the opening closed, sealing in the filling. Then Nana cupped her hands, one atop the other, and circled them in opposite directions, forming a roughly circular shape that came to a gentle point on each end.

I did every step along with her, then held my kibbe out for inspection. Tenderly taking it from my palm, Nana would look it over with a keen eye. Deciding it was just right, she would bring her closed fingers to the center of her mouth. Then, with a smack of her lips, she would pull her hand away from her face, fingers exploding with the sound of her kiss. It was her way of telling me I had done a beautiful job.

Every step of the way, they inundated me with praise. Failure did not exist in their kitchen. If something didn't go exactly as planned, it was simply an opportunity to discover a new and perhaps improved way.

As we cooked, Annie would lead me in song. "God is so gooood," she would sing with a lovely accent. "God is so gooood." In between songs, she would drive home the message. "Mahtob"—I loved the way she pronounced my name—"God is verrry good to us—very, very good. He loves us very much. Don't ever forget."

That Annie and Nana could see God's goodness was a true testament to the power of faith. They had endured this world's cruelty at its worst. Nana was a survivor of the Armenian Genocide. She was orphaned by barbaric violence in the early decades of the twentieth century, when the Turkish government massacred the people of her village. No one knew her exact age. To me, she seemed ancient. In spite of the inane brutality that had marked her early life, Nana exuded warmth and kindness, and she had passed on that same grace to her daughters.

Annie, before moving to Alpena, had lived in Beirut, Lebanon, with her husband and three young sons. When a civil war broke out in 1975, they filed papers seeking permission to immigrate to the United States. They wanted to protect their children from the ugly realities of war. Her family was eventually granted permission to flee the country, but not before Annie's husband had joined the ranks of the more than 150,000 civilians who lost their lives in the battle that raged for the next fifteen years. He had nothing to do with the conflict. He had merely been at the wrong place at the wrong time.

Her husband's needless death solidified Annie's resolve to move her boys to a land where they could grow to know peace. She packed up her sons, moved to America, and didn't look back. No matter what life threw at her, Annie, following in her mother's footsteps, remained full of faith and abounding in joy. And just as Nana had passed those seeds of resiliency on to her, Annie took great care to plant and nurture those seeds in me.

In the summer of 1984, when I was four and a half, my parents and I moved south to the Detroit area—also on the sunrise side of the state, at the joint where the thumb connects to the palm. It was just weeks before my parents and I were to leave for our "two-week vacation" in my father's homeland and one month before I was to begin kindergarten.

Looking back, I can see that move as a stroke of evil genius on my dad's part. Convincing Mom that they would begin building their dream home together once we returned from our trip, he managed to manipulate her into leaving most of our family's belongings neatly packed for easy transport to our future prison.

At the time, though, I was completely oblivious to his schemes. I was engrossed in the carefree details of childhood, like the Strawberry Shortcake sheets Mom had bought for my new bedroom and my Care Bear bouncy ball, which had a picture of my favorite Care Bear—Funshine Bear, the yellow one with a cheerful smiling sun on his belly—and made a hollow vibrating ting when I bounced it in the driveway. Above all, I was happy to have made a new friend, a girl about my age who lived next door. Her name was Stacey, and she introduced me to wondrous delicacies like Kraft macaroni and cheese and Kool-Aid.

The Iranian Revolution, which began around the time I was born, had left the country in shambles. The shah, Iran's ruler, had been overthrown. The hostage crisis at the American embassy in Tehran was still recent history. The country was rife with religious and political unrest. The Ayatollah Khomeini and the radical extremists who made up his party had ushered in a much stricter way of life for everyone. In the new Islamic Republic of Iran, even non-Muslims were forced to live by the edicts of the ayatollah. On top of all the bloodshed suffered during the revolution, Iraq had invaded Iran, and the skirmish had erupted into an all-out war between the two countries.

While I spent sunny afternoons splashing through the sprinkler with Stacey, my mom's mind was occupied with the infinitely darker reality of dangers I had not yet come to know. As she packed for the upcoming visit to my father's homeland, she couldn't shake the nagging question, "Why on earth would we take our daughter into a war zone?"

CHAPTER 3

When my family left our home on August 1, 1984, I had no reason to suspect our trip would be anything other than a two-week vacation with my father's relatives in Iran. Had I possessed the wisdom that comes with age, perhaps I, like my mother, would have had a hunch my father was setting in motion a much more sinister plan.

As my parents busied themselves with their final preparations for our departure, Mr. Bunny and I danced around the living room, joined together by elastic straps that held his hands and feet to mine. He was a handsome stuffed bunny, kelly green with white polka dots, whose height surpassed mine by a tall ear's length. He wore a red felt bow tie that looked like two triangles turned on their sides, points overlapping in the middle. Mom's many attempts at keeping his bow tie in place had only succeeded in leaving it stiff with glue.

A viscous air of tension had descended on our house. I could hear the whispers of a squabble blowing in from the hallway as suitcases accumulated alongside the door. My dad stormed into the room and grabbed his Koran from the table beside the blue paisley wingback chair.

Paisley, my parents had taught me, was a Persian design. Our home clearly reflected my father's heritage. The stand that had held his Koran was home to a forest-green lamp made of camel's skin that had been intricately painted with a yellow and white geometric pattern. Our friends had brought it for us as a gift from Pakistan. On the neck of the lamp, up under the shade, was an ornate brassy key-shaped switch that, when turned, sparked the bulb to life. I loved to watch the light shine through the shade, casting intriguing shapes on the wall as I twisted the switch on and off.

Beneath my toes, the plush Persian carpet magically changed hues as Mr. Bunny and I twirled about the room. My dad said that was how you could tell it was authentic. From one end the colors looked deep and rich; from the other they looked lighter, more vibrant.

My parents and I arrived in Tehran, Iran's capital city, on August 3, a month and a day before my fifth birthday. The first thing I remember about my father's homeland is the stench of the bathroom at the Tehran International Airport. Like most of my memories of our time in Iran, it is a brief, disjointed flash. As Mom and I neared the entrance of the restroom, we were struck by an overwhelming cloud of foulness. I protested. I did *not* want to enter. We went in anyway. It smelled putrid. I had to go so badly I was in pain, but I refused.

Some of my memories of that time are like photographs that I can "see." Others are facts, details, or emotions, things I know but can't quite visualize in my mind's eye. My memory of the airport's bathroom falls into the latter category. I don't remember exactly what it looked like, but I do remember there were no toilets. That was my introduction to the traditional Iranian bathroom. Where a Western bathroom would have a toilet and a roll of toilet paper, in Iran there was a hole in the floor and a hose on the wall. The result was nauseatingly wretched.

Many family members had gathered at the airport to welcome us. They engulfed us like a swarm of bees, crowding us with hugs and cheers. Perhaps there were only dozens of relatives, but for all the commotion, it could have been hundreds. The women wore black *chadors*, long pieces of fabric that wrapped around their bodies, revealing only a portion of the face. The chador was held in place from the inside, so even the skin of their hands was hidden.

My father's parents had both died when he was young, and he had been raised by his older sister, whom I knew as *Ameh* Bozorg. We were driven from the airport to her house. Inside the iron gate, surrounded by a chaotic mass of people, stood a man with a sheep. Mom held me. We paused to watch as he slit the throat of the sheep and let its blood spill out onto the walkway. I buried my face in Mom's shoulder as she and my dad stepped over the blood and entered the house. In my father's culture, this was an extremely high honor, but to me it was traumatic. For a little girl who couldn't stomach the violence of a Disney movie, the slaughter of a sheep in real life was horrifying.

Ameh Bozorg was the matriarch of the family and thus was treated with the highest respect. I was afraid of her. She had stringy shoulder-length hair tinged with henna. Her nose was long and crooked, and she wore dark green nylons and a matching dress. To me, she easily could have been a stand-in for the Wicked Witch of the West. She and her husband, Baba Haji, lived in a once-opulent house that was literally connected to the Chinese embassy. Their home was redolent with marble, ornate chandeliers, and layers upon layers of Persian carpets, yet it was sparse, cold, and lacked the luxurious feel its refined materials would suggest.

Besides smelly and frightening, Iran seemed very noisy to me. Being an unusually quiet child, I found the commotion unsettling. Perhaps it was because I didn't understand the language, or then again, it might have been the sheer volume of their chatter.

I'm not sure how many people actually lived at Ameh Bozorg's house, but there seemed to be people everywhere—grown-ups sitting on the living room floor, drinking tea from miniature glasses, and children running every which way, unsupervised. My dad tried to get me to play with my cousins, but I was overwhelmed by their rambunctiousness and clung all the more to Mom.

For the most part, the adults seemed oblivious to the youngsters as they tore through the house and out into the walled courtyard in back.

From the safety of Mom's side, I watched them cavorting in the backyard among the rosebushes and around the in-ground swimming pool, whose water was green and stagnant. When a child wandered into the kitchen, the nearest woman would tear off a small piece of the previous meal's *lavash* (flatbread), stuff it with feta and a sprig of mint, and hand over a miniature rolled treat along with a pat on the head or a kiss on the cheek.

Ameh Bozorg's house was mostly devoid of furniture. We sat on floors cushioned with handmade Persian carpets. And when it was time for a meal, in traditional Persian style, that is where we dined. A cloth served as the table and families ate in shifts—first men, then women, and lastly children. Despite the social norm, I ate with Mom.

Breakfast was typically served on the floor like the other meals, but there were occasions when we ventured into the dining room. Even at the table, grown-ups sat cross-legged on their chairs. For breakfast we usually ate *nan paneer sabzi*, a sandwich made of Iranian bread layered with feta, sliced tomatoes, cucumbers, and fresh greens like basil or mint. Sometimes we ate *nan paneer gerdu*—bread with lots of butter, feta, and walnuts. Occasionally it was bread with butter and quince, sour cherry, or rose-petal jam.

Fresh fruit and vegetables were abundant. We ate little cucumbers the way people in America eat an apple. Bread was purchased hot from the bakery for each meal, and rice was served twice a day, every day.

In a blur of food and family the visit flew by. Our days of immersion into my father's land had come to an end—or so Mom and I thought. Mr. Bunny and I bounded about the bedroom, excited to go home. Mom did her best to dodge us as she packed, and together we prattled on about those we were eager to see upon our return.

My dad came in. He was quiet. Mom was talking, but an invisible object on the floor held his attention. He stammered something about an issue with our passports. I thought I made out the words *confiscated* and *government.* Then, abandoning the lie, he gripped Mom's upper arms in his fists. Gathering his resolve, he declared, "Betty, I don't know how to tell you this. We're not going home." His voice and his grip intensified with each word. "You are in Iran until you die!" He stood straight, shoulders back, head held high. "Now you're in my country. You'll abide by my rules."

"What are you talking about? Moody, you can't do this to us. Please don't do this," she pleaded. "You promised we would go home in two weeks. You swore on the Koran. You can't do this!"

His blow struck her with such force that she was momentarily stunned into silence. I had never seen my dad hit my mom before, and it terrified me. I was shocked, confused—more than that, utterly bewildered. What did all of this mean? Who was this man? His violent anger obscured him to the point of unrecognizability. What had happened to my loving Baba Jon—my dear daddy?

From that moment forward, even his footsteps lost their familiar lilt. Plodding down the hall, they sounded deliberate, filled with rage. Their horrid pounding turned my stomach.

That was the day my daddy turned into a monster.

CHAPTER 4

D ay after day I clung to Mom crying, "Mommy, I want to go home. Please take me home." Day after day Mom did her best to reassure me, "Don't worry, Mahtob. Everything will be all right. I promise. I'll find a way to take you home." And day after day my dad vowed, amid shouts and flying fists, that we would never leave Iran.

With no provocation, he would tear off into violent tirades directed at my mom: "If you ever touch the telephone, I'll kill you. . . . If you ever walk out that door, I'll kill you. . . . I'll kill you, and I'll send the ashes of a burned American flag back over your body. . . . You'll *never* escape, but if you do, I'll spend the rest of my life looking for you. And when I find you, I'll kill you and bring Mahtob back to Iran."

My life became a blur of screaming matches and crying fits. Then Mom got sick. Although for the first two weeks the food hadn't troubled her, almost immediately upon learning our fate, she was struck with dysentery. Mr. Bunny and I sat helplessly at her bedside and watched as she continued to weaken.

Those were excruciating times. Fading in and out of consciousness, Mom begged me to protect her from my father, the American-educated doctor who now claimed to have returned to Iran to save his people. She would wake with a start and look to be sure I was still manning my post. "Mahtob," she would whisper in part because she was so frail and in part so no one would hear her instructions, "no matter what, don't let your daddy give me a shot. Please, no matter what he says, don't let him give me an injection. He could give me medicine that would hurt me."

"I'll protect you, Mommy," I would promise. "I won't let him hurt you."

It would take all her strength to get the words out. Drained, she would then drift back into a fitful sleep.

Those bitter days turned into weeks and I, like the other children in the family, was left to fend for myself. Without Mom at my side to brush off my father's demands, I had no choice but to interact with the other children.

My parents had each been married once before. My father had no other children, but Mom had two sons. Joe and John, my brothers, predated me by thirteen and nine years, respectively. I remember John sneaking me into the basement to watch cartoons when I was around three. John would have been twelve or so.

In America, I had been forbidden to watch TV unless it was with my father and he picked the program. I was allowed to watch the woman who had a yoga show on PBS. I liked her because she spoke softly and had long brown hair just like mine, except hers was much longer. I hoped mine would be that long one day. Other than the yoga lady, we mostly watched *National Geographic* specials about animals. I would sit on my dad's lap in his recliner, and he would teach me the names of the animals in Farsi. It upset him that anytime I saw a baby animal alone I would whimper, "Where's its mommy?"

"Why don't you ever say 'Where's its daddy?'" he would reprimand.

The day John sneaked me down to the basement, we didn't watch yoga or *National Geographic*. He sprawled on the couch, I leaned over the back of a ceramic zebra that was almost as big as I was, and we watched *The Smurfs*. John and I were so engrossed in the show that we didn't hear my dad come home. Our first clue that we'd been caught was his voice bellowing from the top of the stairs. "What do you think you're doing down there? Shut that TV off this instant!" I ran for cover, but before I could get away, he grabbed me and spanked me. I should have known better than to disobey him, and he would be sure I thought twice before ever exhibiting such disrespect again.

Television is a powerful means of cultural indoctrination. Perhaps that's why it was off limits to me in the States. My dad didn't want me to be influenced by what he saw as a morally corrupt society. In Iran, however, it was a different story. Wanting me to absorb the culture in its entirety, he forced me to watch television. There, even the cartoons took on a dark, menacing tone.

I have very few memories of the shows I watched in Iran, but I do remember fragments of a cartoon about a bee. The bee was indiscriminately kind, even though there was much evil in his harsh world. Danger lurked high and low, and he was frequently called upon to fight not only for his own life, but also for the lives of those who treated him cruelly. The "bad guys"—other insects like wasps and praying mantises—constantly pursued him, but the cheerful bee did not waver in the face of their attacks. The bright spot in the show was the queen bee, who, though obscure, was gentle and loving.

It was validating when years later, I found the cartoon posted on the Internet. The bee was as I remembered from my childhood, sitting in a red flower, eyes cast upward, lost in a daydream. In the background was the scene he longed for. Floating in the distance, in the image from his dream, his mother, the queen bee, clutched his hands in hers and smiled down at him affectionately.

The little bee's name was Hutch. They had been separated when the evil wasps attacked and massacred the beehive, killing the honeybees that fought to defend their queen. The wasps looted and pillaged the hive. Not content merely to consume the honey stores, they even feasted greedily on the honeybee eggs. But one egg fell to the ground and was hidden from view by a leaf. Inside that egg was Hutch. That's how he lived through the invasion. His mother and a small number of survivors flew away in tears, thinking that all the eggs had been devoured by their wicked nemeses.

No wonder I had remembered Hutch. It is surprising that my dad let me watch a program about a bee who spent his life in a tireless quest to be reunited with his mother.

As Mom lay in her bedroom, losing her grasp on life, I would lie on my stomach on the living room floor, head in hands, legs bent at the knees, feet swaying in the air, watching Hutch. I desperately willed him to find his way back to his mom, as if by some miracle his success would translate into my life.

Mr. Bunny and I did our best to stay at Mom's side at all times, but on the occasions when my dad forced me away from my post, the living room served as an acceptable secondary defensive position. From that vantage point, no one could enter or exit our bedroom without my knowledge. Before I retreated, I would leave Mr. Bunny behind with Mom so she wouldn't be alone. And if my dad even looked in her direction, I would leap to my feet and rush to her aid.

A few days before my fifth birthday, I tumbled off a stool while playing, and the overturned leg tore through the flesh of my right arm just below the elbow. Blood gushed, and I wailed. My parents rushed me to the hospital, where my entitled father was offended to be told we would have to wait our turn. We sat in chairs haphazardly placed along the wall of a corridor. My father ranted, spitting insults about the degenerate state of his homeland while Mom, who had mustered her strength to be with us, did her best to insulate me from his rage.

When at last we were ushered into a treatment room, I was placed on a table where the doctor examined my wound. It was quite deep and would require stitches, a diagnosis my dad had made within seconds of my fall. When my father, the anesthesiologist, learned that the hospital's limited supply of anesthesia was rationed, only to be used for victims of the war, he began screaming. But no amount of anger could multiply the scant supply of medicine. I don't remember the doctor suturing my arm without the aid of anesthesia, but I do recall that for some odd reason there was a cat in the room.

Understandably, I was a bit out of sorts on my fifth birthday. My bandaged arm throbbed, and my heart ached. The extended family gathered at Ameh Bozorg's house for a feast, complete with a guitar-shaped birthday cake. Somehow the cake was dropped upside down on the floor. But by coincidence, my favorite uncle on my dad's side arrived at just that moment. He was late, but he hadn't arrived empty handed.

Majid was the uncle who loved to play with the children. He was tall and thin with red hair, a matching mustache, and the glint of a jokester in his eye. He knelt before me with a smile and extended a bakery box with a clear opening in the lid. My eyes widened. Inside the box was a cake—and not just any cake. It was an exact replica of the cake that just moments earlier had been scraped off the floor and dumped into the garbage.

The weeks gave way to months, and Mom's health continued to deteriorate. Mr. Bunny and I remained with her as much as possible. Mom had taken a bottle of White Rain shampoo along for the trip. The shampoo had run out, but the smell lingered in the plastic bottle. I used to fill it with water and drink in its aroma. Sometimes I would squeeze the empty bottle in my face, cherishing the brief blasts of a familiar scent from home.

I sat on the floor leaning against Mom's bed. She slept, and I dreamed of home. I missed the rest of my family terribly and took every opportunity to beg Mom to take me back to them.

I knew better than to discuss such things with my father. Each time I heard his ominous footsteps approaching the door, my stomach gurgled with terror and the beating of my heart echoed in my ears.

What if this time I couldn't stop him from giving my mom an injection? I worried. What if today was the day he killed my mommy?

CHAPTER 5

Who would think that something as seemingly insignificant as a gum wrapper would change our course? After more than two months of slowly inching her way toward the grave, Mom found a crumpled gum wrapper. Smoothing it out, she tried to write her name on it and was shocked to learn she was just too weak. She realized that if something didn't change she would die, leaving me in that household. I would be raised believing that my father's brand of brutality was an acceptable part of life.

She couldn't—*wouldn't*—let that happen.

As Mom lay there feeble and emaciated, she came up with a plan. She would kill everyone with kindness to convince my father and his family that she had accepted life according to his rules. As she set her plan into motion, her attitude improved, and gradually so did her health. She regained her appetite, her strength, and a sliver of my father's trust.

Knowing that any chance of escape hinged on getting out from under the microscope of Ameh Bozorg's house, where surveillance was inescapable, Mom proposed that we move in with my dad's nephew, Mammal, and his wife, Nasserine. Mom, who has always been a hard worker, would lighten Nasserine's load by cooking, cleaning, and taking care of their baby boy, Amir. My father assented. But even separated from the relatives at Ameh Bozorg's house—the ones who, eager to do my father's bidding, served as our guards—we could not evade my father's violent outbursts.

His temper tantrums were so frequent and extreme that shortly after we moved in, Mammal and Nasserine moved out, leaving my father to rage on in their absence. The hierarchical nature of Persian society rendered it improper for them to intervene. My father outranked them on some invisible family totem pole.

The apartment complex was a giant concrete box with sharp angles and drab passages. We lived upstairs in a modest two-bedroom unit. Like Ameh Bozorg's house, the living room was devoid of furniture, and the dining-room table was rarely used for meals. Mom spent her days in the galley-style kitchen, and my parents and I shared a bedroom at the other end of the apartment. My dad's nephew, Reza, lived downstairs with his wife, Essie, and their children. Vines loaded with sour green grapes tangled their way through their courtyard. I enjoyed the pucker that came with eating the unripened grapes off the vine, but it wasn't worth having to be near Reza and Essie's cruel daughter.

Although Iran had been at war with Iraq, early on in our time there the skirmishes had been held to the border regions. That all changed in the course of a night. I was fast asleep between my parents when an air-raid siren pierced the night. Bombs exploded amid flashes of red and orange. The room shook. What terrified me more than Iraq's attack was my parents' reaction. Their eyes were wild with fear. Questions shot questions back and forth: "What's happening?" "What do we do?" "Where do we go?"

No answers.

"I thought we were safe in Tehran!" Mom shouted in a whisper.

"This is your country's fault," my father snarled, pointing angrily. "Who supplies Saddam Hussein with his bombs? The Americans are behind this war."

After that, life really became difficult. Warplanes came more days than not, and our lives were ordered by the sirens. No matter what we were doing, when the alarm sounded, we took cover. Most bombings happened at night, prompting citywide blackouts that made it harder for the pilots to hit their marks. In silence, my family would tiptoe into the blackened corridor, inching our way downstairs to the first floor. There we would sit on the cold floor of the main hallway, shoulder to shoulder with our neighbors, waiting to see if we would be hit.

Much as children count seconds between lightning and thunder to gauge a storm's distance, we counted. I'm not quite sure *what* we counted. Maybe we started with the flash and stopped when we heard the explosion. Perhaps the count began when the bomb was released and ended with detonation. At any rate, we counted. Sometimes a barely audible count would quietly crescendo through the darkness. Close strikes gave us hope that the next blast would be beyond us.

Those were excruciating, anxiety-provoking waits. Sirens shrieked their warning long before the planes could be heard. The longer we waited, the more frightened I became. And whenever I was frightened, I had to go to the bathroom.

"I have to go potty," I whispered to Mom.

"Can you hold it?"

"No," I whispered, shaking my head. "I have to go right now."

"Moody," Mom said softly to my dad, "Mahtob has to go to the bathroom."

Her words sent him into a fit of rage. He insisted that I did *not* have to use the bathroom. I tried to wait, but the added fear of his ire made my need even greater.

"Mommy," I cried, "I have to go potty. I can't wait."

"Moody," Mom pleaded, "Please. Let me take her." Begrudgingly he handed over his penlight, the kind doctors use to examine patients. Mom lifted me silently into her arms and carried me up to our apartment. There we had a modern bathroom that smelled of soap. In the dark I went as quickly as I could, being careful to fight the reflex to flush when I was done. We couldn't risk making that much noise. Then we rushed right back to our spots along the wall with our neighbors and my fuming father.

My parents and I started sleeping in a makeshift bed beneath the dining-room table. They draped layers of blankets over the sides in an attempt to create a protective barrier between us and the shards of glass that they feared would pierce our bodies in the night if an unexpected explosion struck nearby. It was from that bunker beneath the table that I witnessed one of my father's many horrendous attacks.

That afternoon, without warning, my dad turned and grabbed my mom by the hair. He dragged her to the wall that separated the living room from the bedroom that was no longer safe enough for us to use. Other family members were visiting that day, but they did nothing to stop him.

Mom fell to the floor, begging my dad to stop. Screaming at her, he took clumps of her hair in both hands and brutally bashed her head against the wall. Pleading with him, she clutched at his fists with her hands, trying to pry his fingers from her hair. He just kept smashing her head against the wall, over and over again. I crouched on my knees beneath the edge of the dining room table, reaching out to Mom. Tears streaming down my face, I beseeched the family members to help her.

They stood scattered about the living room watching, completely unaffected by my father's savageness. They said nothing. They did nothing. They just stood there.

"Stop it, Daddy! Stop it," I shrieked. He continued lambasting her. He kicked her as he slammed her head against the wall. Sobbing, I scrambled to my feet and charged at him with all my might. "Stop it, Daddy! You're hurting her!" Undeterred, he swatted me away. I charged at him again, trying to wedge my body between him and my bloodied mom. He hit me. I didn't care. I just wanted him to stop hurting her.

One of the women in the room came and pulled me away from him. She cradled me in her arms on the floor until my father, running out of steam, bashed my mom's head into the wall one last time and pulled his fists from her hair. Mom lay sobbing and gasping for air on the carpet, partially propped against the wall. I wriggled free and ran to her. She enveloped me in her embrace and together we wept.

That was how I learned what a goose egg is.

One afternoon I was out on our balcony, splashing in a kiddie pool, when the sirens sounded their alarm. Mom immediately came running with a towel. "Just a few more minutes," I protested. "There's still lots of time before the planes come." That may have been true, but she snatched me from the pool nevertheless, and my parents and I took our standard places in the hallway with our neighbors. I had become so accustomed to the routine bombings that I had become somewhat desensitized to the urgency of their dangers.

Stepping outside after the planes had flown was enough to jolt anyone back to reality. After one particularly close nighttime attack, we went out to inspect the damage. There were people wailing and screaming. Flames shot from toppled buildings. Vehicles were upturned. People ran in all directions. We breathed thick clouds of dust tinged with gunpowder and the acrid smell of burning electrical wires. I imagine hell looks an awful lot like what we saw that night.

At one point I saw grown-ups pointing toward the branches of a tree in disgust. Mom was carrying me. As her eyes came into focus and she recognized what it was she was seeing, she too gasped and quickly turned me away, pressing my face against her shoulder. Only later would I stitch together enough snippets of conversations whispered between wary adults to learn that dismembered body parts were hanging from the tree.

The other thing I didn't immediately understand as a child was that the characteristic stench of a bombing's aftermath wasn't only composed of fire and rubble and gunpowder. Intermingled with all those components was the smell of burning human flesh. Life in a warzone was cruel, wretched, sickening, terrifying, and chillingly inhumane—not unlike my father's increasingly ferocious outbursts.

Even in the States my father had felt that people were out to get him and that the government was watching him. As our months as his captives passed, his paranoia mounted. He watched our every move, eyeing us with more and more suspicion.

The bathroom became our refuge—the place where we whispered our prayers in English, beseeching God to deliver us from my father's hands and return us safely to the family we sorely missed back home in Michigan. Even in the bathroom, we weren't free of my father's surveillance. There were two entrances—one from the living room and one from the bedroom. The latter held a window where he would stand silently, observing to be sure we weren't up to anything.

My dad wouldn't allow us to communicate with our family in America. At the beginning of our captivity he had called them, saying the Iranian government wouldn't let us leave the country. That was a lie, but how were they to know? Later he forced Mom to send letters and pictures that made it seem like we were happy living in Iran. Our loved ones sent us letters and care packages, but I suspect only a small fraction of these made it past my father.

Given the circumstances, items that at other times might have seemed insignificant took on treasured memento status. My former babysitter Patty sent her university ID badge with her picture on it. It was so special to me because she had held the little laminated card in her hands, just as I held it in mine. Someone else sent a toothpaste-like tube of gooey pink bubble gum. Instinctively I rationed it. Holding the closed tube in my hands, I would swish the sticky substance back and forth, feeling it ooze between my fingers inside its plastic container. When I could resist no longer, I would gingerly twist off the cap to smell the pink goo that reminded me of home.

One afternoon I walked with my parents to the market, my treasured tube of bubble gum in hand. It was an affluent neighborhood. The sidewalks were wide and lined with grand houses that boasted manicured lawns, gardens, and mature trees. My parents walked side by side in front of me, making small talk—one of those moments between fits of rage when I could still catch a glimmer of my daddy as he had been before he turned into a monster. I dawdled a step behind and, without thinking, reached into my pocket to give my bubble gum a squeeze. It was gone!

Panic-stricken, I stopped and looked all around. There was no sign of my treasured gift from home. It must have fallen from my pocket. Stinging tears welled in my eyes, and I fought to keep them from falling. The distance was growing between my parents and me. I wanted to run back and retrace my steps but knew I couldn't. Taking one long last look down the path, I quickened my pace and once more fell into step behind them.

Dread swelled within me. If my dad found out I had lost the tube, he would lose his temper for sure. His recurrent belligerent tirades were always on my mind. At best he would scream at me. More likely he would scream at Mom, and when he screamed at Mom, things snowballed far beyond a verbal tantrum. I considered whispering my tragic news to Mom when my dad wasn't looking, but I didn't want to burden her with my sadness. She was so sad already. So I trudged on with my head hanging, tears threatening to flow. I longed to go home, and I hated my dad.

Returning from the market, I kept a hypervigilant watch for my missing trinket hoping it waited to be recovered somewhere along our path. Block after block I scanned the sidewalk, the grass, the bushes. With each step my heart grew heavier. I had all but given up when out of the corner of my eye, in the strip of grass between the sidewalk and the street, I glimpsed something at the base of an old tree. Lagging behind, I scampered over for a closer look. There, to my great joy, was my tube of bubble gum—my treasured connection to home.

CHAPTER 6

For me five was an age filled with fear—fear of my father and his violent temper, fear of being separated from Mom, fear of the bombs that were sure to fall, and fear of never again seeing my loved ones back home. Months came and went; Mom and I remained trapped. We clung desperately to life's little moments of joy—a package from Annie with a letter, a Raggedy Ann doll, and a red dress; a box from Aunt Carolyn bearing a packet of red Jell-O and a Crystal Gayle cassette tape; my favorite view of the city at night from high atop the winding mountain road. Sadly, their solace was elusive and fleeting.

Compounding the fear already consuming my life, late one afternoon my dad made a chilling announcement: the next morning I would be starting school. I clung to Mom, crying. I didn't want to go to school. I didn't want to be away from her. What if there were a bombing and we couldn't find each other? What if my dad killed her while I was away?

Mom protested on my behalf, "We can't send her to school. Moody, let's talk about this. She's not ready. Can't you see she's frightened?"

He was staunchly resolute. I was starting school, and that's all there was to it.

Life in Iran in the mid-1980s was bleak. There must have been some color somewhere, but when I think back, what I see is gray. The streets, the concrete high-rises, the sky itself—all are etched in my memory in grim, polluted shades of bleakness. Outside the home, people wore clothing in solid shades of black, dark blue, brown, or gray. The gutters were malodorous and lined with urine-soaked filth. The air, perpetually heavy with the dust of exploded bombs, covered the city in smog. Even the water cisterns that dotted the sidewalks were made of drab, weathered tin. Mom and I never drank from the small metal ladles that hung from chains, to be shared by all who passed. She carried a portable plastic cup that collapsed into a case.

My new school was not immune from the unremitting bleakness. It looked more like a military compound than a nurturing environment intended to foster creativity and learning. Our identities were stripped from us, as were our rights to speak or even think freely. Classes were segregated by gender, and each student wore a government-sanctioned uniform. For girls, that meant a *montoe*, a shapeless coat that reached to the knees, and a *macknay*, a loose-fitting, billowy head covering long enough to conceal our shoulders. Beneath the *montoe* we wore pants made of the same drab fabric as the rest of our garb. The color of the uniforms at my school, not surprisingly, was gray.

The government of Iran was engaged in an all-out campaign to indoctrinate its citizens. Every country does this to some extent, but Iran's brand of brainwashing was particularly effective. Thinking of the generation of young Iranians who marched alongside me in the gray courtyards of our gray schools, I am reminded of Ronald Reagan's words, "Information is the oxygen of the modern age. . . . It seeps through the walls topped by barbed wire. It wafts across the electrified borders." Did enough information reach my classmates before it was too late—before the government sterilized their minds and stole their souls?

I remember climbing down from the bus and staring at the school gate, desperately wanting to be anywhere else. The smell of diesel fuel mingled with the hot tar that was being mopped onto the street. A uniformed guard stationed at the gate ensured that each person entering the complex treated the American flag with proper contempt. In order to pass, I was required to either stomp or spit on its image, which was painted on the ground. Seeing my flag on the ground was insult enough, but to be mandated to physically defile the symbol of my heritage more than infuriated me. On the outside I may have been small and meek, but inside I seethed with hatred.

After showing disdain for the American flag, we were lined up in military fashion and forced to keep step as we chanted the familiar cadence.

"*Maag barg Amrika.*"

"*Louder!*"

"*Maag barg Amrika!*"

"*Louder!*"

"*Maag barg Amrika!*" I screamed the words with such force my throat burned. My screams mingled in unison with those of the other students echoing off the cheerless walls that confined us, infusing us with the government's bigotry.

"*Maag Barg Amrika.*" Death to America. The words grieved me. Day after torturous day, I called down curses on the land I loved.

Finally reaching my limit, I made an announcement to Mom one day as she fixed me an after-school snack. "Tomorrow," I declared brazenly, "I'm going to shout, 'Death to Khomeini!'"

"No, you will not," she said, firmly. "You can say anything you want to me when no one else can hear, but don't you dare say those things in the presence of others. It would be very dangerous. Do you understand? If your teachers heard you say that, the government would take you away, or they would take your daddy and me away. Promise me you'll say exactly what they tell you to say."

I heeded her warning, knowing she was right. Violence was such a prevalent part of life under Khomeini that not even the youngest children were shielded from it. Khomeini used children as his moles. How better to infiltrate the home? They were the eyes and ears of the government, used to gather intelligence. Teachers asked, "What does your mommy read? What does your daddy listen to on the radio? Do your parents drink alcohol? Is music played in your home? Does your mommy cover inside the house?" Any wrong answer was grounds for government action.

People disappeared on a regular basis. The government was fond of using such disobedient traitors as examples to strike fear in the hearts of its citizens. Sometimes these alleged "criminals" were tortured for months or years before being released to tell the tales of their captivity. Others spoke by their blood. Public executions were commonplace.

I have a memory of watching the scenery of the city pass before me from the backseat of a vehicle. We were driving past a military compound or a prison—I'm not sure which. Through the fence topped with barbed wire, far off in the distance, I saw a group of men standing beside one another. They were wearing blindfolds and their hands were bound behind their backs. Soldiers standing opposite them opened fire and, one by one, the men crumpled to the ground.

I wonder sometimes if that really happened. Maybe I saw it on TV, or maybe I saw it in a dream. It's scary what the mind and body can become accustomed to. The sound of gunshots was as familiar to us as car horns honking in the city or birds singing in the country or waves crashing along the shore. Violence surrounded us on all sides, whether we were within the confines of our home or venturing down the streets of Tehran.

Even at age five, I understood what might happen to my family if I were defiant enough to speak my mind. So in my head I substituted the word *Khomeini* for *Amrika*. With my lips I protected my family, but in my heart I remained loyal to the land of the free—and my hatred grew.

In school, we stood at desks in groups of two or three. The teachers, harsh women in black chadors, paced before us wielding wooden sticks. They asked questions and supplied the answers in a chantlike fashion. Students responded by repeating the answers we had been given in unison, in the same singsong tone—same inflection, same speed, with the emphasis on the same syllables. We were told what to think, and nothing else was tolerated.

I had hours of homework. I was ordered to write pages of a single repeating letter. Each one had to be formed precisely as the teacher had illustrated. Even my dad thought the copious copying was excessive. He meticulously inspected my assignments each night, and my work wasn't complete until he had given his approval.

He was a perfectionist in the most severe sense of the word, especially when it came to his native tongue. When Mom tried to speak with someone in Farsi, he would become incensed, screaming at her to shut up. She had an accent, and he would not tolerate such mediocrity. "If you can't say it right, don't say anything at all," he would rant.

I had the advantage of being immersed in Farsi during a period when my brain was developing language, and the elongated guttural sounds rolled off my tongue with ease. Within weeks I had become fluent to an age-appropriate level. Reading and writing came with practice, and my teachers made sure I got plenty of that.

School was pure agony for me. Among the students, I was an outcast and that's not surprising given that I was too timid to talk and often cried inconsolably—so much that Mom had to come to school with me. On top of that, they saw me as an American. As far as my social struggles went, however, being American was the least of my troubles.

One day Mom managed to get her hands on some peanuts. Food, water, and electricity were rationed due to the war, and luxuries like peanuts didn't exist in our world. Somehow she found some, and she labored all afternoon to fashion her thrilling find into something that resembled the peanut butter we missed so much from home. The end product wasn't exactly the same, but it was close enough. We were elated.

I was especially overjoyed when she packed one of my favorite snacks for me to take to school. My mouth watered as I dreamed of the celery stuffed with peanut butter that was waiting for me in my lunch bag. But when mealtime came, I found myself embarrassed to eat something so foreign in the presence of the other children. I nervously eyed them as I took a bite of my wonderful treat. I could see girls staring, looking perplexed. Some sniggered and pointed. Others seemed genuinely curious. Mom nudged me. "Mahtob, why don't you share some with your friends?"

Obediently, I held a piece out for the closest onlooker to sample. She took it from me and tasted it. The other students watched for her reaction. When she smiled, others found their courage and wanted to taste this strange culinary concoction. I handed out every last piece and in return I was warmed for the first time by their smiles of acceptance.

Outside of school, my father still forced me to play with my cousins. I preferred to sit quietly with the adults, but he was harshly insistent. Playing with the other kids, I would stick to the periphery, watching silently more than participating. They pretended to be grown-ups. Pretend men barking orders to their pretend wives. Pretend wives jumping at the command of their pretend husbands.

The walled courtyard behind Ameh Bozorg's house was our make-believe house, and the stacks of rolled Persian carpets served to separate one imaginary room from the next. The girls would don chadors like the older sisters and aunts they admired. They would squeal with delight as they mischievously let the fabric slip from their heads and then off their shoulders before hesitantly dropping to the floor. Set free from the weight of the government mandated garments, they would bound about their "house," giggling at the thrill of their rebelliousness. That's when one of the boys would pound on the wall as if someone were rapping at the door. The girls would gasp, their eyes wide with feigned fear, hands instinctively covering their exposed hair, as they ran for the chadors they had so jubilantly shed.

When we tired of playing house, my cousins and I would camp out on the living-room floor, coloring pictures while we watched cartoons. They were as quick as the adults to reprimand me when I chose my own colors. The government's brainwashing was so pervasive that it even dictated which shades children were allowed to use when coloring in their own homes. The facing pages in our coloring books were identical except that one was in color and the opposite was in black and white. If the flower in the colored picture was red, then the flower on the opposite page had to be colored red. It didn't matter if purple was my favorite color or if my grandma's favorite color was yellow. Bolstered by a campaign of terror, Khomeini's regime was going to great lengths to raise a generation of submissive, mindless followers.

All around me, grown-ups talked about the trucks that pulled up at school gates to take children off to war. Young boys would gather to listen as uniformed men stood in the backs of pickup trucks and shouted over megaphones, giving rousing pep talks about martyrdom. Children were told that they would make their parents proud by sacrificing their lives for Allah and that dying in this holy war ensured their souls would be immediately welcomed into paradise. To drive the message home, the men gave each boy who volunteered a plastic key—a key to paradise—to wear on a chain around his neck. Rumor had it that those young boys, seen as expendable pieces of military equipment, were sent ahead of the soldiers and artillery vehicles to walk for landmines. The Iranian government knowingly murdered its own children.

CHAPTER 7

Why is it that hardworking women often end up with lazy men? Whatever the reason, I thank God for that dynamic in my family. I shudder to think what my life would be like had things been reversed.

In Iran, shopping was done on a daily basis, and the markets were specialized. When we needed bread, we had to wait in line at the bread market. If we needed cheese, that was a different market and a different line. The same was true for produce, meat, spices and so on. My dad, afraid Mom would try to escape with me, let us out of his sight only when there was a suitable guard to stand in for him. When it was time to do the day's shopping, he went along to keep watchful eye.

Mom knew that eventually the day would come when he would grow weary of this menial task that he saw as beneath his station in life. She prayed for that day, hoping that then he would let her go to the markets on her own. Perhaps then she could finally find a way out of our prison.

Mom was right. She knew my father well. He was arrogant, self-important, and above all lazy. He despised wasting his valuable time fetching basic necessities. He was more of a luxury-item shopper. He liked expensive cars, original artwork, fine jewelry, designer clothes. Whatever he bought had to be the biggest and the best, and he bought in excess. If he purchased a Lacoste shirt, he didn't buy just one—he bought one in every color. To be demoted to a common errand boy, waiting his turn in countless lines filled with common folk to buy soap or cheese or tomatoes was insufferable to him.

Driven by his pride and his laziness, he eventually acquiesced and began loosening the reins. But he did so by degrees—very small degrees. He began by sending Mom to the markets with a shopping list and no money. She was to return with the precise cost of each item. While she was out gathering prices, he timed her to ensure she didn't have a moment for any unauthorized stops along the way. When Mom returned, he would give her the exact change and restart the timer. Again she would make her rounds, this time gathering the items for which she had been sent.

She had gained an ounce of freedom. Still, it was absolutely out of the question for her to leave the house, unsupervised, with me. My dad knew my mom well too. He knew that even if she managed to find a way to escape, she would never leave without me. He could set her loose on the unfamiliar streets of Tehran, confident that as long as he held me as ransom she would do exactly as told.

He judged her loyalty accurately. What he underestimated was Mom's resourcefulness and determination, both learned from her father. When she was growing up in central Michigan, my grandpa, a warm-hearted lumberjack of a man, used to take her for walks in the woods. Once they were deep in the heart of the forest, he would turn to her and say, "Okay, show me the way. How do we get out of here?" Mom says he would follow her down one wrong path after another until she got her bearings and figured out how to lead them home.

That real-world instruction had honed her sense of direction and taught her perseverance. Wandering through the trees, my grandpa had infused his philosophy of life into his little girl. "Where there's a will, there's a way. Don't ever give up. If you want something badly enough, keep working. There's always a way."

I don't believe in coincidences. I believe in miracles. And so it was that a stranger, an Iranian man no less, made it his mission to help Mom and me escape. On one of Mom's early solo shopping trips, she asked around like a beggar for the special coin required to use a payphone. Holding her hand out, she pleaded with passersby, "*Dozari? Dozari?*" She stepped into a shop and asked again, "*Dozari?*" The shopkeeper, recognizing her accent, said with enthusiasm, "You're American! Please come in. Use my phone." In awe, Mom accepted his compassionate offer.

Since the Iranian rebels had ensured there was no American embassy in Tehran, she called the Swiss Embassy, which housed the American-interest section, in the hope that they would find a way to free us. Though they knew of our situation, they could offer no assistance. When Mom hung up, the shopkeeper, who had listened to the conversation, said to her, "You're in trouble. I want to help you." He didn't want her to think all Iranians were like my dad and his family. He said that he knew people and would do some checking to see what arrangements could be made. We couldn't have known it then, but that chance meeting would be a pivotal step on our journey toward freedom.

Our shopkeeper truly was a godsend. In an environment where it seemed that everyone spied for someone and no one could be trusted, he remained faithful to his word. As often as Mom was able, she stopped by to check in with him. Sometimes weeks would pass between her visits as my father's paranoia waxed and waned. But each time, the kind shopkeeper offered hope. He had mobilized a grassroots network to help us. He talked secretly with people, and they talked with people, and he remained steadfast in his mission to free us from my father's oppression.

Over time, my dad began to believe that Mom had become a broken woman, accepting life under his rule in Iran. Only then did he permit me to leave the house with her. Mom made the most of every opportunity to touch base with her underground network of angels. We raced to see the shopkeeper for his latest update. We rushed to meet with others whom Mom had come to know through the shopkeeper. We sped to the embassy to swap messages and beg them to intervene on our behalf.

The Swiss embassy was enormously intimidating, with its heavily armed sentries and the weighty metal bars that clanged shut behind us with finality. No matter how many times Mom and I entered that gate, no matter how prepared I was for the chilling sound, it always made me quiver with fear.

Once inside the stately building, we were taken by an armed guard to a small room where we were searched before finally being led into the tangle of offices. Our case had been assigned to a woman named Helen. She was gentle and sympathetic, and she desperately wanted to help us. At the same time, her hands were tied. In America we were considered dual nationals, but Iran recognized only our Iranian citizenship. We were outside her jurisdiction and considered the legal property of my father. If anything should happen to him, we would become the property of his family.

There was a man working at the embassy who kept a drawer of his desk stocked with Toblerone chocolate bars. Passing by, I always shot a glance in his direction, hoping to see him sitting there. If he was, he would surely invite me to sit with him and share a chocolate bar while Mom talked with Helen. I would carefully break off one alpine chunk at a time and drink in its every detail—its aroma, its glistening angles, the letter etched onto its side in the alphabet of my homeland. Only then would I slip a bite into my mouth.

I would savor every bit of the experience as I cautioned myself not to ever tell anyone but Mom of this secret joy. If my dad found out, he would never let me see her again. His constant threats to kill her had not lessened. Mom was doing everything in her power to find a way to take me home, and I had to do everything in my power to protect us from my dad. So with every splendid, creamy bite I took of the Toblerone, I reminded myself this never happened.

Our excursions were rife with danger. The Pasdar, or morality police, roamed the streets armed with machine guns, specifically looking for wardrobe offenses. Their job was to make sure women were dressed in a way that protected them from the lustful glances of men. Women were required to cover all flesh except for their faces and hands. No hair was allowed to be visible. No nail polish was permissible, and absolutely no makeup was tolerated . . . for the woman's protection, of course.

Mom had several run-ins with the Pasdar. One day when we had just left a store and were waiting to cross the street, a woman wearing a black chador and carrying an automatic rifle jumped from the back of a truck. My heart caught in my throat as she charged at us. Mom's grip tightened on my hand. The woman was shouting at Mom because her socks had sagged below the hem of her montoe, revealing a sliver of skin on her shin. Mom, in an uncharacteristic and foolhardy show of boldness, yelled right back at her about the worthless elastic in the socks available to her in Iran. If she could find decent socks, she would gladly wear them. The guard, in an astounding act of kindness, agreed and let us go.

It was, without a doubt, the grace of God that saved us that day. That little display of flesh would have been cause enough to warrant Mom's arrest or execution, and arguing with the Pasdar, by all accounts, should have had grave consequences.

The teachers at my school, once they had learned of our plight, also showed us unexpected benevolence, even at the risk of jeopardizing their own safety. They wouldn't let us leave once we had arrived at school, but they did allow us to come late to class, giving us even more opportunity to focus on our top-secret quest.

One morning Mom and I went to check in with the shopkeeper on our way to school. As the months elapsed and one escape plan after another fell apart, our pleas had become more urgent. We cut through an alleyway and happened upon a flock of birds pecking at the dirt along the road. I was happy to see them because they reminded me of the birds I loved so much at home. We took a moment to enjoy them before scurrying to meet the shopkeeper and then heading to school.

That evening my dad walked with us to the market to buy bread for dinner. The bakers worked in an open pit. They wore sandals and hats that were flat on the top. They crouched on the floor kneading dough in mounds of flour and passing the loaf from one person to the next at different stages of production. The last man in the assembly line placed the flat loaf of dough on a long-handled wooden paddle and poked it with his fingers, lining its surface with divots. Then it was thrust into the fire, where it baked on a bed of tiny pebbles. Another man tended the bread with a long stick, flipping it as the edges singed from the intense heat. When the bread was golden, it was retrieved from the oven with one deft twist of the stick, bringing with it a sprinkling of renegade stones that had baked into the bottom of the massive loaf. This was *sangyak*, my favorite Persian bread. Its loaves were oblong and almost as big as I was.

Mom tore off big hunks of steaming bread for us to eat on our way home. She carefully picked out the hot stones from my piece before handing it over. After our treat, my parents each took one of my hands in theirs and swung me between them as we walked. "One, two, three," we would count in unison and then, "Whee!" Their arms lifted me from the ground, and my feet swung out in front of me.

"Do it again," I begged.

"One, two, three . . . whee!"

"Again," I giggled.

We were still walking hand in hand as we turned down the alley that would lead us back to our apartment. There before us were the birds, the same birds Mom and I had enjoyed that morning. In my excitement, I forgot to forget that I had seen them. "Look," I said with glee, "The birds are still here!"

"What birds?" my dad asked suspiciously.

"Those birds. We saw them this morning on our way to school. They're still here. This must be their home." Mom squeezed my hand. I looked at her, confused, as my dad continued his interrogation.

"You passed these birds on your way to school this morning?"

"Yes," I announced cheerfully, "Aren't they pretty?" Mom squeezed my hand again, harder this time. "Ouch!" I cried, turning my head sharply toward her, not understanding her signal, "Why did you squeeze my hand?"

"What were you doing on this street this morning?" my dad interrupted. "Where were you going? You weren't going to school. This is not on your way to school." He was using his angry voice. His footsteps were his angry footsteps.

I recognized my mistake, but it was too late. I stared anxiously at my feet while Mom tried to run interference. I can't remember now if she told him I had mixed up the times or if she said we had gotten lost. I do remember that he was furious and that I was even more furious with myself for making such a devastating blunder. I had worked so hard at remembering what I could and couldn't say. Mom had trained me well, and I knew that if I wanted to go home, I could never make a mistake like this.

Not a day passed without my begging Mom to take me home and her promising that she would. We prayed continually for God to open a door for us and trusted that somehow he would. Now I was certain that I had destroyed any chance of escape. Even worse than not being able to go home was the fear that now my dad was going to kill Mom because I had forgotten to forget and had said something I wasn't supposed to say.

I hate you! I hate you! I hate you! I seethed in my heart. I loathed my dad for doing this to us.

I wasn't the only one infected with hatred. Back home in Michigan, my brothers, grandparents, aunts and uncles, and family friends kept a bitter and agonizing vigil. The messages we got from them were disheartening. My grandpa's long battle with colon cancer was claiming his life, and we were trapped in Iran as his last days were slipping away.

Family members called my dad, pleading with him to send us to see my grandpa before it was too late. Standing at my father's side in our living room, Mom begged with utter desperation. "Let's all go as a family to see him, and then Mahtob and I will come back to Iran with you. Just let us go see him one last time before he dies."

I watched silently from the floor.

"You're right. You should be with your family right now. They need you. You will go to see him," he announced.

"What?" Mom asked, breathless. "Really, we can go? We can go see him? Thank you, Moody!"

He cut her thanks short. "I said *you* can go. Mahtob will stay here with me."

"What?" she whispered, timidly staring at the ground and bracing for his fist. "Moody, I can't go without Mahtob. I won't leave her."

Thus began a confusing time. My dad threw himself headlong into making preparations for Mom's departure. All the while, Mom promised that she wasn't leaving me. But I saw the preparations being made. How could she say she wasn't leaving?

My dad said she was. He told me she was going home because she wanted to see my grandparents and brothers. I knew that was true. I knew she wanted to see them as much as I did. I also knew that what my dad said was the law. If he said Mom was going to America, then she had no choice. The more she protested that she wasn't abandoning me, that she would find a way out of this mess, the more I pulled away from her. I was angry with her for leaving me and even angrier that she had the nerve to lie to me about it.

Even after my dad declared he was sending Mom to America, his threats on her life continued. He oscillated between shouting that he would kill her and pronouncing that he would lock her in a basement and she would never again see me or the light of day.

By then our family had moved into our own apartment. I had my own room filled with toys. For my sixth birthday, my parents had given me a ballerina that sat daintily upon a swing suspended from my bedroom ceiling by ropes adorned with pink bows. The bombings still came at night, and I hated my dad for making me sleep in my own room. I felt much safer tucked in between my parents. There I could protect Mom from my dad if he lost his temper, and Mom could protect me from the bombs.

I remember lying in bed at night, sobbing because I felt so betrayed by Mom. For eighteen months she had promised me every day that she would take me home, that she would never leave Iran without me. Even as the final preparations were made for her departure, she kept telling me what I was sure were lies.

CHAPTER 8

Mere days before Mom was to leave for the States, an ambulance arrived at our apartment to take my dad to the hospital where he was employed as an anesthesiologist. Because of the war, the purchase of automobiles was rationed. We did not have a vehicle, so when his services were needed he was driven to the hospital by ambulance.

In the days preceding he had become increasingly violent and suspicious of Mom's every move. And he was right to be suspicious. Just that morning he had unknowingly thwarted our most recent escape plot.

Through the shopkeeper, Mom had met a man who had dedicated himself in earnest to helping us. Over the months he had staged several well-intentioned but unsuccessful escape attempts. That morning, as Mom walked me to the bus stop, someone was supposed to snatch us off the street. But my dad, throwing one of his customary tantrums, had taken me instead. Now he refused to go with the ambulance, even though there was a woman visiting who said she would stay with us until he returned. There was no way he was letting us out of his sight.

The ambulance driver was insistent, though, and my dad reluctantly gave in to his urging. This must have been an uncomfortable exchange for our unsuspecting visitor. The woman, who had been thrust into the unsought role of prison guard by my father, had a daughter around my age. We played on the floor while our moms sat on the couch making small talk.

Shortly after my dad left, Mom excused herself and went upstairs. She was gone for what felt like an eternity.

One thing both of my parents agreed on was the importance of being a good host. My anxiety grew as the minutes passed and Mom hadn't returned to sit with our guests. I shot furtive glances towards the stairs hoping to see Mom emerge. Finally I, too, excused myself and ran to see what had happened.

Mom was in her bedroom frantically shoving items into a giant purse. I climbed onto the stationary bike at the end of the bed and watched as I pedaled. I was confused. We had guests in the house. Why was she not visiting with them? Mom brushed off my concerns and shooed me back downstairs to announce that she would soon follow.

When at long last I spotted Mom tiptoeing down the stairs, I was greatly relieved, until I realized she was carrying the bag I had just seen her pack. My dad wasn't the only one whose suspicions were growing.

During our entire time in captivity, Mom and I had been a team. We had counted on each other and had trusted each other implicitly. We had talked about our dreams of freedom and the lengths to which she was going to find a way to take me home. I knew the people who were trying to help us. I had often been at Mom's side when she went to see them. We had kept no secrets from each other. But now, all of a sudden, I could tell she was hiding things from me, and I didn't like it. Maybe my dad was right. Maybe I couldn't trust her anymore. Maybe she really was abandoning me to go back to America.

"We've been invited to dinner this evening," Mom briskly announced to our guests, "I need to go buy the flowers." There may have been a war going on, but when someone was invited to dinner, it was unconscionable to show up without a bouquet of flowers.

"That's no problem," she offered graciously. "I'll drive you."

"Thank you," Mom answered. "Mahtob, *bia inja*. Come here," she directed, holding out my montoe and macknay. Her eyes did not meet mine. She hurried to put on her own montoe and covered her head with a *roosarie*, a large scarf that she knotted below her chin. Taking me by the hand, she marched toward the door.

Our guard was a gentle woman, and she suspected nothing. To her, going to buy flowers was an established custom. There was no reason for her to question. Without complaint, she and her daughter joined us at the door.

When we pulled up to the curb directly in front of the flower shop, Mom motioned for me to get out of the car. "Thank you," she said to the woman. "We will walk home."

"No," the woman countered, "I will wait for you."

"No," came Mom's polite reply, "That's not necessary, We'll can walk."

"No, really, I don't mind."

"No, please, go on. We'll be fine."

They went on like this until finally Mom leaned over and hugged her, saying, "Thank you for everything."

I wonder sometimes if, in that moment, the woman may have understood. If she did, she gave no indication. Mom stepped out of the car and took me by the hand. We walked toward the flower shop, and our gentle guard drove away.

There was a pay phone at the corner, and as soon as the coast was clear, Mom turned and sprinted for the booth. As she turned, a silvery hand-crocheted silk skirt fell from her bag. An old man passing by stopped and picked it up. He handed it to me, and I ran after Mom, more befuddled than ever. We were going to buy flowers. Why had she brought a skirt along?

She was fishing in her pocket for a dozari when I handed her the skirt. Taking it from me with no explanation, she stuffed it back into the bag. She dialed the familiar number and waited impatiently for the man who was helping us to answer. There was a resolute desperation in her voice when she whispered into the receiver, "I have Mahtob. I'm out of the house, and I'm not going back." There was a pause as Mom listened to his response. Her eyes darted nervously about, scanning for any signs of danger.

There was no plan in place. The man who was helping us wanted us to return to our apartment and wait while he tried to organize something. Mom argued back. There was no time to wait. We might not get another chance. Every day my dad insisted even more vehemently that Mom's days were numbered. At that point it was immaterial whether he locked her in the basement to die, killed her outright, or forced her onto a plane bound for the United States. It was clear that time was of the essence.

The man knew our situation well, and he understood the urgency in Mom's voice. He had no reason to help us except that his heart was filled with compassion. He had no responsibility to us except that we were fellow human beings who were suffering a cruel injustice. Despite his initial hesitation, he gave Mom an address and said he would meet us there.

Returning the receiver to its cradle, Mom knelt to talk with me. She looked me straight in the eye, and I knew instantly that I had been foolish to doubt her intentions. She was not leaving me. She was fighting harder than ever to find a way for both of us to escape.

"Mahtob, we may have an opportunity to go home. Do you want to go home?"

I nodded enthusiastically.

"But if we leave now, I don't know when or if you'll ever see your daddy again."

As her words sank in, tears filled my eyes. I tried to hold them in, but they spilled over and rolled down my cheeks. My shoulders rose toward my ears as I fought to control the sobs that were building inside.

"I will understand if you want to go back to your daddy," Mom offered with loving sincerity. "It's okay if that's what you want. But if we go back now, I don't know if we'll have another chance to go to America."

My chin quivered, and my body heaved with sobs that had broken free despite my best efforts to contain them.

"We'll do whatever you want to do," Mom gently assured me.

"I want my bunny." I finally managed to utter between gasps. "I want my bunny." I wasn't concerned about my dad. I wanted more than anything to be free of him. But aside from Mom, my bunny was my closest companion. I couldn't just leave him behind.

I could see in Mom's eyes that she understood how much my bunny meant to me. She thought carefully before responding. "If we go back to get him, we won't be able to get out of the house again. If you want to stay here, that's what we'll do. If we're going to go to America, we have to leave your bunny. When we get home, I'll buy you a new one." She let the options sink in before she asked for my decision. "What do you want to do?"

The choice was mine and mine alone.

It was a bitter decision to make. I wanted my bunny, and I wanted to go home to my brothers and my grandparents and aunts and uncles and friends. More than all of that, I wanted to get away from my dad and his threats, his beatings and the terrifying sound of his angry footsteps. I wanted to go home where I could go to sleep at night and know no bombs would fall under the cover of darkness. I wanted to go to a school with no more marching, no more stomping on my flag, no more screaming, "Maag barg Amrika."

I wanted to go home.

Mom's question hung between us. "What do you want to do?"

I was too emotional to form the words.

"Do you want to stay here?"

Silently, I shook my head.

"Do you want to go home?"

Tears streaming down my face, I nodded resolutely.

CHAPTER 9

Mom and I stand at the phone booth.

Click.

We sit in the back seat of a taxi. The driver stands outside, shaking his finger accusingly at another man.

Click.

Before we went to Iran, I was captivated by my View-Master. Each pull on the lever brought into focus a new snapshot with a satisfying click. Click by click, the circular disk studded with slides rotated, bringing my favorite fairy tales to life. This red plastic toy that nearly every child in America played with is a good analogy for those memories for which I had no frame of reference. My mind is filled with a similar series of disjointed snapshots. The images are timeworn and distant, almost as if belonging to some other child who bears a striking resemblance to me. Some scenes are remarkably clear, while others prove almost entirely elusive—like glimpsing a dim star in my peripheral vision, only to turn my head and find it has vanished. There are details of our escape that I remember, yet much has mercifully been erased from my consciousness. There are experiences I know I endured but can't quite visualize today . . .

Crossing town to meet the man who was helping us, our taxi collided with another vehicle. In true Iranian fashion, both drivers jumped out and began to argue. This meant trouble. Horns were honking. Traffic was backing up. Authorities would be arriving at any moment. My dad might have already sounded the alarm. We couldn't risk being spotted by the police.

Quietly we slipped out of the car and blended into throngs of people hurrying on their way in the metropolitan darkness. It was a cold night in the dead of winter, and we weren't dressed for the elements.

An announcement blared over the city's loudspeakers. Mom's grasp of Farsi was limited to the words she had gleaned by observation or through makeshift sign-language exchanges with well-intentioned neighbors. I was fluent, but only at a first grade level. The announcement was troubling but neither of us was sure what it had said. It was either a message about a woman who was on the run with a child or it was a message about a bathtub. Judging by the seriousness of the tone, it wasn't likely about a bathtub.

Click.

I see myself kneeling backward on the sofa in the dark apartment. Silhouettes of two figures huddle in conversation near the window.

The presence of the man who was helping us soothed me. He and Mom were speaking softly but with urgency. The apartment was high up in an urban building, and below the world went on, oblivious to our angst.

The couch delineated the border between sitting rooms. I knelt on the soft cushions and played with delicate glass figurines that lined the sofa table. Years later, I still hesitate to reveal further details of that apartment for fear I could inadvertently endanger the selfless man who came to our aid. Describing the figurines should be harmless, and yet I will not take that risk. They put me at ease, as did the hushed sounds of the brainstorming session wafting in from the next room.

A silent witness to many such conversations over the months, I was filled with hope. The man who was helping us had pledged to get us out of Iran and, listening to him, I felt confident he would keep his promise.

Others had offered to get Mom out of the country, but smuggling a child was far too dangerous. If caught, they would be executed. Despite the dangers, this man wanted me to grow up to be happy and safe. To him, risking his life to improve the quality of mine was a calling, not a decision.

Click.

I gaze apprehensively over my left shoulder as a woman slips in through the barely open front door. The hallway's brightness renders her nothing more than a dark shadow.

The door was quickly closed and bolted behind her. The atmosphere was tense and secretive. We were all aware of the danger we shared by virtue of our joint mission. Her greeting came as a clipped whisper.

Click.

The woman sits sideways beside me, her heavily bangled arm leaning over the back of the sofa. Together we play with the table decorations.

I found comfort in the jingle of her bracelets. I hoped that someday my arm would be lined with beautiful jingling gold bangles just like the women on the Persian side of my family. At the moment I wore two.

The woman spoke tenderly to me, running her fingers through my thick curls, assuring me that everything would be all right and that soon Mom and I would be safe at home with our family in America.

Click.

Everything is dark save for what is within the window's boxy frame, illumined by the city lights from outside. The man sits leaning forward, his hands held before him, pleading with Mom to remain calm. Mom, the base of a rotary phone in one hand and the clunky receiver pressed to her ear with the other, paces anxiously. The long, coiling cord droops out of sight below the window's ledge.

"No, *you* listen to me!" she growled.

The words woke me with a start. In an instant, I was leaning over the back of the sofa to see what was wrong. Confused and frightened, I wondered who was on the other end of the line. I recognized by Mom's tone that the danger was escalating.

"I have a lawyer," she warned, her voice firm and unyielding.

She had a lawyer? How could I not know that? Doug and Karen, our friends from Michigan, were the only lawyers I knew. Were they here? Had they come to help?

"No, Moody. I'm not bringing Mahtob back until we've settled things."

What? She was talking to my dad? How could she? And how could she say she would take me back?

"My lawyer and I will meet you on Saturday."

How could this be? Plans had already been made. We were departing for home on Friday, going over the mountains into Turkey even though the peaks were covered with snow.

It was common knowledge that when snow was visible atop the Zagros Mountains from Tehran, the passage was closed for winter. We were going over the mountains anyway.

Click.

The man who is helping us rushes Mom and me out of the apartment and toward a car that waits with its back door open.

It was Friday. The man who was helping us was saying good-bye. I could tell that he was sad to see us go. One last time he raced through our instructions. He seemed to be under great pressure to tell us everything we needed to know without delay. There was no time to linger on an emotional farewell. He hugged us both as we climbed into the car.

"How can I ever repay you?" Mom asked.

"The only payment I want is to know that there's a smile on Mahtob's face."

With that he closed the door, and we sped off. Desperately longing for him to make the journey with us, I never would have dared to say so.

Click.

A busy square—or perhaps a circle—in Tabriz. Traffic everywhere, absolute chaos. Mom and I sit in the backseat.

Screeching to a halt, our driver jumped out and began arguing with a police officer. Simultaneously, another man opened the back door and grabbed Mom by the arm. Raising his index finger to his lips, he ordered us to remain silent as he whisked us from the car. "*Zood bash.* Hurry." He put us in a truck, and off we went.

We changed vehicles repeatedly. Sometimes we were crammed in among many other people, staged to look like one big, happy family. Mom held me close as she hid in plain sight behind her flowing black chador.

Click.

Mom and I hunker on the side of a mountain. A blizzard swirls around us. Everything is white. Above us is a road, but no vehicles in sight.

The jagged, powdery peaks of the Zagros Mountains were our refuge. The snow that signaled the end of travel for the season now hid us from view. Shivering, we huddled together to conserve our warmth and we waited.

We had been riding in the back of a Red Cross vehicle when a bullet rang through the air, narrowly missing us. Our guides had stopped and made us get out. Not speaking Farsi or English, they'd used hand gestures to instruct us to hide and to wait. It felt like hours had passed since then. Mom and I were nervous. Were they coming back?

We waited.

Just as Grandpa had taught Mom to find her way home from deep in the heart of the forest, she had taught me what to do if I were ever lost. Through the tale of Hansel and Gretel, who left a trail of crumbs in the woods, Mom had coached me to sit and wait. She would come to me. How would two people ever find each other, she had asked, if both kept moving? Likewise, if both sat still, they wouldn't find each other. So if I ever get lost, I should stay still, and Mom would locate me. Whatever it took, she would find me. She would never stop looking.

"Mahtob, what do you think we should do?" Mom asked now as sleet and snow stung our bare faces. "I don't know if they're coming back. Should we stay here, or should we start walking?"

"We should wait. Otherwise, they won't know where to find us."

And so we waited.

And waited.

We listened with growing desperation for the distant rumble of a vehicle that would signal our rescue. And when we did hear one approaching, we were torn between the impulse to jump up and wave our arms in an urgent plea for help and the instinct to stay hidden to protect ourselves from being discovered and sent back to my father.

Click.

Mom and I are alone in a ramshackle stable, sitting on the dirt floor.

Chickens ran in and out at will, pecking at the ground in their characteristic frenetic way. Outside, sheep were bleating. Sheep had become a familiar sight to me in Iran. It was quite common to see a shepherd, stick in hand, leading a flock down the bustling urban streets.

Mom had been given clothes to change into. We were high atop the mountains in Kurdish territory now and must blend into our surroundings.

For the first time in days, we had been given food—one small handful of sunflower seeds still in their shells. My mouth watered as I gazed at this most welcome feast. Mom insisted that I eat the first seed. Even then, I knew her to be generous to a fault, giving beyond her capacity. I refused, certain that if I ate the first seed, she would force me to eat every seed, saving none for herself. Instead, I separated the tiny black kernels with the side of my hand into two portions. Half we would share immediately, and the other half we would save for later. Only after I had taken a seed and placed it in Mom's mouth did I eat one myself. My greatest fear was being separated from her, whether by my father, the police, or death. She had grown gaunt and frail, her hair stringy and gray, and the decrepit nature of her countenance was of great concern to me.

I heard a commotion outside the stable. Our guides were busy with preparations—for what, I did not know. I felt an unexplainable attachment to the undisputed leader of our smugglers. He rarely spoke to us, and when he did his words were in a language Mom and I didn't understand. Still, there was something reassuring in his manner. A large network of men had been leading us through the mountains. Each time Mom and I were handed off, my eyes darted anxiously about in hope of spotting the leader. He wasn't always with us, though strangely I felt he was always near, overseeing, though sometimes from a distance.

Click.

Darkness.

Outside, the slick ice crunched beneath our feet. A man hoisted Mom onto the bare back of a small horse. Nervously, I waited to be handed to her. To my horror, I was passed to a stranger on a different horse. Silently I squirmed, reaching for her. I wanted to ride with Mom.

We don't always get what we want.

Click.

Riding gingerly along the narrow, icy edge of the mountain, I don't know if it's the same night or the same horse or if I'm riding with the same stranger. What I do know is that Mom and I are still separated, and I don't like it.

Feeling as if I were far ahead of Mom, I worried we wouldn't find each other in the all-encompassing blackness. I couldn't see the steep drop-off to our left, but I sensed its treacherous void.

My small contingent moved slowly and with great care. Abruptly a shot rang out, crashing into the rocky ledge near us. We set off at a gallop. Horse still in motion, my rider dismounted, cradling me in his arms. He ran for a shallow cave etched into the side of the cliff. Others followed. I searched the shadows for Mom. Had she been shot? I listened for her and heard only faint whispers of a language I could not understand.

And then, silence.

Click.

I stand at the top of a snowy peak with a group of exhausted men who are gazing apprehensively into the darkness beneath us.

I had been delivered safely over the mountains. Mom was nowhere to be found. We waited and listened. There was no movement. A sense of dejected gloom grew among my rescuers. My heart ached. Anxiously they checked their watches and peered into the darkness. Their expressions looked as bleak as I felt.

I can't remember if one of Mom's guides ran ahead for help or if one of mine went back in search of them. Things were not going according to plan. I didn't understand what was happening, but somehow I knew Mom was in danger.

Later I would learn that Mom's body had given out. The last summit had been too much for her. Exhaustion had prevailed.

There is a limit to the power of the human will. There is no limit, however, to the power of God's grace. In an act of selflessness, the drug smugglers who had been paid in advance to transport us over the mountains into Turkey had picked up Mom's listless body and carried her to me.

Click.

The leader stands before us. He brushes his hands together
as if wiping them clean.

"*Tamoom*," he sighed. It is finished. Then he pointed to the ground. "Turkey." My momentary elation vanished the instant I realized he was not smiling.

This was as far as he would be traveling with us. He had been hired to get us over the border. His job was complete. Now we were on our own, but the perils of our voyage were far from over.

As he struggled for words in a language he did not speak, tears filled his eyes. He wanted Mom to know she was like a sister to him. For the second time in a week, I wanted desperately to beg one of our liberators to continue this journey with us. Once more, I held my tongue.

These are the images that have been preserved through my lens. Time and distance have reduced them to matter-of-fact snapshots, random glimpses of a life that only vaguely feels like it was once mine. I see the images. I know they are real, that they happened to *me*, in fact. And yet I feel a surreal sense of detachment from them. It is with awestruck amazement that I think back and know the pictures on the View-Master's circular disk truly belong to me.

CHAPTER 10

"Passport!" the attendant demanded. We were at the bus station in Van, on the Turkish side of the Iranian border.

Mom looked bewildered, holding out her hands and tilting her head in feigned ignorance. We needed two tickets to Ankara, and she wasn't stepping aside without them. "Passport!" the attendant insisted. Mom played dumb.

Earlier, she had warned me not to translate for her. Knowing my propensity for languages, she knew I would quickly absorb the words spoken around me and, being overly helpful, I would want to assist.

"Passport!" the attendant bellowed with obvious frustration, as if shouting would make Mom understand.

Mom persisted. I tugged on her sleeve, letting her know that I understood and would gladly explain. Taking my hand, she gave a gentle squeeze. This time I knew the meaning of her signal and kept my mouth shut. Finally, exasperated, the man handed over two bus tickets and waved us on.

We were already five hundred miles from Tehran, but a journey of nearly six hundred miles still separated us from our dream of freedom. The bus wound its way on the outer edge of treacherous cliffs that bore no guardrails. The road was covered with ice and snow, at times nearly impassable. Having gone so many days without a meal, we had lost our appetites. Though we struggled to stay awake and be on alert, the cushioned seats, the rocking motion of the bus and the hum of its engine, coupled with utter mental and physical exhaustion, lulled us both to sleep.

From a deep slumber, my eyes suddenly shot open. I frantically searched my surroundings to get my bearings. Our erratic travels had left me disoriented. As my senses came into focus I realized I was on a bus—toward the back, on the left side—*dasta chap*. Mom was asleep beside me.

A man was making his way down the aisle with a worn shaker bottle. He paused at each row to sprinkle a little of its liquid on the hands of the passengers. A lemony scent tickled my nostrils. Glancing quickly from Mom to the man and back again, I wondered if I should wake her for this. We were caked in grime. My hair was a snarled mess. We looked like the homeless refugees that lined the streets of Tehran because of the war.

I sat up straight in my seat, awaiting my turn. Looking out the window on the right—*dasta ras*—I spotted another bus pulled to the side of the road, its passengers standing in the cold holding their travel documents to be inspected by heavily armed soldiers. I had witnessed this sight many times since we crossed into Turkey.

I shivered, knowing we didn't have the necessary travel documents. My dad had our real passports. The ones we carried, while authentic, were not valid. They had been issued the previous autumn by the American embassy in Bern, Switzerland, and came to us via the Swiss embassy in Tehran. Without the proper stamps, our passports were worthless little books bearing our pictures, and they would stay that way until we reached the American embassy in Ankara. If the soldiers looked at them before then, we would be sent back to Iran—to prison or to my dad. Either way I would never see my mommy again.

The refreshing aroma of lemon intensified as the man with the bottle approached. I turned back to Mom, still asleep. She looked so peaceful. I felt torn. Maybe I should let her sleep.

When he reached me, I kept my eyes averted while I held out my hands. He gave them a generous misting. A smile spread over my face that went all the way to my eyes. Ever so timidly, I whispered my thanks as I raised my hands to my face and inhaled deeply, drinking in the sunny, energizing bouquet of lemon. To my great joy, Mom awoke just in time to join me.

The man with the bottle couldn't have known how much his modest act of service cheered our hearts that day. In the context of our lives, it was a pampering beyond words. For hours we delighted in the glorious scent of lemon on our skin.

I dozed again and awoke to find our bus had stopped. Looking around to see what had happened, I saw the driver reach for the handle to open the door. Instinctively my gaze followed the swinging doors and there, to my great horror, stood a soldier.

Recoiling, I clutched at Mom. I would not let them take her from me. We watched the driver get off the bus and confer with the soldier. Both men talked with their hands. There was pointing and talking and more pointing. Mom and I held our breath, awaiting the outcome, fearing the worst. At last the soldier stood down, and our driver climbed back aboard his vehicle. Giving no explanation, he dropped into his seat and the bus chugging to life, carried us farther down the road. By the grace of God we had been spared yet again.

It was dark when Mom and I reached Ankara. Turkey was under martial law at the time, and a strict curfew was in force. We rushed to a row of waiting taxis. When the driver asked where we were headed, Mom said in heavily accented English, "Ho-tel—Hy-att, Sher-a-ton, Hil-ton."

Understanding Mom's request and perhaps recognizing our distress, he drove us past the American embassy. As we approached, he pointed to draw our attention. There, waving proudly high atop the building, was the most magnificent sight—our flag! My heart leapt with gladness. *We're home!* I thought. *We must be in America.* I turned to watch it through the back window of the cab as we drove by and, even in the midst of my exhaustion, my joy was complete.

The taxi driver dropped us at a hotel across the street from the embassy where, with much trepidation, Mom was forced to hand over our invalid passports. It really was nothing short of a miracle that this was the first time since the bus station in Van that we had been asked for our identification. In exchange for our passports we were given a key to a room where, for a few precious hours, Mom and I could rest in relative peace behind the reassuring solidity of a bolted door. Mom and I hustled hand in hand to our room, giddy at the prospect of finally getting to take a bath and brush our teeth. We felt freer than we had in ages.

The roar of the water echoed in the bathroom as Mom filled the tub with warm water for me. We were ecstatic to be across the street from the embassy. In the morning we would simply go there. The officials would validate our passports and put us on a plane to America. Our short-order plan had actually worked.

But our bubble was burst just minutes after we reached our hotel room by a firm pounding on the door. Our cover had been blown. The hotel clerk ordered us to leave at once. Mom pleaded with him to let us stay until morning. The embassy would stamp our passports, and everything would be fine. There was, however, no persuading him. We were illegal aliens, and he would not risk harboring us even for a night.

From the lobby, he let Mom use the phone to call the embassy. A night-duty guard answered. Mom briefly explained our situation. He demanded to know how we had entered the country if our passports were unstamped and scoffed when Mom told him we had crossed the border on horseback, a seemingly impossible feat. He hung up without affording us refuge.

Dejected, Mom begged the clerk to permit her to make one more call. We hadn't notified our family in Michigan of our escape attempt because Mom didn't want them to worry. She knew my grandpa had been scarcely holding on to life, and she didn't want his last hours to be spent contemplating visions of us dead in the middle of the mountains.

When Grandma answered, Mom was relieved to learn that Grandpa was still holding on. Breathlessly she pleaded with Grandma to call the US State Department. I stood by Mom's side, listening, as she hurried to update her. Mom's tone was all business. The State Department needed to know that we were out of Iran and in Ankara, literally across the street from the embassy. We had been refused entry that night but would go there in the morning, hoping to receive a warmer reception.

The call ended too soon, and Mom again pleaded with the desk clerk. "Can't we just sit in the lobby until morning? It's only a few hours."

Still he refused.

"What are we supposed to do? We can't be on the street. It's past curfew. We'll be arrested."

Our other fear, the one Mom didn't bother explaining to the clerk, was that my dad was on our trail. He was intelligent and resourceful. His family had connections. We were certain he wouldn't be far behind us, and this would be a logical place to look.

The clerk's solution was that we could either ride around in a taxi all night or find another hotel. He called a cab and sent us on our way.

Mom did her best to reassure me, but this was a stinging defeat. We had come so close to reaching safety, only to be thrust back into the dangers that lurked in the night. The taxi drove us to another hotel, where Mom woefully explained our predicament. This time we met a more compassionate response. The clerk took pity on us and let Mom register under a different name.

The next morning, embassy officials were immensely relieved to see us. During the night, the American embassy in Ankara had been bombarded with calls from the State Department in Washington, DC, and the Swiss embassies in Bern and Tehran, all of which had been monitoring our situation for nearly eighteen months. Thankful that our blood was not on their hands, they jumped into action.

At lunchtime we were taken to a formal dining hall with an impressively long table, where we were presented with a feast of hamburgers and fresh raspberries. But after five days of being deprived of food, our stomachs wouldn't accept this splendid offering. Despite our best efforts and our excitement at seeing American food, we simply could not eat it.

Mom and I spent that day waiting. At one point we were taken to a dim and hushed room, where we were introduced to a very serious woman sitting behind a formidable desk. Without hinting at a smile, she handed me a child's art pad, an activity book, and a metal case of colored pencils. She looked me straight in the eye as she gave her instructions. "These are not for you to keep. You may use them only while you are here. Before you leave, you must return them to me."

I sat beside Mom and busied myself drawing. One of my pictures was sketched in pencil on stationery from the hotel where we had spent the previous night. The letterhead, on which I drew upside-down, was embossed with an oval navy-blue logo that depicted an eagle perched atop two elongated letters: *HD*—Hotel Dedeman.

I stopped and examined my handiwork. Nearly the entire page was covered in overlapping rows of imposing peaks, sharp zigzags scrawled with such force that they deeply scored the paper. In the bottom corner, removed from the mountains, lay a lake shaped like a mitten—the unmistakable shape of Michigan, my home. In the middle of that lake floated a boat with a striped flag. Along the northeastern shore of the lake, near the spot on the mitten where my family had lived before Iran, rested a house. Like countless houses I had seen in Tehran and on our trek through the mountains into Turkey, it was riddled with bullet holes. Smoke billowed from its chimney, and a large antenna protruded from its roof. Also jutting from the house was a massive flagpole bearing another striped flag that almost surpassed the building in size.

I quietly broke the heavy silence of our wait. "Mommy, how do you spell America?" Our voices echoed faintly down the corridor of wood and marble as she patiently told me the letters, one at a time, pausing between each one, so that I could carefully inscribe it above my flag: A M E r I C A.

Above the scene, in spite of the ominous mountains and the bullet holes, I added a sun, a reminder of the song Mom and I had often sung during our time in captivity: "The sun'll come out tomorrow . . ."

Maybe tomorrow wasn't "always a day away." Against all odds, it seemed that Mom and I were basking in the proverbial sunshine of tomorrow as we waited for the embassy officials to finalize our travel plans.

From nowhere came a great flurry of activity to get us on the plane that would take us one step closer to home. In the excitement, I wasn't able to get Mom's attention to return the art supplies. They were still in my hands when we were rushed out the door. For nearly three decades it has weighed on me that I didn't get to return them to the dour woman at the desk.

The rest of our journey was a blur. We flew from Ankara to Munich and then to Switzerland, or perhaps the other way around. Mom continued to call my grandparents with updates as she was able. At some point, she handed the phone over to me.

"Grandma, we're coming home," I said cheerfully. "We'll be there soon."

"Well, then, I'd better start baking pies for my little Tobby. What kind do you want?"

It was a dizzying thought. My grandma's pies were delectable. Blueberry, banana cream, lemon meringue, raspberry, cherry, rhubarb—I loved them all. I ordered one of each and probably asked for a batch of her sour-cream sugar cookies and molasses cookies with raisins too.

We flew to New York, where we landed late and missed our connecting flight. We spent the night in the airport with no food, no money except a quarter that fell out of a payphone, and no way to communicate with our family, who was waiting nervously for us to walk off a plane at the airport in Detroit. None of that seemed to matter at the time. We were back in America, but still we did not feel safe. We were plagued with visions of my dad disembarking from a plane in search of us.

I don't remember landing in Detroit. My first memory of being reunited with my family is of riding in the backseat of my aunt and uncle's car. Beside me sat a toy baby carrier holding the Cabbage Patch doll they had brought me. She was bald save for a small tuft of yellow yarn atop her head. The lovely scent of baby powder emanated from her smooth plastic face. She wore a white nightgown with pale-blue rosebuds similar to the dress I had worn home from the hospital, except mine had sported pale pink rosebuds and white lace. Before we went to Iran, I had put the dress on my favorite doll, a Gerber Baby doll I had affectionately named Jenny

J after my cousin. *Is she still wearing it?* I wondered as we made our way to my grandparents' house in the middle of the state.

I'm not sure what time of day it was, but there is no doubt that the sun was shining.

The door opened, and before me stretched the familiar stairs I had been longing to climb for eighteen months. It was Friday, February 7, 1986. I was six years old and weighed just thirty-six pounds—the same as when I had last set foot on this landing at the age of four. A good deal of that weight had to have come from my snarled mess of curly, waist-length, auburn hair. Mom was right behind me. We were both far beyond the point of exhaustion, but at the sight of that rickety old staircase, my sleepy eyes opened wide in anticipation. I knew what was to come next. It was tradition. Surely, he would still remember.

I climbed the first few steps and paused. Nothing. A few more steps. Silence. Gingerly I tiptoed to the top of the stairs and—"Boo!"

I jumped with a giggle. He remembered!

His voice was hardly more than a raspy whisper. An emaciated body laboriously appeared through the bathroom doorway on the left. Wearing a hospital gown and tethered to an IV pole, he was so weak he had to be supported by my brother John under one arm and my cousin under the other. But the mischievous glint was still bright in his eyes. There he stood—my grandpa.

At long last, we were home!

Grandma was waiting in the kitchen, which was filled with the mouth-watering aroma of my favorite pies. She had filled my order. I was in heaven.

Mom was one of six children, and most of her big family showed up to celebrate our return. The exception was my older brother, Joe. We got home just two days before his twentieth birthday. He lived on his own and, as was common in rural Michigan in the mid-1980s, Joe didn't have a home phone. Although he lived and worked within miles of my grandparents, no one had notified him of our escape, so he wasn't there when we arrived. It was otherwise a joyous time of hugs, laughter, and food.

That evening I was tucked snugly into my grandparents' warm bed, layers of soft blankets pulled up to my chin. Mom sat beside me. Taking my hands in hers, she began our bedtime prayers. "Dear God," she said, for the first time in a year and a half, not having to hide the fact that we were praying. "Thank you for bringing us back home to our family in America. Thank you for keeping us safe during our escape. Please continue to watch over us. Let nothing separate us. In Jesus' name we pray. Amen." Wearily she bent down and kissed me gently on the forehead. *"Shab be khair,"* she sighed. Good night.

Instantly my body went rigid with anger. Every inch of my being was filled with bitter, icy hatred. "Mommy," I spat, looking her defiantly in the eye, "I told you. I *never* want to hear Khomeini's language again!"

It was in Khomeini's language that I had first learned to hate. I hated my dad for hurting my mom. I hated his family for letting it happen. I hated the school in Iran for making me curse my country. I hated Khomeini for killing people who didn't believe his lies. I hated the Pasdar who roamed the streets of Tehran with their machine guns, looking for wardrobe offenses. I hated Iraq's bombs.

I hated.

CHAPTER 11

The next day my Aunt Carolyn, a Mary Kay independent beauty consultant, came back—this time with her boxy pink makeup case in hand. She set up shop at the dining room table and lived the Mary Kay mission of "enriching women's lives." By the time she was done, I had been given my mom back—the vibrant and beautiful woman who had vanished the day my dad turned us into prisoners. My brother John had been conned into doing a facial along with Mom. It hadn't seemed like such a bad idea to him until someone pulled out a camera. He ran for cover, but Mom caught him rounding the kitchen table. When the picture was snapped, he was snickering as he tried to wriggle free of her grasp. Mom had his arms pinned behind his back. Her head was thrown back in jubilant laughter. It was good to be home.

Later that evening, Mom took John and me to meet our friends Doug and Karen for dinner. I didn't know it then, but the framework for my double life was already being put into place. Hearing the particulars of our ordeal, Karen told Mom she had to write a book. Mom had brazenly told people in Iran that we would escape and that someday they would read about this. People needed to know this type of danger existed in our world. First, though, we had to put our lives back together. Karen asked if she could share our story with her brother, who worked in the publishing industry. Mom said yes. The ball was rolling.

On Sunday Mom and Grandma spent the day preparing for Joe's birthday celebration. As they cooked, Grandpa's condition worsened. Against all odds, he had managed to stave off death awaiting our return—a feat his doctors said was nothing short of a miracle. When Mom and I came home, he was nothing more than an eighty-pound bag of skin and bones, though his jolly gruffness hadn't suffered an ounce's loss. He was confined to a hospital bed in his living room, where he passed his time enjoying the birds at the feeder and dreaming of hunting and fishing. Always a lighthearted and jovial soul, now he begged us not to make him laugh because it was just too painful. His doctor still made house calls, but even that didn't keep the ambulance away. Before Joe's birthday meal was ready, Grandpa had to be rushed to the hospital.

That week brought with it one implausible scenario after another. Mom received an unlikely call from an agent at the William Morris Agency in New York. He was eager for her to write a book. She was exhausted from being up all night with Grandpa on top of the trauma of our escape, the pressure of not knowing how to rebuild our lives, and the fear of my father's retribution. She told him she would definitely write a book someday, but now was not the time.

The next day he called back, this time offering rebuttals to all Mom's objections. He could arrange for an advance on royalties. That meant writing could be Mom's job. The advance would allow her to get a house and work from home. She could spend all her time with me, ensuring my safety. How could she possibly say no?

By midweek the media had become aware of our story. One afternoon Uncle Jim drove Grandma home from the hospital for some rest. She, like much of the family, had been keeping a constant vigil at Grandpa's side. The emotional and physical strain was taking its toll on everyone.

The phone rang, and Grandma answered, expecting it to be a nurse calling her back to the hospital or a concerned loved one calling to check in. Instead it was Barbara Walters, asking to speak with Mom. Grandma gave her the number for the hospital. You can imagine the stir a call from the most famous female journalist in America, the coanchor of the renowned news program *20/20*, caused in rural Carson City, Michigan, a town with a population of around a thousand. Ms. Walters explained to Mom that she would like very much to interview us. It was clear, even then, that simply stepping into the routine of our past lives would not be an option.

From an extremely young age, the minutiae of the world had intrigued me. Soaking in a tub filled with toys, I would focus instead on the water dripping from the faucet—the drip that swelled and stretched into a tear shape before falling into the pool of water, the drop that leapt from the surface, bringing with it some of the liquid from below, only to fall once more and dissolve into ripples. Springy doorstops held a similar enchantment—the blur brought on by the spring oscillating faster than my eyes could focus, the boing reverberating in time with the movement, the magical moment when the fuzziness of the coil gave way to crispness as it slowed. These were just some of my earliest fascinations.

To say I was observant is an understatement. Things others overlooked were glaringly obvious to me. Whether a blessing or a curse, this quiet attentiveness quickly became a mandatory safety precaution. Every sound, movement, unspoken word meant something, and even as a very small child I sensed the vital importance of noticing all that happened around me.

Whenever the phone rang in those days following our escape, I saw the panic in the eyes of my aunts and uncles, my grandparents, and my mom. No one had to explain the fear to me. I felt it too. A knock on the door or a car turning in to the driveway, expected or not, had the same momentarily paralyzing effect.

One might expect that our reunion with our family would mark the end of our struggles and the beginning of a new, peace-filled existence. That simply wasn't the case. Even though Mom and I were home, there was no finality to the previous chapter of our lives. My dad's vow to find us— to kill Mom and take me back to Iran—hung over us and our loved ones.

Returning to America, Mom quickly learned that, while we were in Iran, my dad had sent his nephew Mammal back to the States to liquidate our assets. He had transferred all my parents' money into Swiss bank accounts. Mom and I were penniless. Without hesitation, however, my grandparents welcomed us into their home.

The St. Patrick's Day Parade was in full swing the day Mom, John, and I met Barbara Walters at the Mayflower Hotel in New York City. Feeling very grown-up to be wearing a pair of Mom's pearl earrings, I sat beside her on the couch, surrounded by lights, cameras, booms, makeup artists, producers, and sound technicians. In the midst of the chaos, calm as could be, sat Barbara Walters. Elegant and poised, she was a beacon of refinement. She leaned in as she softly asked her questions, creating a sense of intimacy. As usual I said nothing, only observed. She tried her best to engage me in conversation, and although I felt an instant affinity toward her, I was too shy to utter a word. She respected my silence, and her approving smile assured me that there was no shame in remaining mum.

It was a question about school that finally elicited a response. Mom got as far as describing our morning chant, *"Maag barg Amrika,"* before I could take no more and gently reached up to cover her mouth with my hand. Words aren't always necessary for communicating the heaviness of our hearts. Acknowledging that she had touched on a topic that was still too painful, Ms. Walters artfully moved on.

When the interview was finished, she treated us to a night on the town. We ate at Benihana, a Japanese restaurant where the food was prepared at the table. Although I was no stranger to the theater, that evening I had my first Broadway experience with front-row tickets to the musical *Cats*. Everything about it was sensational—the music, the dancing, the costumes. Then we took a ride in a horse-drawn carriage through Central Park, and I felt like a princess listening to the hypnotic clippity-clop of the horse's hooves.

For John's sixteenth birthday, *20/20* sent a production team to capture additional footage of our family. Joe wanted nothing to do with the interview process, and Mom didn't force the issue. Others in the family were only slightly less reluctant, with the exception of Grandpa. He was his usual to-the-point self. A member of "the greatest generation," he showed himself to be both stoic and a true optimist, asserting that he'd never doubted Mom would find a way to escape. Grandma was overcome by emotion and struggled to get the words out. John, perhaps most articulately, gave voice to our family's shared pain when he frankly described the anguish of going to bed each night not knowing if Mom and I were dead or alive. It was our loved ones, waiting helplessly for our return, who bore the brunt of the hurt caused by my dad's actions. I had Mom at my side fighting for me. My brothers suffered this brutal injustice on their own.

That interview was the *only* time we as an extended family discussed our experiences. Even then, we didn't speak about it with each other, only with Barbara Walters and her producers. Mom had grown up in a culture of avoidance, where painful issues weren't discussed and problems weren't dealt with. But starting with me, she broke the cycle of silent suffering.

My life was destined to be lived in extremes. Swirling in a sea of turmoil and upheaval, I was nevertheless, in many ways, experiencing an idyllic childhood. At my grandparents' house I was surrounded by an extended family who doted on me. They lived along a rural highway in the middle of Michigan's mitten. The sprawling front yard was densely packed with trees Grandpa had planted years earlier. My cousins and I inundated Grandma with bouquets of wild flowers—light-purple clover blossoms, deep yellow dandelions, velvety cattails, and snowy Queen Anne's lace.

In the evenings, the grown-ups played euchre or pinochle on the dining room table while my cousins and I tried our hands at crazy eights or go fish at the kids' table. When we tired of playing cards, we raided the coffee table in the living room for coloring books and crayons. Sometimes Uncle Jim, the jokester of the family and a big kid at heart, would usher the children outside for a game of Wiffle ball.

My cousin Jenny, two weeks my senior and the namesake of my favorite doll, liked to stay over at my grandparents' house. We slept together in our matching Rainbow Brite nighties. Happy to have me home, the grown-ups tended to indulge me, but Jenny, being a child, wasn't burdened by the need for tact.

One afternoon, I was trying to tell her that something tasted bitter. Even though I had sworn off Khomeini's language, some words still eluded me in English. Desperate to find a way to communicate, I resorted to mixing languages. "It was *talkh*." Jenny gave me a sideways glance that clearly meant she didn't understand what I was saying. So I said it again. "Talkh."

"Huh?" She tilted her head and scrunched her nose.

"Talkh. It was talkh," I repeated, frustrated with her for not understanding.

"Where'd you learn to talk anyway?" she asked, then ran away giggling at the absurdity of my frustration.

I sought comfort and felt most rooted in the familiar. One of the first things I spotted at my grandparents' house after our return was the purple vase I had painted with Patty. Grandma had it on the shelf reserved for special treasures that were too precious to risk being broken by curious little fingers. She saw me looking at it and asked if I wanted it back. I pondered for a moment, then answered cheerfully, "No, you keep it, but when you die, can I have it?"

I was not yet seven, but I had been on this earth long enough to know that Grandma thought she was dying. She was one of those people who just seemed to always have one foot in the grave. In reality, it was my grandpa who was inching toward the grave. Many of our early days of freedom were spent at his bedside at Carson City Hospital. It was the hospital where both of my brothers had been born, the hospital where my parents had met, and the hospital where my grandpa now fought for his life.

Sometimes, while Grandpa slept, we went to the local diner for lunch. Joe liked to treat me to songs on the diner's old-fashioned jukebox. He would pull a chair over so I could climb up and watch as he dropped in the coins and pushed the buttons to select the songs. My favorite was Ronnie Milsap singing "Happy, Happy Birthday Baby." It was not a cool song by big-brother standards, but he always played it for me without complaint because that was the one I liked.

On the surface we seemed like a normal family, but our collective distress could easily become apparent. Everyone was constantly on high alert. The men in my family, feeling the burden of the responsibility to keep us safe, huddled together furiously whispering about what they would do to "that worthless SOB" if he ever came after us. The children were given strict orders not to touch the loaded shotgun that stood behind my grandparents' bedroom door. Someone always had a protective eye on me, and on the rare occasions when they realized no one was pulling guard duty, panic ensued.

On one such afternoon the adults in the house suddenly realized that no one knew where I was, and a frantic search commenced. I was discovered huddled in a corner in the fetal position. I had heard an airplane and taken cover. That was what life in a war zone had trained me to do. How was I to know that in America planes didn't drop bombs?

Another day I was riding in the car with Aunt Carolyn when sirens sounded behind us. Trembling and shrieking in terror, I clung to her. My experience with authorities included machine guns and death threats. I was certain they would kill us on the spot, send me back to my dad, or imprison Aunt Carolyn. But to my surprise, when the officer approached the car, he spoke gently and sent us on our way, telling us to have a nice day. There was a lot I had to relearn about life in America.

That August Grandpa's battle came to an end. He died in peace, knowing that Mom and I were back home where we belonged. His death marked a perplexing milestone in my life. I was old enough to miss him instantly and yet young enough to wholeheartedly rejoice in the fact that he was in heaven where he suffered no more. I didn't understand the tears that accompanied Mom's grief. One evening during a visitation at the funeral home, after watching Mom cry for days, I finally had to ask. "Mommy, Grandpa's with Jesus. Why are you crying?"

"I know," she answered feebly, "I'm just sad that he won't be here with us anymore. It's okay to cry when you're sad."

Still, I didn't cry.

Grandpa was given a military burial. At the cemetery we gathered around his flag-draped coffin. I recoiled when I caught sight of the uniformed soldiers who had come to carry out the honors. Two soldiers folded Grandpa's flag with precision, their motions crisp and exact. Then one turned sharply, clapped his heels together, and marched with purpose toward Grandma. Kneeling humbly, he held out the neatly folded triangle of blue studded with white stars. His gentleness was perplexing to me. In Iran I had come into contact with countless soldiers. Never before had I seen one behave in such a way.

By the time of Grandpa's death, the manuscript for *Not Without My Daughter* was well underway. Mom had used part of the advance money to rent a small house on the outskirts of the town that I would later come to think of as my hometown. The broken chain-link fence on the side of the house served as my play set. The mesh of fencing had pulled off just enough of the frame to leave me ample room for twirling around the bar or hanging upside down, my long, unruly hair dragging on the ground. Wanting to bring some vitality to our humble dwelling, I proudly filled mom's beautiful blue vase from Japan with weeds that grew in the unkempt flowerbeds.

What stands out most in my mind about the months Mom was writing is the amount of pizza we ate. I don't know how she did everything she did—setting up a new home, taking care of me and my brothers, and spending every possible second with Grandpa and the rest of our family, all while throwing herself headlong into the writing process. Something had to be overlooked, and that something was cooking. For the first time ever, we lived on junk food.

Mom's coauthor, William Hoffer, lived with his wife, Marilyn, and their children outside of Washington, DC. He spent a great deal of time with us in Michigan, but Mom and I also traveled to his home to collaborate. With disheveled hair and the bushy beard of an eccentric genius, Bill looked like an author to me. He was a jolly man who smoked a pipe and liked to be silly with the kids. At the same time he was a profound thinker, a man thirsting for a more thorough understanding of the world around him. This quest to learn had led him to become knowledgeable on a vast array of topics. It was perhaps in watching Bill and Marilyn passionately expound upon relevant philosophical issues with Mom that my love affair with deep intellectual conversation was born. Knowing how much I missed Mr. Bunny and how much I loved books, they gave me a beautifully illustrated copy of *The Velveteen Rabbit,* along with a matching plush rabbit. It didn't replace the bunny I had left behind in Iran, but it was a kind gesture intended to validate my loss and assuage my grief.

When Mom and I went to work with Bill and Marilyn, we usually stayed at their home, but once we stayed in a hotel and were confronted with the fear that was omnipresent in our lives. Mom and Bill had worked late into the night, and we returned to the hotel room exhausted. Half asleep, Mom slid the key into the lock and turned the knob. Abruptly the chain caught stopping the door from opening fully.

Mom grabbed me and raced to the hotel lobby, where she breathlessly explained to the clerk that someone was in our room. Rushing back to the room with us he hesitantly turned the key and unlatched the door. This time it opened. The chain had been released, and whoever was inside had vanished. A quick inventory of our belongings revealed that nothing had been taken save for our already feeble sense of security.

When we first escaped, Mom had thought we would change our names and go into hiding. But upon learning that I couldn't legally change my name without the consent of both parents and that going into hiding meant completely cutting all ties with our friends and family, she'd decided that wasn't an option. My father had made us prisoners long enough; we wouldn't sacrifice the rest of our lives to his rule. Writing the book proved to be the perfect solution, giving us the extra one-on-one time we needed to adjust to our new circumstances. Instead of going into hiding, we embraced the opposite extreme. Mom told our story to anyone who would listen, hoping that the public attention would serve as an added measure of security.

Whenever she could take a short break from writing, Mom diligently made her way through our belongings from before we went to Iran. When my parents and I hadn't returned from "vacation," everything had been packed up and put into storage. Now Mom faced the monumental task of sorting through the relics of our past lives and deciding which items belonged in our present.

It was painful for me to see piles of our old belongings going into the trash. The more Mom sorted, the more she pitched. And as soon as she turned her attention back to writing, I would pilfer through the garbage, ferreting away worthless treasures that I wasn't yet ready to part with. One was a giant aqua-colored pen that had belonged to my dad. I don't know why I felt compelled to keep it. I was angry with him. I feared him. I hated him. Yet I was drawn to the things that represented who he had been when he was still my beloved Baba Jon. I also kept his medical bag and two of his scrub jackets. One became my painting smock, and the other hung in the back of my closet for years.

Then there was my Care Bear bouncy ball. Taking it in my hands, I brought it to my nose and inhaled deeply. "Mommy, it smells like Stacey!"

The aroma had transported me back to the summer days spent running through the sprinkler and playing on the swing set, the days before the innocence of my childhood was shattered.

CHAPTER 12

As summer drew to a close, so did my opportunity to remain at Mom's protective side. I needed to start school, and Mom decided to enroll me in a private school where the teachers, she hoped, would be able to keep an eye on me and any suspicious activity on my dad's part would easily set off warning bells. She enrolled me at Salem, the local Lutheran school. In order to protect myself and the other students, I would use a different name. In August of 1986, the embassy hostage crisis had not been forgotten, and the Iran Contra Affair was about to capture the world's attention. Aside from violence and hatred toward America and American ideals, not much was known in the United States about Iran, and school officials were understandably cautious.

Further complicating our situation was the fact that the legal systems had not caught up with our globalizing society. When Mom inquired about filing for divorce, she was told that she would be required to serve notice on my father so he could defend himself in court. If my dad knew where we were, it would be easier for him to make good on his threats. We were going to great lengths to stay hidden from him, so her divorce would have to wait.

While I couldn't officially change my name, however, nothing prevented me from simply *using* a different name. The night before my first day of school, Mom sat me down and taught me my new name, explaining that my real name would now be our secret. I would be known as Amanda Smith, Mandy for short, just like her first doll.

I took easily to my new name. I did not take easily, however, to relating with other children my age. I was quiet and awkward, an easy target for the other kids in my neighborhood. They teased me because I was different, because I didn't talk, because I wasn't any good at riding a bike, and especially because I had trouble staying in my seat. Used to standing at a desk for the duration of the school day, I had difficulty adjusting to sitting while I worked. At times, engrossed in a task, I would forget to remain in my seat, only realizing I had risen when the giggles of the other children reached my ears. Self-consciously, I would slump into my seat and fold in on myself.

Things soon got better, though. A girl named Jamie was one of the first classmates to reach out to me. She offered her chunky Care Bear pencil and a smile, signaling to the others that I was now officially one of the family.

My seventh birthday arrived a month, almost to the day, after my grandpa died. To mark the occasion, Joe gave me his stereo and a Ronnie Milsap cassette tape so I could listen to "Happy, Happy Birthday Baby," otherwise known as "my song." whenever I wanted. Just as in Iran, even after our escape, it was the things that connected me to my loved ones in some tangible way that I held most dear.

That autumn we moved to a house in an adjacent town. It was my tenth move, but I didn't mind it. Our new house was across the street from a golf course, the yard was filled with beautiful old trees eager to drop mountains of leaves for me to jump in. Joe and John were both living with us, and life was good. Salem had become my sanctuary, my source of structure and stability. The consistent routine of school life provided a sense of security that I desperately needed.

The eight o'clock bell rang, and we were all seated quietly with our hands folded atop our desks. Mrs. Hatzung stood at the front of the class in her cornflower-blue dress, cinched at the waist with a thick matching belt. She wore camel-colored shoes with the slightest hint of a heel. She was tender and kind like a grandma.

Punctual as ever, in marched the principal. He was fit for a middle-aged man, with hair and a goatee that matched his gray suit. He paused at the front of the room and greeted Mrs. Hatzung. Turning, he added, "Good morning, first graders."

"Good morning, Mr. Schultz," we answered in unison, just as we'd practiced.

Mrs. Hatzung beamed approvingly. And with that, he was off to pay his morning visit to the second graders next door.

"Okay, children, join me up front for our opening devotion. Today we're going to talk about Joseph," Mrs. Hatzung announced. She took the devotional calendar down from the sunny yellow wall and flipped the page.

Each morning brought with it a new calendar picture and an accompanying Bible lesson. There was David, the young shepherd who, armed only with a slingshot and his faith in God, had defeated Goliath, a fierce Philistine giant. Then there was Daniel, who'd been thrown into the lions' den for praying to his God, which was forbidden by the government, just like in Iran. God had sent an angel to close the mouths of the lions so Daniel wouldn't be eaten. Even better, the king had seen this miracle and believed.

Even though she was a grown-up, Mrs. Hatzung sat on a first-grade-sized red plastic chair with metal legs. We formed a tight half circle around her in our matching chairs. This was my favorite part of the school day. Fearing that each lesson could be the last before my dad snatched me back to Iran, where the Bible was forbidden, I hungered to store up every kernel of God's Word.

It turned out that Joseph and I had much in common. He'd been taken away from his family, too, though I'd had it better than he did. I'd had my mom with me, while Joseph, sold as a slave by his brothers, had been all alone. I wondered if he'd watched the moon the way I had when my dad took me away from my mom. Had he known that no matter where you are, you can look at the moon and know that your family is looking at the same moon and thinking of you?

God had protected Joseph just as he'd protected Daniel and David— just as he had protected Mom and me. Years later, when Joseph's family was starving because of famine, Joseph had forgiven his brothers for being jealous of his colorful coat and their father's love. He'd had pity on them and given them food.

That's where Joseph and I differed. I could never forgive my dad for what he did to us. I hated him. I never wanted to see him again—ever.

"You've done a very nice job listening today. Now you may return to your desks, but please remain standing." Mrs. Hatzung's words broke into my thoughts, bringing me back to our cheerful yellow classroom.

Each day after devotion, we watched with excitement as Mrs. Hatzung took her yardstick from the ledge beneath the chalkboard and made her way across the room. Sandwiched on the wall between our most recent artistic creations and an oversized poster of a box of crayons in a rainbow of colors ran two rows of numbers. They would be the focus of our next exercise.

I surveyed our drawings as Mrs. Hatzung approached the wall. They were as unique and varied as the pupils who filled the room. Here, unlike in Iran, we were free to color our pictures any hue we chose.

With the yardstick, Mrs. Hatzung pointed to our number for the day. On the first day of school, back in August, she had started with the number one. Each day we added a number. She liked to ask us if we thought we would get all the way to two hundred before summer. I had a hunch she knew the answer, but she wouldn't tell. She just grinned and said, "You'll have to wait and see."

"It's time to count," she said today. "First let's count by twos." She pointed to the numbers as we said them.

"Two, four, six," we recited.

"Nicely done, students. Now by fives."

When the 3:15 the bell rang, we were dismissed for the day. Mrs. Hatzung waited at the door with a hug for each student as she sent us on our way. Our teachers took turns waiting outside with us until our parents arrived. That day it was Miss Neujahr's turn. She would be my teacher the next year. The bigger kids said she sometimes played her guitar when her class sang hymns instead of the piano like the other teachers. My favorite hymn so far was "Now Thank We All Our God," which we were learning for Thanksgiving.

"Now thank we all our God," I sang in my head,

> With hearts and hands and voices,
> Who wondrous things hath done,
> In whom his world rejoices;
> Who from our mothers' arms
> hath blessed us on our way . . .

(That was my favorite line, the one about our mothers' arms.)

> With countless gifts of love,
> And still is ours today.

We lined up along the brick wall of the school, looked beyond the kickball field and through the fence, and watched for our parents' cars to appear on the street. The other kids took off running at the first glimpse of their car. Not I. None of the students knew about my dad, but all the teachers were aware of the danger he posed and so were ever vigilant.

I continued in my head with verse two of the hymn, which ends with the promise that God will

> . . . keep us in his grace,
> And guide us when perplexed,
> And free us from all ills
> In this world and the next.

Mrs. Hatzung said *perplexed* meant confused and that when we found ourselves unsure of what to do in life, we could go to God in prayer. She said he heard our prayers and he'd make everything work out for our good. That didn't mean we'd always get what we wanted. God was wiser than we were, and we could trust that what he gave us was always in our best interest, even if we didn't recognize it right away. I thought about this as I scanned the cars that stopped on the edge of the schoolyard.

My mind wandered back to Joseph. His brothers had intended to harm him, but God had used Joseph to save his family and many others. Mrs. Hatzung said that God worked the same way in our lives today. Sometimes things looked really bad on the surface, but God could use even the bad things for our good down the road.

I was contemplating Mrs. Hatzung's words when Mom drove up. Quietly I tugged on Miss Neujahr's sleeve and pointed.

"Okay, go ahead, Mandy," she said after confirming that it was Mom behind the wheel, "have a nice night."

Then and only then was I permitted to leave my post along the wall. Miss Neujahr watched until I was safely in the car.

Mom was not wearing her typical smile. "I've got some sad news, Mahtob," she said softly. "Today there was a plane crash in Iran, and a lot of Iranian people died." She was obviously shaken.

I looked past her out the window and said nothing.

"Did you hear what I said?" Mom asked quietly. "A lot of Iranian people died today."

Still staring blankly ahead, I crossed my arms over my chest, "Good," I huffed. "I hope my dad was one of them."

Rarely can one look back and know at precisely which moment one's life was set on a different course. Generally, such shifts happen gradually and go somewhat unnoticed. Yet in all our lives, there are key moments that stand out as life altering. That conversation in the car with Mom on November 3, 1986, proved to be one of the clearly evident crossroads in my life.

It was a startling wakeup call for Mom to see that I had mutated into someone cold and bitter. That was not the life she wanted for me. She hadn't fought to free us so that I could waste my life wallowing in anger and hostility. As long as hatred ruled my heart, my father would imprison me even in his absence. Mom was not going to stand idly by and let that happen. That very day she jumped into action.

For her, writing *Not Without My Daughter* had been deeply cathartic. She'd been forced to explain to the reader all the sides of my father—not only the bad that was foremost in our minds, but also the good that had drawn her to him in the first place. Mom recognized that if I were to have any chance of being free, I needed to be forced, as she had been, to remember the endearing qualities of the daddy I had once loved.

That night she pulled out the photo albums bursting with images my father had captured for posterity, many of which flagrantly boasted a red fox on the reverse. We flipped through photos of birthdays, holidays, vacations, dinner parties, even quiet everyday moments. There were pictures of me on the day I was born, at my first Halloween (dressed as an angel and sleeping on Mom's shoulder), crawling, standing, taking my first steps, eating my first strawberry, posing by the haft sin each No-ruz.

Each picture offered a glimpse into my past, but not just mine. Each was also, in some way, a reflection of the photographer. My dad had adored me so wholeheartedly that he was compelled to capture and hold on to every possible moment of my life. There was nothing about me that didn't fill him with joy to the point of wanting to carry the memory with him in a tangible way.

With the turn of each page, Mom regaled me examples of my father's love. "Remember how you used to love gardening with your daddy?" she would ask, flipping to an image of me as a toddler squatting beside him in our garden. "Remember how much fun you and your daddy had swimming?" She'd point to me timidly leaping from the edge of the pool into his outstretched arms.

When Patty got married, I had been her flower girl. Mom had put my hair in ringlets and I had worn a handmade white lace dress with a crinoline and delicate pink satin accents. A picture of that day showed my dad, looking handsome in his crisp gray suit and his chunky-framed glasses, kneeling beside me in the church aisle. He wrapped his arm around me, and together we grinned at the camera.

Page by page, Mom forced me to confront our past. Image by image, she told me the stories of our family life together before Iran. But with each story, I pressed myself to hold on to my hatred even more resolutely. I would not allow myself to love him.

It was the pictures of him that I most abhorred because in looking at his image, there was no denying he was part of me. The resemblance was undeniable. No matter how violently I fought it, my father and I were inextricably bound to one another. I couldn't hate him without hating a part of myself. But I tried.

My disdain wasn't confined to him alone. I wanted to run as far away as humanly possible from any remembrance of my past. I despised anything and everything that had to do with him or our time in Iran.

Mom was tireless in her efforts. Every day she offered up reminders of good times with my dad and my Persian heritage. She read me the books that he had read to me. She sang me his songs and told me his nursery rhymes. She cooked Persian food. It was a slow process but she was persistent.

Over time, despite my best efforts, more palatable memories of my father began to resurface. In the years before we had gone to Iran, I had been a daddy's girl. If he was reading at his desk, I was almost certainly sitting at his feet, often surrounded by old medical journals and a pair of children's scissors. My favorite organ was the heart. While he analyzed the latest scientific advances, I would carefully cut out images of the human heart. Periodically he would lean forward to inspect my work. "Very good, *Azzi zam*," he would praise, going on to educate me about how the organ worked. He was almost as passionate about instilling his scientific knowledge in me as he was about the science itself.

If he was in the kitchen, I was standing at his side, eager to learn the nutritional value of each ingredient. "*Narenge*," he would say, holding up an orange he was about to peel. "Oranges are very nutritious, Mahtob Jon. They are high in Vitamin C." I loved it when he held the rind in front of my face and folded it backward, showering me in a glorious mist of orange essence.

My dad also swore by yogurt, which we made on a regular basis. I loved the *ruh*, the stretchy white film that developed on top of the milk when it was heated. Also high on his list of healing agents was saliva. Whether I bit my cheek, burned my finger, or had a paper cut, saliva was the answer. "Just suck on it," he'd instruct. "Your saliva will provide everything that's needed for cleansing and healing. Hippocrates was right when he said the body was designed to heal itself."

CHAPTER 13

I was still wrestling with my slowly softening heart when Mom, spurred on by the transformative power of her makeover in the hours following our homecoming, became a Mary Kay consultant. When our "Armenian side of the family" heard the news, they were eager to show their support. Vergine gathered the ladies at her house for a skin-care class. Ever poised to help despite my bashful nature, I was Mom's assistant. When it was time for blush, I begged Mom to dab a little on my cheeks. Next came the eyeliner. Mom put it on me just like the diagram showed—at the outside corner of the eye above the top lashes and below the bottom ones.

"There, how's that?" she asked, handing me the mirror.

I took one look and told her she didn't do it right.

"I did," she protested. "It's just like the drawing."

"That's not how I want it," I whined. "I want it the Iranian way."

"I don't know the Iranian way, Mahtob."

"Yes, you do," I argued, on the verge of an uncharacteristic meltdown.

Vergine, knowing what I was asking for, stepped in. "Come here, Mahtob. I'll show you, honey."

Still pouting, I walked around the table and stood before her. Vergine removed the eyeliner from below my lashes. With a charcoal-black eye pencil she traced my eyelid, following the curve in one fluid stroke.

Then, telling me to look up, she started at the outside and followed the ridge above my lower lashes all the way to the tear duct. After she did the same with the other eye, she turned me toward the mirror.

Examining my reflection, I saw a pair of dark-brown, almond-shaped eyes that testified to my Iranian ancestry. That was exactly what I had wanted.

Why would I want to look Iranian when I was so purposefully separating myself from all such reminders? I do not know. I cannot even say why I associated any form of makeup with my Persian heritage. During our time in Iran, makeup had been strictly forbidden. But before we went to Iran, my dad had kept albums filled with pictures of his family from the time of the shah. The women wore vibrantly colored, ultrashort, sleeveless dresses. Their hair was dyed and piled high atop their heads in the updos that were so fashionable in the late 1960s and early 1970s. And their eyes were embellished with intense green eye shadow and black eyeliner drawn on just as Vergine had done for me.

So perhaps Mom's lessons were taking root. Perhaps, in my own way, I was struggling to connect with my Persian heritage. Even though I continued to fight her every step of the way, occasionally I could be caught secretly celebrating my dad's enriching contributions to my life.

That winter Mrs. Hatzung asked our first grade class, "Who has been baptized?"

Arms shot enthusiastically into the air. I glanced around sheepishly, wondering whether or not to join my classmates with their hands waving above their heads. I noticed only two other students who hid their hands, looking as confused as I felt. Still, I wasn't alone, and that was reassuring. I didn't know if I'd been baptized. In truth, I didn't know what baptism was.

That afternoon, before I even climbed into the car, the question burst from my lips.

"Mommy, am I baptized?"

"What?"

"Have I been baptized?" I was too thrilled to wait for her answer. "Mrs. Hatzung says it's really important. God gives us baptism as a gift, and when we're baptized he washes our sins away and strengthens our faith so we can go to heaven. Jesus was baptized by John the Baptist. And all three persons of the Trinity were there. God the Father spoke from heaven and said Jesus was his Son and he was 'well pleased' with him. The Holy Spirit was there as a dove. He landed on Jesus when he came out of the water. And well, Jesus was there as Jesus. And even though there are three persons in the Trinity, there's just one God. It's a miracle, something our simple human minds can't quite understand, but we believe it because it's in the Bible and everything in the Bible is true."

I couldn't contain my fervor. This newfound knowledge was so earth-shattering that the words just poured out. I couldn't wait to tell Mom every bit of what I had just learned.

"Mrs. Hatzung asked us to raise our hands if we'd been baptized," I continued breathlessly. "I didn't raise mine because I didn't know. So have I been baptized?"

Mom was still explaining that I hadn't been when I interrupted and announced matter-of-factly, "I want to be baptized."

"Okay. If you want to you can be baptized."

"When?"

"I don't know. I'll talk with Pastor and see what he says."

"Good. Mrs. Hatzung says that through baptism, God plants the seed of faith in our hearts and that just like seeds need sunshine and water to grow, God grows our faith when we hear his Word in the Bible. That's why even once I'm baptized, it's important to keep studying the Bible and going to church . . ." In my elation, my mouth just couldn't stop moving.

The next morning at school, eager to share the grand news, I excitedly announced, "Mrs. Hatzung, I haven't been baptized, but Mom says I can be. She'll talk with Pastor."

"Well, that *is* great news, Mandy." She gave me a hug. "I'm very happy for you, dear."

That afternoon I ran to the car, excited to hear when the big day would be. Opening the door, I asked, "Did you talk with Pastor?"

"No, Mahtob, not yet. I had a busy day. Don't worry, I will."

Mom's plate was overflowing at the time. She had good intentions of scheduling my baptism; she was just stretched too thin. Days turned into weeks. Christmas came and went, and still I was not baptized. By the time Mom and Bill finished the manuscript on January 2, I had grown weary of waiting for the arrangements to be made. "Mommy," I threatened, "if you don't talk with Pastor, I will."

Knowing me to be true to my word, Mom talked with Pastor. He chose a Thursday in January for the baptism. To mark the occasion, my whole class joined me for a field trip to our church across town. They filled the pews at the front of the sanctuary wrapped in their bulky winter coats, feet dangling in the space between the padded wooden benches and the floor.

I stood beside Mom on the edge of the chancel, wearing a frilly white dress and matching crocheted socks pulled up over my calves. Mom had pulled my hair back with a bow, but my curls, stubborn as ever, stuck out in all directions. Around my neck hung a gold cross, a gift from Mom in honor of my big day.

It felt funny to stand in the pastor's territory. This was God's house. Children didn't generally enter that area. That may have been the first time I set foot beyond the pews that lined the nave, a fact that added to the reverence I felt that afternoon.

Pastor Schaller, wearing his black robe and white stole, opened with prayer and talked with all of us about the meaning of baptism, through which I would become a child of God. He addressed Mom on her responsibility as a parent to instruct me in God's Word and then turned his attention to me.

"Receive the sign of the cross on the head and heart to mark you as a redeemed child of Christ." Using his thumb and first two fingers, to represent the Trinity, he traced a cross in the air above my head and another above my heart. When it was time for me to lean over the baptismal font so he could pour water on my head, a ripple of laughter echoed through the pews as, one by one, the small congregation realized I was too short to reach.

Chuckling, Pastor Schaller tenderly bent down and picked me up. Holding me in one arm, he cupped his other hand and dipped into the font. A trail of water dripped from his hand as he brought it to my forehead. "Amanda Sue Smith, I baptize you in the name of the Father." He poured the water over my head and dipped his hand again into the basin. "And of the Son," he continued as he applied the second handful of water to my forehead and reached for a third. "And of the Holy Spirit." Then he dabbed the drops from my eyes with the crisp linen handkerchief embroidered with a white dove like the one that landed on Jesus after his baptism. "The Almighty God—Father, Son, and Holy Spirit—has forgiven all your sins. By your baptism you are born again and made a dear child of your Father in heaven. May God strengthen you to live in your baptismal grace all the days of your life. Peace be with you."

Just like that I was baptized, and I was ecstatic. The service concluded with prayer and compulsory pictures at the front of the church. As was common for much of my youth, I looked miserable, though I felt elated. In shot after shot, everyone beamed while I frowned. The exception was a photo of just my beloved teacher and me. In her presence it was safe to think, to speak, even to feel. With her standing behind me, the tiniest hint of a smile pushed its way to the surface.

That randomly picked Thursday happened to be January 29, 1987. When Pastor Schaller chose the date, he didn't know that it would be one year to the day from when Mom and I left our house in Iran. January 29 was our freedom day. It seems somehow fitting that the day I celebrate freedom from my dad's oppression is also the day I celebrate my freedom from the oppression of sin, death, and the power of the devil.

If not for the first, I certainly wouldn't be able to celebrate the second. "God is so gooood."

At the beginning of my second grade year, we moved yet again, this time to a charming two-story, white pre–Civil War era house back in my "hometown." Mom and I shared an upstairs bedroom. She had long since given up on forcing me to sleep in my own room. Sleep was as torturous for her as it was for me. We fought the same demon, except in her dreams he wasn't cloaked as a fox.

I used to will myself to fall asleep as quickly as possible in the hope of slumbering through her screams. I knew the stages of Mom's sleep: first came the snoring, and when the snoring stopped the screaming began.

"Moody, no," she'd beg. "Don't take her from me. Mahtob, run." She kicked, scratched, and pleaded. She wrestled her demon tirelessly, and just when her body began to quiet, it seemed the monster would once again intensify his assault. "You stay away from her," she would growl, her voice icy and steeled with the determination that stems only from a mother's desperate struggle to protect her child. "Help! Somebody help!"

I would nudge her arm gently, whispering, "It's only a dream, Mommy. We're safe." But my small voice was usually too soft to break through to her. Eventually her frenetic screaming would give way to bitter wailing. My head would pound. My stomach would churn. I would roll on my side, turning my back to her, burying my head beneath the pillow, pressing with all my might in a vain attempt to drown out the terror that still lurked in every corner of our lives.

When I could take no more, I would nudge her hard enough to make her stir. I didn't want to wake her, but I needed it to stop. Sometimes I could feel her sit up and look over my shoulder to see if I was sleeping. "Mahtob, are you awake?" she would ask. I would steady my breathing and peek through my eyelashes, pretending to sleep, just as she had taught me in Iran. That's how we had watched my dad to see what he was doing, in search of any clue that would protect us or aid in our escape efforts.

I hated my dad for doing this to us. "I hate you. *I hate* you. *I hate you!*" I screamed night after night inside my head as if he could hear me, as if even the furthest recesses of my mind were within his realm of control.

Every day seemed to bring more fear of my father's retribution. Without a divorce, Mom couldn't get permanent custody of me, which meant that even if my dad were caught at the airport attempting to remove me from the country, no one could stop him.

As a precaution she started carrying a handgun and had an alarm system installed in our house. Once it was armed, invisible lasers scanned for movement and would immediately trip the sirens to notify the police if any was detected. We had a secret code that could be punched into a keypad to send a silent distress signal without alerting a potential intruder. And I was given a panic button to wear as a necklace any time I left the safety of our locked doors.

One evening the doorbell rang, and I was happy to see a family from our church. They had a teenage daughter who had been my babysitter on a couple of occasions. With the exception of the pastors, teachers, our family, and the close friends who had known us before we went to Iran, no one knew yet about our ordeal or that Mom had written a book. That all changed the day Mom appeared on *Good Morning America*. *Not Without My Daughter* had been released early in the fall of 1987, and Mom had begun a book tour.

The family that showed up unannounced at our home that evening was in a rage. They felt betrayed by our secrecy and angry for being kept in the dark. The daughter and I were sent to my room, but through the closed door we could hear the muffled shouts of her irate parents. We didn't get to be friends anymore after that. I could understand why her parents felt I posed a risk, and it saddened me to be a danger to others.

I joined Mom on her book tour as often as possible, but it quickly became too much for me to travel and keep up with school. So we were separated more and more. Early on, Grandma stayed with me. She taught me to crochet. In the evenings we made blankets. I enjoyed ripping the stitches out and winding the yarn into a ball as much as I did adding to the length of my creation. Hence, most of my attempts ended up as giant balls of yarn. When we weren't crocheting, we played cards or watched Grandma's favorite country singers on TV. My life went on as normal—my version of normal, anyway.

Late one evening, returning from a trip, Mom gently sat on the side of our bed and woke me with a kiss on the forehead.

"Mommy, you're home!" I said sleepily, giving her a hug.

"I have something for you." She beamed and held out a small gray-velvet bag.

Yawning and blinking in the bright light that spilled in from the hall-way, I took the pouch from her. It fit in the palm of my hand. Gingerly I pulled at the center of the closure, and the drawstring gave way, revealing a glint of something shiny. I reached in and pulled out a beautiful gold bangle. She couldn't have given me a more perfect gift.

Since I was a toddler, I had worn gold bangles. I was enamored by the collection of delicate, jingling bands of gold that adorned the arms of our international friends—women from India, Pakistan, Armenia, and even my relatives in Iran. I longed to be grown-up and wear oodles of bangles just like them. Even as I renounced my father and the heritage he gave me, I had clung to my gold bracelets. With time I outgrew them, and still I refused to let them be removed. But when they threatened to interfere with my circulation, Mom had taken me to a jeweler and had them cut off.

First my bunny and then my bangles. Mom empathized with the grief that came with having to part with a piece of my identity before I was ready. She also recognized an opportunity to encourage my appreci-ation for an aspect of my Persian culture.

"Look at this." Mom now pointed to an almost imperceptible button along the side of the bracelet. "Push it and see what happens."

I did, and to my surprise the bracelet expanded. Mom, wanting to be sure to avoid future standoffs, had gotten me a bracelet with a built-in safety mechanism. I could wear it without ever again having to worry about outgrowing it. With a simple push of the button, I could easily remove my new bangle whenever I was ready.

CHAPTER 14

My thoughts still on the woman I met on the plane to Atlanta, I page through my half-filled photo album. She was quite surprised to learn that I hadn't read *Not Without My Daughter* or Mom's second book *For the Love of a Child*. That seems to be the standard response. People who know our story assume I have read the books. But why would I read them? I lived them.

I suppose if it wasn't for Anja, I might have considered reading the books at some point, perhaps during my adolescence. But God is good and puts just the right people in our lives at just the right moments. He sent Anja Kleinlein to me as a child.

Anja, the editor of Mom's books in Germany, quickly became family to me. She had experienced life at its fullest and knew well the extremes of immense joy and abhorrent evil. Yet somehow she had managed to embrace joy—to bask in the sunshine instead of wallowing in the pain of the tragedy she had endured. As a loving grandmother would, she nuzzled me by her side and taught me her secrets of survival.

With wisdom refined through the fires of life, Anja recognized that it would be important for me to keep my memories untarnished. And so at the age of just eight or nine, under Anja's guidance, I made a conscious decision to not read Mom's books.

Side by side, Mom and I climbed the same mountains in Iran,

literally and figuratively, but our experiences were immeasurably different and understandably so. After all, we were looking through vastly different lenses. I have no doubt that the memories in my head are my own. They are the pictures of my past captured through the lens of youth and understood first from a child's perspective.

Feeling a chill, I set the album beside the box and look for my favorite sweater, an oversized cream cardigan with oblong wooden buttons that belonged to my dad before we went to Iran. It hangs down to my knees and the sleeves are rolled and bulky, but there's no better sweater for lounging at home. Spotting it in the closet, I part the sea of clothes, hangers squeaking along the metal bar. Out of the corner of my eye, I glimpse something shimmery and gray poking out from the shadows.

It's funny how something can be invisible, yet in plain sight. I don't know when I last noticed the skirt that fell from Mom's bag that night outside the flower shop in Iran. Why has it hung unworn in the back of my closet all these years? I run my fingers over its stitches, delicate and precise. It was handmade for Mom in Iran. I had one too. I wonder what my dad did with mine once he realized I wouldn't be back to wear it. How long did it hang in my closet in his house?

Looking at this skirt reminds me of the pivotal moment when Mom and I made the joint decision to escape. As a student of developmental psychology, I have learned that children typically become autonomous from their parents during adolescence. That is when they develop their sense of self—their identity, their individuality, their independence. That's why teenagers rebel and test boundaries. That's why they tend to cling to their friends and push away from their parents.

From the start, however, my developmental milestones were destined to keep their own pace. Because of the hurricane, I was born a month early. Despite that, Mom says I learned to sit, roll over, walk, and even talk ahead of schedule. My parents invested a great deal of time and effort into parenting me. They—especially my dad—had high expectations for me, and at a young age, I learned to have even higher expectations for myself. To this day, I believe one of the worst things we can do to people is to have low expectations for them.

Even when I was six years old, Mom appreciated my ability to comprehend the gravity of our situation and the implications of the decision to flee. As desperately as she longed to escape, she never would have left without me. And yet, regardless of her desperation, she had enough respect for me as an individual to let me choose if we would stay or go. It was not only the path of her life in the balance, but mine as well. She wouldn't make such a far-reaching decision on my behalf without consulting me, even when there was no time for talking, even when delay could literally mean life or death for her.

Had I said I wanted to go back to my dad, we would have gone back. If ever there was a moment that typifies our relationship, it is that one. I didn't have to wait for adolescence to fight for autonomy. Mom gave it to me freely and generously a decade ahead of schedule.

Cozy in my dad's old sweater, I return to the open box in my sunroom. Sinking to the floor beside it, I gaze up at my haft sin. Everything on the table carrries a symbolic meaning. *Sib* and *sir*—apples and garlic—convey wishes for beauty and health. *Serkeh*—vinegar—symbolizes wisdom. *Samanu*, represented on my table by *halva*, a delicacy made of sesame-seed paste, honey, and pistachios, stands for the pleasant things life has to offer. And so on. Each item nestles in a gold-rimmed clear-glass saucer from a Persian tea set that belonged to my parents.

On the haft sin, life and rebirth are represented by greens—*sabzi*. In my childhood home, the haft sin wasn't complete without loads of spring flowers: cheerful yellow daffodils, fragrant hyacinths, and vibrant tulips with their powdery, pollen-coated stamens. As a child, I liked to collect the bright dust on my finger and swept it across my eyelid, creating my own eye shadow. The purple hyacinth on my table now fills the room with its sweet smell. That, to me, is the scent of No-ruz.

Wheatgrass is another staple. Each spring Mom would retrieve the container of wheat berries from the pantry. The rest of the year we ate them in soups or other dishes, but at No-ruz they were for planting.

Transferring a handful to a shallow bowl, she would cover them with warm water and let them soak overnight. The next day we would fill trays with dirt, scatter the tops with the rehydrated seeds, sprinkle on a bit more soil, and wait for them to grow.

No-ruz is a time for making a fresh start, for leaving behind all the negativity of the previous year and moving forward with a blank slate. If you've wronged someone, No-ruz is the time to make amends. If you've been hurt by someone, No-ruz is the time to forgive.

The first sprouts of wheat start to appear around day three. They grow so quickly, you can almost sit and watch it happen. First the seeds germinate and tiny roots begin to form. I like to use a clear container so I can watch the roots extend and intertwine to support the fresh green blades of grass. In a dish as shallow as an inch, wheatgrass can grow to be eight to ten inches tall, if not taller, a phenomenon that speaks to the importance of strong roots. Some of the blades sprout with such vigor that they carry a clump of dirt right up into the air and hold on to it for days. Looking closely, you may even catch a single gleaming droplet of water clinging to the grass.

As the grass grows, you transfer any negativity you're harboring from the previous year to the plant. At the end of the two weeks, tradition holds that you throw it into the river, and with it last year's ill will. I've never actually tossed my plant into a river, but an emotional tug of war happens when I throw away a healthy, thriving plant that I've cared for.

The symbolism is clear. We hold on to the things we nurture—all the more reason to choose the object of our tending wisely. A nursed grudge, if not released, can infect our lives and relationships for a lifetime.

Throughout my life, Mom and I have enthusiastically shared No-ruz customs with our friends. I've even been known to take the practices into the workplace. One year I stocked our break room with all the necessary supplies and a flyer explaining the idea. My coworkers loved the concept that I called "sowing seeds of peace." It was fun to walk down the hallways and see glasses of spring green growing on desks and windowsills.

Like me, some weren't ready to let their plants go at the end of the two weeks. When it was time for the "throw it in the river party," my inbox was flooded with e-mails asking if the plants could be kept. After all, it was raining that day, and it wouldn't be fun to go outside in the rain. One coworker, not wanting to waste the life, took her wheat grass home and fed it to her turtle. Others gladly cut the ties, eager to rid themselves of the psychological burden. Forgiveness can be a tricky thing.

As hard as I fought to hold on to my anger, to continue to hate my dad, the tugging of the good memories eventually found an inroad to my heart. No one is all good or all bad. The reality that my father would forever be a part of me was inescapable. A big part of making peace with myself was rediscovering the good in him and claiming that as my inheritance.

The act of forgiving wasn't like flipping a switch—forgiven . . . unforgiven . . . forgiven . . . unforgiven . . . forgiven. It was a gradual progression, a slow softening of the heart aided by the guidance of Mom and teachers like Mrs. Hatzung. I'm not sure exactly how or when I forgave my dad, but I do know why. Starting on my first day at Salem and continuing every single day I was there, I was taught the incredible redeeming power of love. Its mysteries were revealed to me not just in the lessons my teachers shared with me about God's love for all people, but also in the unconditional love they modeled.

Along the way, I was also taught about the destructive, lethal impact of hatred on our lives and, more importantly, on our souls. "Anyone who hates his brother," the Bible says, "is a murderer" (1 John 3:15). Plain and simple, hatred is a sin—a sin that, like all sin, separates us from God and his forgiveness. Hatred is a cancer, and as I had seen cancer destroy my grandpa's body and ultimately steal his life, I was blessed to have adults in my life who recognized that unless I was taught the dangers of this sin I harbored, it would destroy me and condemn me to an eternity in hell.

My teachers gave me permission to forgive my father. Mom gave me permission to love him. That was one of the greatest gifts she gave me. While the rest of our family was quite vocal about their hatred for my father, Mom found a way to strike a gracious balance between being realistic and being complimentary. It wasn't just with me that she spoke kindly of him; it was with everyone. This selfless act on her part had a lasting impact in my life—and not just mine. If not for her inexhaustible commitment to helping me heal, perhaps it would have been easier for her to linger in the darkness. But she couldn't pull me out of my dark hole of hatred without first digging her own way out.

Turning to the box at my side, I reach in like an archeologist on the brink of unearthing a relic from days of old, only to turn up a timeworn spiral-bound notebook. Opening its yellow cover, I discover the familiar writing of my former self. There are pages and pages of entries written in the sloppy penmanship of a child. In the space above the lines on the first page, words are scrawled in pencil: "By Amanda Smith." Some of the massive letters curve down, while others curve up. Those three words alone take up almost the entire width of the paper.

The first entry is dated September 2, 1988, two days before my ninth birthday. "I read that if you take your finger and meeger [measure] your arms that is how tall you are." Regrettably my spelling has improved only marginally since the third grade. On September 28 I wrote, "I read about Woodsy Owl. He says not to pollute. He says if you go on a hike not to leav [leave] a tral [trail] of something but to draw on a rock." That little tidbit of information I had filed away in the recesses of my mind, just in case I was ever kidnapped and had to leave clues for Mom to find me.

On October 12 I wrote about the Statue of Liberty, "She stands for world peace," a topic close to my heart. And November 30's entry is most telling: "Today I read about She-Ra. I found out that she was wonce [once] kidnapped. She-Ra has tow [two] identities one is She-Ra and the other is Adora." That was all I wrote on the issue, a matter-of-fact recounting of our similarities. She-Ra was my favorite cartoon character at the time. I even took on her superhero persona for Halloween. By then, it appears, I had come to terms with my dual selves. Touring with Mom, no doubt, played a vital role by giving me an outlet for releasing my original identity.

As *Not Without My Daughter* flourished, Mom's travels intensified. She and my teachers agreed that I could join her for some of the travel. Midyear trips in the fifth and seventh grades took me to Australia, and in third grade I traveled to Utah.

Mrs. Tackebury, my third grade teacher, loved music and movement and regularly combined the two in our classroom. As a treat, she often led us in song with her ukulele or a tambourine, and on special occasions she dragged out the pogo sticks. She was also passionate about God's grace. There wasn't a day that she didn't remind us of it. "Grace is God's undeserved love for us sinners," she would say, in awe that even though we're sinful, God loved us enough to send his Son to redeem us. "We don't do anything to earn it, and yet God gives it to us free and clear. That's grace."

Her other passion was literacy. So it came as no surprise, when I went with Mom to Utah, that Mrs. Tackebury's special assignment for me was to journal each day. Nearly a quarter of a century has washed away the memory of that trip, save for the evenings I spent sitting in a hotel room carefully chronicling the day's adventures. The only thing I remember about what I wrote is that I wished my mommy wasn't so tired all the time. Why couldn't she be peppy like Mrs. Tackebury?

When I returned to school, I turned in my stack of journal pages, and Mrs. Tackebury surprised me by binding them in wallpaper-wrapped cardboard and presenting me with my very first book.

CHAPTER 15

Though my trips during the school year were limited, I spent my summers at Mom's side, traveling the world to promote her book, which had quickly become an international bestseller and had even been nominated for a Pulitzer Prize. I loved seeing new places, meeting fascinating people, and experiencing their cultures and culinary delights.

In London, around the age of nine, I encountered for the first time a black swan, a teenager wearing a dog collar around his neck with a Mohawk of lime-green spikes, and the thrill of creating wax rubbings at Westminster Abbey. That was a normal day for me. My life was eclectic to the extreme, and I thoroughly enjoyed drinking everything in.

In each new city Mom and I ran the gamut of media experiences. Press junkets in Scandinavia were arranged for the sake of time. Mom and I sat in a hotel room and a revolving door of journalists appeared, each asking the same questions as the ones who had come before.

Wanting me to be free to answer questions as I chose, Mom and I sometimes did our interviews separately, in adjacent rooms. Most of the reporters were very gracious, asking me silly questions to lighten the mood and put me at ease. I was still shy, but I didn't mind doing the interviews, especially for print media, where my awkwardness was less likely to be apparent to the reader.

Once, in Copenhagen, I encountered a journalist who made me

immediately uneasy. He treated me like a five-year-old when I was nine and tried to get me to let down my guard. He started off with standard questions but it soon became clear that he had an agenda—to get me to tell him the real identity of the man who had helped us escape.

Mom had taught me the art of tactfully choosing not to answer a question. Instead of revealing the name of our rescuer, I told the reporter why it was important to protect his identity. Again he asked who our helper was. I expounded on the methods we had used over the years to protect him. The reporter remained undeterred, certain that eventually I would reveal just enough for him to put the pieces together. Each time he asked, I deflected the question.

I was relieved when we were interrupted for lunch. As soon as I saw Mom, I privately told her that I was done with interviews for the day.

"Okay, you can be done. You never have to do interviews if you don't want to. Did something happen?"

"He wants me to tell him who helped us escape. I told him I won't say, but he keeps asking me," I fumed. "I won't talk to him anymore."

Mom immediately informed the organizers that I would grant no more interviews that day and would spend the afternoon with her.

Every night when the interviews had finished, representatives from the publishing company took us out for dinner. These were extravagant meals with an endless procession of courses. Even as a child I relished the opportunity to try new dishes. On our Scandinavian trip, though, my tolerance was tested to the extreme.

Scandinavians are proud of their abundance of fresh seafood, and every entree we were served, it seemed to me, was raw. Actually, most of the fish was smoked, but in a way that left it looking and tasting uncooked to a young girl from the American Midwest. The one night we weren't served fish, we were served steak tartare, which I found surprisingly delicious.

On our last night in Sweden, the publicist complimented me on what a good sport I had been on the Scandinavian tour and said, "Tonight is all about you. We'll go anywhere you want. What would you like to eat?"

Typically I would have thanked her and said I'd gladly go anywhere she chose. But I had eaten my fill of "smoked" meat, and before I could stop myself, the words had slipped out. "I don't care—as long as it's *cooked*," I said with a deep sigh.

The innocence of my response was met with a belly-busting round of laughter. "Very well, then," the publicist said once she could again speak, "We shall go for Swedish pancakes with lingonberry sauce. That, too, is a local specialty, and I promise you it will be cooked."

In London, I found the traditional afternoon tea most enchanting. It was all so dainty and refined—tiny cucumber sandwiches, elaborately decorated bites of cake, miniature fruit tarts, scones with clotted cream and jam. It was a grand experience. Mom and I sat in the hotel lobby, surrounded by colossal arrangements of flowers, sipping tea while a harpist filled the room with elegant classical music.

In Paris, I was introduced to crepes, baguettes stuffed with brie and ham, and steaks accompanied by thin golden French fries served with the most delicious mustard. But nothing I ate in France or anywhere else in the world could compare with breakfast at Hôtel Balzac—croissants still hot from the oven, freshly squeezed orange juice, coffee for Mom, hot chocolate for me. My favorites were the croissants with a line of rich dark chocolate running through the center—*pain au chocolat*.

Also a wonderful discovery was the fact that hot chocolate was not the same everywhere in the world. In France it was not very sweet. It was rich and bitter like the centers of the pain au chocolat, so I added my own sugar. In Spain, it was slightly sweeter, but it was also thick, almost like cooked pudding before it sets.

It was in Spain that I came to love gazpacho, although my first experience eating it wasn't entirely pleasant. There was a large group that evening for dinner—people from the publishing company, I suppose, and perhaps some representatives of the media. As was the custom at such meals, Mom and I weren't seated near each other. The meal began with bowls of chilled tomato soup placed before each guest. I watched the others at the table for the cue to begin eating. No one reached for their spoons, so I waited. Before I knew it, there was a waiter at my side offering me some diced cucumbers for my soup. Liking cucumbers and wanting to oblige the custom, I nodded. When he had dished a spoonful into my bowl, I thanked him, and he moved to the next guest. Then I was presented with a bowl of onions, which was followed by tomatoes and peppers and I don't recall what else. Thinking it the polite thing to do, I graciously accepted each offering.

One of the guests seated across from me watched in amazement as my bowl heaped with toppings. Leaning to the man at his side, he chuckled, nodding in my direction and whispering something under his breath. Instantly I understood it wasn't customary to accept each topping. I was mortified. The deep sense of embarrassment I felt was almost more than I could hide. I wanted to cry. I wanted to melt into my chair and pool into a puddle beneath the table. I felt fat, self-conscious, and awkward. I couldn't raise my eyes to meet any of their stares.

In retrospect, I'm sure they weren't staring at me, but at the time I felt every eye in the restaurant boring into me disapprovingly. In my Middle Eastern culture, where food is offered in excess as a symbol of abundant hospitality, it would have been rude for me to turn down the offerings. It could have been seen as an insult to our hosts. Acutely aware of my gaffe, I had lost my appetite, something I find most regrettable now. The soup was scrumptious. Why should I have let my humiliation rob me of enjoying it?

During our travels, our hectic schedules rarely allowed for sightseeing, which was fine with me. What I found most alluring about a nation was its food and its people. My fondest memories of our journeys are of hours spent sharing meals with the strangers who welcomed us into their lives for a day or two or a lifetime.

Whether abroad or at home, people went out of their way to shower us with kindness. Thousands of letters from people who had read the book offered support and encouragement. Children sent me their pictures and invited me to be their pen pal. Many said they would name their daughters Mahtob. The letters that touched me the most were those from other children like me who lived with the constant fear of being kidnapped by a parent. Each served as a reminder of the vital importance of raising awareness of international parental child abduction. And so we continued granting interviews.

While Mom was exceedingly vocal in her quest to raise awareness, my bashfulness rendered me virtually silent, much to the frustration of media legends such as Larry King, Maria Shriver, and Barbara Walters.

When Mom was scheduled for a second interview with Barbara Walters—this time on *Good Morning America*—I watched from the periphery. Ms. Walters greeted Mom on the set amidst a flurry of activity. A makeup artist ran over to touch up their powder, and the audio guy wired Mom with a mic. The two women chatted familiarly despite the commotion, as if they were the only two in the room. "So, how's Mahtob?" Ms. Walters inquired.

"She's fine," Mom said pointing to me. "She's right over there."

"Oh, my goodness." Barbara Walters beamed, waving for me to draw near. "Bring her over."

It was seconds before they were to go on air, and the crew went into a tizzy. There was no chair for me. I hadn't been through hair and makeup. I wasn't wearing a mic. The prepared questions didn't include me.

Our host would hear none of it. Giving me a hug, she motioned for me to sit beside her. Wrapping her arm around me, she shooed everyone off as we were counted in.

The segment opened with Barbara Walters smiling warmly into the camera. "Welcome back. I'm here with my good friend, Mahtob. We go way back . . ." She was in complete control of the interview. Having not yet recovered from the fright of causing the staff such grief, I'm not sure I said a word on camera. I may be the only person ever to be interviewed twice by Barbara Walters and not answer a single question.

CHAPTER 16

I don't regret that Mom went public with our story. The book's success provided us with many unique opportunities while also providing an unforeseen level of security. Wherever we went people recognized our names and expressed their support, which meant that even strangers played a role in my protection. Several times customs officials acknowledged that they knew who we were. One even told us not to worry, because she would recognize my dad just as easily as she had recognized us.

Not only did Mom's candor shine the spotlight on us, it also brought to light broader issues that were going unaddressed. Before we went to Iran, instinctively fearing my dad would do what he did, Mom had sought legal advice from friends who were attorneys. They had told her the truth—that no judge would believe her and that if she left my father, no judge would order his visits with me to be supervised. Even then, international parental child abduction was a scourge on society, but no one talked about it, and our legal system was not equipped to deal with it.

The situation hadn't changed after we escaped. Having recognized that she couldn't safely petition the courts for divorce under the current laws, Mom began talking about the issue, making use of every opportunity to get the information in front of anyone who would listen. Increasingly, others approached her for help, and she quickly recognized that this form of abuse was much more pervasive than even she had imagined. Both men and women kidnapped their children to and from every country in the world, and yet, until we experienced it firsthand, she had never heard of another such incident. How could the entire world turn a blind eye and leave these families to suffer in silence?

Informally at first, Mom began working with some of the left-behind parents who came to her begging for guidance. Soon she was involved with hundreds of cases, and those hundreds quickly swelled to more than a thousand. Feeling it her duty to take action, she cofounded an organization called One World: For Children and hired a staff to join in her calling.

Mom had never been politically active, yet now she found herself at the forefront of a battle to protect the children of the world. Tackling international parental child abduction consumed her life and mine by association. It was empowering to live in the midst of such activism. I traveled with Mom to Washington, DC, to meet with members of congress and officials in the US State Department and the Department of Justice. In Michigan she was on a first-name basis with the staff of our state representative's office.

No obstacle seemed too daunting for my mom in her quest to give me a world where I could live without fear. If state and federal laws didn't do their job of protecting me, then she would get the government to change the laws. She testified in court on behalf of other children who, like me, were in danger of being abducted by a parent and explained to judges that this threat was real. When parents called in the middle of the night crying because their hope was gone, she listened to their heartache, knowing she could easily be in their position.

On Christmas Eve the year I was thirteen, we received a call from an area police department. A family of six was in extreme danger and needed a place to stay. Could we help them? Without hesitation, Mom welcomed them into our home. There were three sisters, one of whom had three young children. They had fled the family's home in America because their father planned to sell the youngest sister, who was just sixteen, as a bride to a middle-aged man in Palestine, their native land.

Being Muslim, this family had never experienced a Christmas celebration before. The little children were in awe when they spotted the decorated tree with wrapped packages beneath it.

"Is Santa coming for us too?" they asked.

"Have you been good this year?" Mom inquired.

Their eyes sparkled as they dared to hope. Jumping up and down they exclaimed, "Yes, we've been good! We've been very good!"

"Well, then," Mom said with a smile, "you must be on Santa's list."

That evening, as was our tradition, Mom and I went to a Christmas Eve candlelight service. It was one of my favorite services of the year. Near the end of the service, we would each hold an unlit candle, and as we began to sing *Silent Night* in German, the pastor would light the ushers' candles using the Christ Candle from the Advent wreath. The ushers would then make their way down the aisle, passing the flame from one person to the next, until the whole church sparkled in the glow of flickering candles. The church lights would dim, and together we'd sing of heavenly peace.

The Palestinian family joined us that evening, and it was there that they heard for the first time about the Savior that was born to them and all people in a stable in Bethlehem. In fact, the greatest gift I received that year was given to me at that service—by the youngest member of the family. During the sermon, when the pastor explained that this baby whose birth we were celebrating would grow up to die for our sakes, the little girl was distraught. She had been standing quietly at the balcony railing, listening intently to the pastor's every word. At the news of Jesus' death, she turned to us in a panic. "Jesus died!" she cried. She might have been young, but she recognized the true meaning of Christmas.

Church ended at midnight, officially Christmas day. We made our exit amid joyous rounds of yuletide greetings. Mom took us all home, figuratively tucked us all in, and then raced to the only twenty-four-hour store in town. She feverishly filled a cart with gifts for our new guests, then stayed up all night wrapping them. In our home, everyone was family, and everyone had presents to open on Christmas morning. When Joe and John arrived with their families, they were unfazed to find six more places set at the table.

At times I felt frustrated by such disruptions in our family time. For years, family vacations consisted of my brothers, their families, and me. No Mom. She would have good intentions of going with us, but at the last minute there would be a break in a case, or some other emergency would demand her attention. If she did go along, she would spend the whole time on the phone or flipping through case files.

I wanted her to get a "real job," one where she could punch the clock and be done, one that would allow for uninterrupted family time. But I was torn because I understood the important nature of the work and took great comfort in the recovery of a child. Over the years, Mom helped to rescue seventy-eight children. Each success story served as a reminder that there was hope.

The week Grandpa died, in August 1986, Mom had signed a movie contract. The book had yet to be penned and Mom had yet to find her calling as an advocate. But by way of Hollywood, God was already providing a means to bring the issue of international parental child abduction to a worldwide stage. Mom would help with the screenplay and work as a consultant for the project.

Filming began in Israel in February 1990, and we arrived in March. I hadn't been prepared for the shock of seeing armed guards posted at the airport in Tel Aviv. Not since our days in Iran had I come face-to-face with a machine-gun-toting soldier.

It was sunny and warm, much balmier than in Michigan. Spring was at its peak as we rode from the airport to the movie set. The windows were down, and the fragrance of orange blossoms filled the air. We were told that a skyscraper-sized painting of the Ayatollah Khomeini, unveiled for filming, had caused a collective panic. The police had come to investigate, and a press conference had been required to ease the fears of the public. I was grateful for the advance warning but even so, the painting was an unsettling sight.

It was in the shadow of Khomeini that Mom and I met the cast and crew. I was most excited to meet Sheila, the young actress who played me. Sally Field, who had been Mom's first choice for the role of Betty, worked on elaborate embroidery projects between takes. Alfred Molina, who played my dad, was extremely social and approachable. Often he would sit and talk with us.

I was on the set the day they filmed a scene of my parents fighting at school. The script called for Alfred to hit Sheila while screaming at her and Sally. Then he was to drag Sally out through the courtyard by her hair. They performed the scene as directed. When Alfred realized I was standing alongside the producers watching, he came over and apologized to me. "I'm not really hurting them. It's all just acting. I'm only pretending to hit Sheila, and even though it looks like I'm pulling Sally by her hair, I'm not really. I promise you."

When they filmed the scene a second time, it was Alfred who was left in pain when Sally, arms and legs flailing, mistakenly kicked him in the groin. "See," he said to me afterward, "I couldn't hurt her if I tried. She's the one who's beating me."

Sally's makeup artist, Lee, became my favorite person on the set. It became his personal quest to break me out of my shell, and his methods were not exactly conventional. One afternoon, during a lull in the action, Lee offered to give me a black eye—with makeup of course. So Mom and I followed him to his trailer, where he unleashed his artistic abilities. Not only did I end up with a black eye, but a gnarly scar to boot. A black eye from Lee was a true honor.

The producers invited me to be an extra in the movie. So for the first time since Iran, I donned a montoe and macknay and became an Iranian schoolgirl. I sat at a desk in a classroom repeating sentences in Farsi with other pretend Iranian schoolgirls. I huddled in a bomb shelter among a crowd of students. I followed Sally and Sheila ("Betty" and "Mahtob") off a bus and ran through the corridors of the school in the frenzy that followed an explosion. Mostly, though, I waited, because that's life on a movie set.

At night we joined the cast in a small room with a projector to watch the dailies—the footage that was filmed that day. I didn't know it then, but with the exception of one small clip, that was the only time I would see myself on the big screen. I may have been the real daughter, but my scenes still ended up on the cutting room floor.

Our time in Israel wasn't all work. We toured Jericho and saw the Jordan River. We went to Gethsemane and the Mount of Olives, where we were swarmed by young children hawking olive branches. We visited one of the places that claimed to be the burial site of Jesus and saw the Wailing Wall in Jerusalem. We even managed to visit Bethlehem, though we'd been told it was too dangerous, and spent a day floating in the Dead Sea.

Our hotel overlooked the Mediterranean Sea. One afternoon Mom and I went for a walk along the white sand, and a strange thing happened. Within minutes my whole body hurt. Every inch of my skin felt like it was being stabbed by fiery hot needles—a penetrating, unscratchable itch mixed with violent, shooting pain. We didn't stay out long, but by evening I had turned red as a lobster. Most of my skin was blistered, and I was in agony. It didn't seem possible that I could be so badly burned so quickly. I had always been sensitive to the sun, but this was different.

Before we left Israel, the movie's still photographer invited us to her parents' house for a Seder. Ever eager to experience a culture from the inside out, Mom and I accepted without hesitation. They shared the centuries-old Passover tradition with us amid the passing of dishes of bitter herbs and the reading of ancient texts—a fitting conclusion to our time in Israel.

It was an unfortunate turn of events that the movie was released in January 1991, just as conflict in the Middle East was coming to a head. The film drew criticism from people who saw the timing and subject matter as a political statement. Death threats were issued against those involved with the production. Suddenly it wasn't only my dad that posed a danger. We were caught in the crosshairs of the Iranian government and Muslim extremists the world over.

Although they were vocal, the fierce challengers were few. The vast majority of the feedback was encouraging and supportive. At one of the premiers, the audience reaction was so strong that Alfred had to be removed from the theater for his safety. I think it was a testament to his skill as an actor that the audience struggled to distinguish between him as a person and him as the monster on the screen.

It was baffling to me that some people viewed our story as an anti-Iranian or anti-Muslim statement. That simply was not the case. The story is nothing more than an account of a piece of my family's journey. If anyone reflects poorly on Iran and Islam, it is my dad for doing what he did, not Mom or me for talking about it. Even so, it's unfair to judge Iranians or Muslims by my dad's behavior.

Although the timing of the release was in many ways problematic, it was actually a blessing in disguise. Because of the political climate, the US government was more ready to lend a listening ear. A congressional screening held in Washington, DC, helped bring the issue of international parental child abduction to the attention of our nation's lawmakers.

To help raise awareness further, Mom began work on her second book, *For the Love of a Child*. She and her coauthor, Arnold Dunchock—Arnie, as I knew him—did much of their research in Paris, so I spent part of one summer living there. By far my favorite spot was Montmartre, the artists' district built atop a hill that overlooked the city. Painters congregated there, creating their works in the open air for all to see. I found them mesmerizing—their concentration, their attention to detail, the way they stood back to examine their work and then continued to add layer upon layer of thick paint to their canvases. Some did watercolors; others created charcoal sketches.

To me, watching the artists at work was much more exciting than seeing the finished masterpieces hanging on a museum wall. I felt as if I were witnessing history in the making. Perhaps one day I would hobble through the halls of a museum telling my grandchildren about my days of youth when I sipped Coca-Cola poured from a small glass bottle and saw these creations given life.

As the weeks in Paris passed, however, my energy waned. Some days I was too tired to go anywhere. Mom thought I was getting lazy, always wanting to sleep in and begging to spend my days sitting around. It became a mild source of conflict between us. She was on a mission to change the world, and I was content to nap on the couch with an unopened book on my lap. We had no way of knowing then that a much more ominous problem was lurking under the surface.

CHAPTER 17

I enjoyed traveling the world, but there was never any doubt in my mind that my real life was lived at home with my family and friends. We had moved yet again, this time to a house across the street from a sleepy park with old trees and a meandering river. The water brought ducks to feed, though I rarely walked across the street to feed them.

Mom was determined to find a way to give me the typical experiences of youth I longed for while still defending against the constant threat of my father's return. Determined to create an oasis for me, she fenced the backyard so I could play outside and redesigned the house so that virtually the entire back of the building was windows, making it easy for her to keep a watchful eye on me. Because I loved to swim, she put in a pool. And whether Mom was home or not, the door was always open to my friends.

Because she was traveling too frequently for Grandma to keep staying with me, Mom hired someone to help. By day Lori worked in a law office, and by night she took care of me. Lori laughed easily and often. She didn't like any of the usual titles that went with her role, so instead of "babysitter" or "nanny" she called herself "the lady who stayed with me when Mom was out of town." In reality, she was more like a big sister. She was playful and unencumbered and precisely the type of influence I needed to help me start to break free from my shy and rule-bound tendencies.

Lori's whole family adopted me as their own—even her boyfriend, Bob, who quickly became one of my favorite people. He was quirky in the best possible way. He drank chocolate milk and called the remote control a biviter. He greeted people enthusiastically with three hellos—"hello, hello, hello"—instead of just one. For no reason at all other than to break the silence, he would cup his hands together at his lips and whistle the song of the dove. And whenever he traveled, even if only for a day, he sent me a postcard.

Years had passed since we'd gotten any word from or about my dad. As I grew older, we had relaxed a bit, though the fear had not gone away. And we remained extra cautious around special days. My dad was sentimental and thus, we believed, more likely to reappear on my birthday, Christmas, or another holiday.

Halloween was especially anxiety provoking. What better time to gain entrance to someone's house than on a holiday when it was standard procedure to open the door for strangers in disguise? Still, Mom did her best to give me the normal Halloween experience. She let me dress up and go out trick-or-treating. And because I didn't want ours to be the one house on the block that didn't hand out candy, for a couple of years, against Mom's better judgment, we did just that. The year we handed out candy with a gun hidden in the candy bowl forced us to admit there were some experiences I just didn't need to have.

There were still plenty of other outlets for enjoying a typical childhood in spite of my atypical circumstances. I played basketball and volleyball. I was a cheerleader. I took piano lessons. When Mom was home, she never missed a game or a recital, and when she was on the road, Bob and Lori took her place on the sidelines. They were extremely social, and we spent Friday nights at home surrounded by friends. We played cards or board games or just sat around laughing into the wee hours. They didn't treat me like a child, which I appreciated.

For several years I'd had occasional headaches, but by the time I was twelve or thirteen, they started striking more regularly and intensified into full-blown migraines. I spent many of those Friday nights lying on the couch in the dark, enjoying the distant sounds of Bob and Lori's merriment and drifting in and out of sleep, willing the throbbing and the nausea to subside.

When Mom came home, film crews often followed her, doing pieces on us or on the abduction cases Mom was working to solve. Typically, journalists coming from great distances used a local production company rather than bringing an entire crew. That is how Mom and I came to know Bob Bishop of Future Media Corporation. A master at putting people at ease, helping them open up and speak freely, he was one of the few people who could actually get me to talk on camera when I was young. Although I remained shy, I offered up more for Bob than I did for most.

He asked me once how I felt about my dad. It was a question I had fielded many times over the years, and I struggled to find ways to convey my feelings. In my experience, journalists often walked into interviews with their story already mentally written. In their versions I was bitter and angry, and hatred for him ruled my life. Bob knew me well enough to prod for a deeper explanation, and I knew him well enough to give it.

"I don't hate him," I said matter-of-factly. "I have forgiven him for what he did to us in Iran, but I don't think of him as my dad anymore."

"Do you sometimes feel as if you are missing out on something because you don't have a dad who's an active part of your life?"

"It is his loss, not mine. 'If you abuse a privilege, you lose the privilege,'" I said, quoting the sage wisdom of my sixth grade teacher, Mr. Voeltz. "Having a family is a privilege, not a right. My father abused that privilege—literally—and so he lost it. It's as simple as that."

"Would you like to see him again someday?"

"No. I'm not holding a grudge, but that doesn't mean I have to expose myself to any more of his abuse."

"Do you think your father loves you, that he misses you? Do you think he's suffering because you're not part of his life?"

"Yes, and he has only himself to blame."

"How does that make you feel?"

"I don't feel sorry for him. He had his chance, and he blew it. Now we've all got to live with the consequences of the decisions he made. I've moved on. I hope he has, too, and that he'll leave me alone to live in peace. I hope his life is so full that he doesn't have time to think about missing me or coming to take me back."

My teachers helped me cope in ways they didn't even intend. There's no way Mr. Voeltz could have known that his oft-repeated warning, "If you abuse a privilege, you'll lose the privilege," would help me make sense of my complex family dynamics. He had used the phrase in reference to recess or to the privilege of spending a few minutes in the afternoon playing board games. He'd been eager to treat us to an afternoon of chess and checkers, but first we'd had to earn the privilege. Later, I'd decided Mr. Voeltz's lesson applied to more than just recess and board games. Perhaps it was Bob's questioning that helped bring the pieces of the puzzle together in my mind.

In the early 1990s, when Maria Shriver came to our house to interview us for *Dateline*, Bob did part of the filming. He had become interested in the work of *One World: For Children* and closely followed the progress on international abduction cases. My friends were giddy because Arnold Schwarzenegger's wife, who was also a real live Kennedy, was coming to our house. Mom appreciated the opportunity to further the cause. And I was happy because my friend Bob would be doing the filming.

Other families whose lives had been impacted by abduction also participated in the interview. When we wrapped up after an extremely long day of filming, Mom invited Marian, one of the mothers, to spend the night. Mom had been actively working Marian's case for many months.

A few years earlier, while Marian was out of town on business, her husband had kidnapped their two children from their home in Michigan and taken them to his home country of Iraq. Weeks later, war broke out in Iraq. The governments of both nations, which had initially been poised to find a diplomatic solution to the kidnappings, found their attention turned to the more pressing issues of the military conflict. Eight-year-old Adam and four-year-old Adora were left on the sidelines with little hope of rescue.

Months turned into years, carrying both mother and children on an emotional roller-coaster ride. Each time it seemed there was a glimmer of hope, things would fall through yet again. Marian even filed for a visa to enter Iraq. She was willing to risk being held hostage by her husband, imprisoned, or even killed for a chance to see her son and daughter. Her heart was absolutely shattered when her request was denied.

The night of the Maria Shriver interview, while Marian was staying at our house, the call came from the US State Department that her husband had taken their son to Amman, Jordan, and from there was requesting a visa to come to America. The State Department, after consulting with Mom and Marian, agreed to issue him a visa on the condition that he return with the children.

Immediately, everything that didn't directly relate to saving Adam and Adora became of secondary importance. Marian's husband was ambushed at the airport in Flint, Michigan, by a representative of the sheriff's department, who served him with a court order giving Marian custody. Unfortunately, he came only with Adam, not Adora. The *Dateline* film crew was there to capture the heart-wrenching reunion. Adam sobbed with joy as he embraced his grandparents, his aunts and uncles and cousins, and his mom. But Adora's absence made the moment bittersweet.

Marian had asked the court to issue an arrest warrant so that her husband could be held for kidnapping their children. But the judge's hands were tied. No law existed on which he could base such a warrant. A gaping hole remained in the justice system. And poor Adora remained in Iraq.

These cases were personal to us. The children who were stolen from their homes were real to us. We saw their pictures, we knew their names, we listened to their stories, we wept with their left-behind parents. I understood why Mom couldn't rest knowing that there were still so many young people waiting to be rescued. Adora became a painful symbol to us of all the children around the world suffering this senseless, unrecognized crime. And so Mom was spurred on in her mission.

This was widespread work, and it brought with it widespread

opportunities. Mom's life was dedicated to a cause much broader than the quiet life I dreamed of living. It wasn't that I didn't wholeheartedly agree with the importance of the issue. I did *and* I also needed the structure a stable home environment could provide. There were few things more inherently threatening to me in those days than the threat of losing my home—my haven, my symbol of structure, security, family, comfort, all things familiar.

This is one of the rare areas where Mom and I struggled to come to an agreement. The root of the issue was that the concept of home meant something different to each of us.

For Mom, coming back to the United States from Iran meant returning to freedom. She has said repeatedly over the years that she could have lived in Iran if she hadn't been a prisoner. So once our freedom was restored, it wasn't so important to her where we lived. We were free to go where we wanted, do what we wanted, spend time with whomever we wanted. Where we lived was inconsequential, so moving around as the opportunities presented themselves made perfect sense—to her.

"Mahtob, if we move the One World: For Children office to the Washington, DC, area, and work with the National Center for Missing and Exploited Children, think of all the families that could be helped and all the kidnapped children that could be rescued."

"No, our family is here. We fought to escape so we could come back to them. My friends are here. My school is here. I'm not leaving."

My ability to express my objections grew with age and, by the grace of God, Mom passed up many opportunities so that I could stay in my home and more importantly, my school.

In September 1992, shortly after my thirteenth birthday, my friends Cathie, Angie, Jamie, and I were preparing to go to our first high school football game. The "fearsome foursome," as we had been dubbed by our fourth grade teacher, Mr. Milbrath, were sleeping over at my house. We had rushed home from school to begin our primping. My bedroom was filled with the giddiness of young girls about to get their first taste of the high school experiences that awaited them. We curled our bangs amid cough-inducing clouds of aerosol hairspray and spackled our faces with blush, eye shadow, and lip gloss. My bedroom floor was littered with mounds of clothes that had been rejected in our quest to find just the right outfits for the occasion.

Minutes before kickoff, we pried ourselves away from the mirror and raced to put on shoes and load our purses with all the essentials—cash for our tickets, lip gloss, bubble gum—the important things. Just then Mom, who had been in Alpena and wasn't expected back until late that evening, burst through the door in a frenzy. She had found the perfect house, she informed me, and we were moving. I needed to pack a bag right away because she was taking me to see it.

I don't know if she wasn't aware of my plans for the evening or if she just didn't comprehend how important they were to me, but her sudden announcement was not well received.

There had been a time when I would have been thrilled at the possibility of moving back to Alpena. At thirteen, it was the last thing I wanted to do. Alpena was a four-hour drive away—too great a distance to put between my friends and me. Leaving Salem at the end of eighth grade was inevitable but there was no way I was going to lose my school, my friends, my church, my home, and my town simultaneously.

"You can do whatever you want, but there is no way I'm moving to Alpena," I sassed, "and right now I'm going to a football game. You can't just waltz in here and change my life like that with no warning."

"Fine, go to the game," she shot back. "Then come home and pack a bag. We'll leave in the morning."

"I am not moving to Alpena."

"We won't move until you graduate from Salem. After that, there's nothing holding us here."

"This is my home. I'm not moving!" I shouted. "You're gone all the time anyway. What difference does it make to you where we live? You're never around. I'm the one that's here."

"We'll talk about it later."

I don't remember the game. All I remember is the immense sadness and frustration I felt at the unfairness of the situation.

The next morning, as we made the long drive to Alpena, I sat silently with my arms folded across my chest in protest. The house was even more beautiful in reality than in Mom's description. Built on the banks of Lake Huron, it was a stately mansion. But despite its grandeur, I remained steadfast in my determination to hold on to the home I knew. Underestimating my stubbornness, Mom bought the house despite my insistence that I would never live there.

The debate continued. Pushed beyond the point of frustration after one particularly infuriating argument, I stormed into my bedroom and kicked my door to shut it. Missing, I caught the end of the door with my toes. There was a loud crack, to which I paid no heed. In my fury I kicked the door again, this time slamming it shut with a decisive crash. I hobbled to my stereo and turned it up full blast to drown out Mom's pleas for me to open the locked door and talk to her. My foot throbbed, my head ached.

My toes swelled and turned black and blue, but in my pride, I refused to show any sign of weakness. I did not limp. I did not complain. I never once mentioned my injury. Each painful step served only to feed my stubborn will to avoid another move. It was only years later, when I had X-rays for some other reason, that we discovered more than my heart was broken that night.

CHAPTER 18

Mom's work continued despite the opportunities she passed up on my behalf, and the world took notice. In the Netherlands she was awarded the Prize of the Public. In Germany she was named Woman of the Year. She was presented with an honorary degree from Alma College, a private school in the town of her birth. We were both recipients of the America's Freedom Award, and in 1992 we learned that the president of France would be presenting Mom with the prestigious gold medal of the City of Paris.

Mom was on tour in Europe at the time, so she asked Bob Bishop, our videographer friend and the unofficial *One World: For Children* historian, to accompany me to meet her in Paris for the honor. Mom's French publishers would be there. Her literary agent, Michael Carlisle, was flying in from New York. Best of all, Mom's German editor, Anja Kleinlein, would be there.

The anticipation of going to a palace and meeting the president was nice, but it paled in comparison to the joy of seeing Anja again. I loved Anja. She was wild and exuberant, with a gift for turning life into a party. Whenever we sat down to eat, we would say grace and then, motioning for everyone to clasp hands with those beside them, Anja would lead us in unison to say, "*Guten Appetit.* En-joy-your-meal!" Our hands would rise and fall with each slowly articulated syllable. Inevitably we dissolved into laughter.

With Anja, we ate languidly and with great merriment. She ended each meal by reapplying her signature coral Christian Dior lipstick and ever so gracefully drawing on a cigarette. She credited old Hollywood movies with teaching her to smoke cigarettes so glamorously. Although Mom and I jokingly referred to her as the *Schnapsdrossel*—the Schnapps drinker—when I thought of Anja, I thought of champagne. It was with her that I would drink my first champagne in the stately lounge of Munich's Hotel Vier Jahreszeiten.

Still extremely shy in those days, I often looked miserable. Shoulders stooped, I avoided eye contact. Uttering even the briefest statement was torture for me. In stark contrast to Anja's elegance, I felt garishly awkward and uncomfortable in my body. I studied her every movement, wanting to emulate her refinement.

One would never know from her lighthearted manner that Anja had lived through the horrors of World War II in Germany. How could someone who had seen such hell on earth embrace life with such joyful abandon? "We've got to be tough," she was fond of saying, and she was.

Anja was waiting with Mom at the Charles de Gaulle airport when Bob and I emerged from customs. They gasped when they saw me. I was expecting smiles and hugs and instead received expressions of shock and concern.

Mom carefully examined my face, turning my head from side to side. "What happened?" she whispered, taking in my red and blistered appearance.

"It's nothing," I insisted, "Just a little sunburn."

Both women stared at me, aghast. Their motherly instincts told them otherwise. Mom scheduled an appointment with a dermatologist as soon as I returned to Michigan a few days later. She was still on tour, however, so Lori took me to the doctor. Dr. Wegman's concern was evident the instant he opened the door.

He sat on a stool wearing a lab coat, with a pair of tapered binoculars perched atop his head. He was goofy in a good way—extremely intelligent yet approachable. I warmed to him immediately. Examining the rash that cascaded over my nose and down my cheeks, he ran through a whole host of symptoms.

"Headaches?"

"Yes."

"Joint pain?"

"Yes."

"Low-grade fevers?"

"Yes."

"Sensitivity to the sun?"

"Yes."

"Changes in appetite, hair loss, fatigue, tiny splinters under your nails?"

"Yes, yes, yes, and yes." I was confused. I was there for a skin rash. What did all this have to do with anything?

"Hmm," he said, studying his clipboard. "Tell me a little about your family's health history."

"You're going to need more paper," I joked.

"My grandpa died of colon cancer," I started and kept rattling off one ailment after another.

When I paused he patiently prompted, "What else?"

"Mom has ulcers. My uncle has heart disease. My aunt has diabetes. I think someone has glaucoma."

"Think really hard. There must be something else."

"I think everyone has arthritis. Oh, and my grandma has lupus."

I'd barely uttered the word *lupus* when he exclaimed, "There it is! I knew it." He had suspected that diagnosis the second he laid eyes on me.

"We'll have to run some tests," he told me. "You'll need a rheumatologist. The best in the business is Carol Beals. She'll take excellent care of you, but it's hard to get an appointment with her. The last I heard she had a six-month wait list, and we can't let this go that long. But don't worry; we're friends. I'm sure she'll be more than happy to discuss your case with me. In the meantime . . ."

Dr. Wegman was a talker. It says something wonderful about him that he went into such a lengthy discourse with a thirteen-year-old.

Suddenly so many things made sense. It was almost a relief to know that the random list of minor maladies that had plagued me over the years had a central cause. I even took comfort in knowing that it was lupus and not teenage laziness causing my fatigue. In my naïveté, I assumed one disease was all a person would get in life and it was inevitable that each person would eventually get one. So it wasn't so bad to know what mine was. At least I didn't have to wonder anymore.

Mom's reaction couldn't have been more different from mine. She had witnessed Grandma's suffering with this autoimmune disorder. My parents were friends with a family whose young daughter had died from it. So Mom had enough experience to know that lupus was capable of robbing me of much more than quality of life. Her mind jumped directly to the worst-case scenario.

Lupus is difficult to diagnose. There are three types, and no two people present with exactly the same symptoms. To further complicate the issue, many symptoms are also indicative of other autoimmune diseases. There's a lot to rule out, and often it can take years to get a clear picture of what's going on inside a person's body. I was incredibly blessed to stumble into Dr. Wegman's office and receive a diagnosis on my very first visit. I was even more blessed that his friend, Dr. Beals, as a courtesy to him, got me in for an appointment in less than two weeks.

In Dr. Beals's office, I sat on the end of the exam table wearing a threadbare hospital gown and trying to look calm as I waited to meet her for the first time. My fidgeting fingers and swinging feet betrayed me. Mom, who had flown home as soon as she heard my initial diagnosis, sat in one of the room's teal wingback chairs. Lori occupied the other.

The instant Dr. Beals entered the room, my fears were allayed. She was a sharp woman, extraordinarily warm and yet in complete control. When I left her office that day, I felt energized and optimistic—we had a plan.

First we would do thorough lab testing to get a handle on what we were up against. Then, together, we would review the information and decide which treatment approaches were in order. I would certainly require medication, at least for a period of time. I would also need some lifestyle changes and, above all, a positive attitude. Dr. Beals assured me that we would be decisive in our attack on the disease, and together we would find a way to make living with lupus manageable. In short, we would face my diagnosis the same way Mom and I had faced our security risks over the years. Lupus was something I would have to learn to account for on a daily basis, but it would not stop me from living my life.

The lab results were shocking. By all accounts I should have been much sicker than I actually felt, which told Dr. Beals that we had caught the disease just as it was poised to ravage my body. Our approach would have to be more aggressive than she'd hoped.

It was clear by the progression of the disease that it had been simmering under the surface for quite some time. In hindsight, we were able to pinpoint unexplained symptoms that dated back at least five years. Abnormalities that we had brushed off as inconsequential suddenly took on a whole new significance.

In a matter of weeks, my body began to give out. A trip to the Mayo Clinic revealed that I had the most serious form of the disease, systemic lupus erythematosus, the type that attacks both the skin and the internal organs. There was no part of my body that was beyond its reach.

They say disease is representative. If that's true, it should come as no surprise that even within my body I was quite literally under the constant threat of attack from my own flesh and blood. My dad remained quiet, but the threat he posed was ever present. The same was true of my lupus. Just as my family had spent years guarding me with hypervigilance against an attack from my father, they now scrutinized me for any sign of an attack from within.

Anja took the news of my diagnosis especially hard. I was like a granddaughter to her, and by her estimation I had already suffered more than enough. After receiving the news of my declining health, Anja was visited by Dr. Franke, a German doctor who was seeking to have his book published. He had multiple sclerosis and had been completely bedridden when he developed a treatment that gave him back his life.

"What do you know about lupus?" Anja asked.

"Well," he told her, "lupus and MS are in the same family of diseases." Although it had never been tested, he was certain his treatment could cure both. In fact, he was convinced with further experimentation it would be found to cure all autoimmune diseases.

Hearing that I was the patient, he was eager to treat me. *Not Without My Daughter* was a bestseller in Germany, and Dr. Franke believed that if he could successfully treat me and write about it, he would have no trouble getting his own book published.

Anja eagerly shared her discovery with us, and for months Mom, Dr. Beals, and I waffled over whether or not to try the treatment. It was experimental. No one with lupus had ever used it. It hadn't been empirically studied, and the long-term effects were unknown. Maybe it wouldn't work. Maybe it would only hasten my death.

Dr. Franke assured us that deoxyspergualin (DSG) was all natural. There would be no negative side effects, and if we found the right combination of dosage and frequency, he felt confident it could cure me. Still, it was a risk we weren't ready to take. First we would try more established treatments.

I set out to continue my life as normally as possible despite the added challenges of living with a rapidly progressing autoimmune disease. Mom, however, began to treat me as a patient, and a very ill one at that. She stopped chastising me for being lazy and instead nagged me to rest around the clock. She was also troubled by the fact that I refused to say I was sick. Instead I would say, "I have lupus." She took that to mean I was in denial, so she took every opportunity to remind me. I saw things differently. I was trying to put a healthy spin on the situation. I pushed her to continue with our normal routine, which for her meant resuming her business travels and for me meant school, sports, and friends.

My brothers were devastated by the news of my failing health. They worried excessively about me. They kept track of my doctor's appointments and stayed on top of the rise and fall of my lab results. And they made a point of spending more time with me.

One day Joe picked me up to take me to his house for the night.

We drove through farm country with the windows rolled down. Heavy metal blared over the speakers as we sped past cornfields and dairy farms. Suddenly he brought the car to a screeching halt, opened his door, and hopped out.

"What are you doing?" I asked, confused.

"You're driving the rest of the way," he announced as he made his way to the passenger side of the car.

"Awesome!" I exclaimed, bounding out of the passenger seat and practically skipping to the driver's side. I had to pull the seat forward to reach the pedals. Gripping the steering wheel with both hands, I put the car in drive. *Okay*, I thought, *so far so good*. I stepped too zealously on the gas pedal. The car lurched forward. Overcompensating, I slammed on the brakes, and the car jerked to a stop.

Laughing hysterically and probably rethinking his decision, Joe talked me through the steps, and I tried it again. It went much more smoothly the second time around. My confidence increased, and my foot grew heavier on the accelerator as I aimed the car straight down the road. When we came to Joe's corner, I turned the wheel. What I didn't know was that it is generally advisable to slow down before making a sharp turn.

"The brake—hit the brake!" Joe yelled as he grabbed for the wheel. "Keep turning! Slow down! What are you trying to do, kill us?" The tires squealed, fighting to cling to the pavement as we whipped around the corner. I was still swerving from side to side, trying to straighten the car when we came to an abrupt stop in Joe's driveway. We were both relieved to have survived our adventure.

John made it his mission to keep me laughing. Of all his comedic stunts, perhaps my favorite was when he juggled eggs. As soon as he started for the refrigerator with that silly sideways grin of his, I knew what would follow, and so did Mom.

"John," Mom warned, "don't you dare!"

We all knew there was no stopping him. He liked to get Mom going just as much as he liked to send me into uncontrollable fits of giggles. I sat at the kitchen counter watching, my vision blurred by tears of laughter as he juggled two eggs with one hand and extended the other in front of him to fend off Mom's attempts at protecting her freshly mopped floor.

"Mom, leave him alone," I begged. "You'll make him drop the eggs." Knowing it was a lost cause, Mom stepped aside with a wry grin. Deep down, she enjoyed John's silliness as much as I did. Free from Mom's interference, John added more eggs and juggled with both hands, making goofy faces and telling jokes as he went. Rarely did he drop an egg, but if he did, we happily cleaned it up, the whole time laughing about the look on Mom's face when John reached for the refrigerator door.

In November 1993, Mom wanted me to join her on a business trip to Japan. "Japan will always be there," I told her. "This will be my last chance to play in a basketball tournament with my team. Mr. Roecker says we've got a good shot at winning, and there's no way I'm missing it."

Ever since Mom announced our move to Alpena, I had agonized over finding a way out of it. I didn't know it yet, but that basketball tournament would show me the answer.

Salem was part of the WELS (Wisconsin Evangelical Lutheran Synod), and basketball teams from WELS grade schools all over the state had come to Michigan Lutheran Seminary (MLS) in Saginaw to vie for the championship. MLS was not a seminary in the familiar modern sense. It was our synod's high school—a boarding school where classes were taught at a college-prep level and aimed at preparing young people for future careers in the ministry.

Mr. Roecker, our coach, had been my seventh grade teacher. He had a gift for making his students want to learn. He was the reason I played basketball. I was not athletic, but I loved being on Mr. Roecker's team.

We won the championship, and as with many other moments of my life, Mom celebrated with me from afar. No matter where she was in the world, she remained attuned to the details of my life. Regardless of hectic schedules and time differences, she found a way to call me every day, and in between phone calls she even managed to send me little notes to let me know she cared. From Japan she sent me a postcard with a picture of two young women, dressed in traditional Japanese style, having tea in a garden beneath a red umbrella.

11–12–93

Dear Mahtob,
    I saw many little girls dressed in kimonos + wearing makeup for a special holiday. Really beautiful.
    CONGRATULATIONS on your championship.
    Miss you, love you, see you soon.

Love,

Mom

At school the following week, Mr. Roecker complimented me on the job I had done at the tournament.

"Have you thought about going to MLS? I think you'd have a chance at making their basketball team."

"Do you really think so?"

"Sure. And you want to be a teacher, right?"

"That's all I've ever wanted to be, since first grade."

"Then you should definitely consider MLS. I really think it would be a good fit for you."

"There's no way Mom would let me go. She'll say I'm too sick or it's too dangerous for me to be on my own if my dad shows up."

"Well, think about it. If you want, I'll talk it over with your mom. Maybe we can find a way to make it work."

I did think about it. That was all I thought about for days, and the more I thought, the more confident I became that Mr. Roecker had offered me the perfect solution.

Moving, it seemed, was inevitable. Mom still insisted that after my eighth grade graduation, we were going to live in Alpena. If I was going to have to move, why not do it on my terms? If I went to MLS I would live in the dorms and Mom could live wherever she wanted. That was exactly what I told her when she called from Japan.

"I'm going to MLS."

"What?" she asked in disbelief. "You don't want to go to MLS."

"Yes, I do."

"But you'd have to live in the dorms. You don't want to live in the dorms."

"Yes, I do."

"You'd have to share a room with someone you don't even know, and you'd have to share a bathroom with a whole floor of girls."

"My mind's already made up. Mr. Roecker says I should try out for basketball. He thinks I could make the cut."

Wise enough not to tell me no immediately, she said we would talk about it when she got home.

By the time Mom returned, I had honed my argument and enlisted the support of not only Mr. Roecker, but also my pastor and my principal. Mom reluctantly agreed to allow me to attend MLS—*if* I was healthy enough. I resolved to be healthy by then.

CHAPTER 19

I did my best to continue with my normal life, but despite all our efforts, by Christmas lupus had attacked my kidneys. I was a little more than a year into my battle and had tried virtually every available treatment, but I continued to lose ground rapidly. I looked like a giant red tomato from taking such high doses of steroids. My stomach was bloated and painful. My joints ached. My hair was falling out. I experienced excruciating migraines.

My skin alternated between an unremitting itchiness and a dreadful stinging, burning sensation. The instant the sun's rays touched my body, I felt as if I were being pricked by hundreds of hot pins. Even five minutes outside was often enough for any exposed flesh to blister; then it would flake off in thick crusty layers and ooze. I would stand in the shower for an hour or more, letting the cool water soothe my irritated skin. Eventually, though, I would have to get out of the shower, and the agonizing pain would return with the first touch of the towel. The only true relief was sleep. And so I slept.

When the last half of my eighth grade year came around, I was too sick to attend school full time, some days sleeping around the clock. Mom would wake me every four hours to swallow more pills and take a few sips of milk. The combination of milk and the warm pastiness of my mouth turned my stomach. I would have preferred water, but Mom insisted I needed the nutrition. I was taking twenty-six pills a day at that point. I knew them all—spellings, dosages, frequency, and purpose. I also knew their many side effects, which medications I took to counteract them, and which necessitated special dietary restrictions.

Even though school was more than my body could handle, my teachers made sure I kept up with my coursework and my catechism lessons. On occasion I was able to attend classes for an entire week. More often than not, though, my attendance was more sporadic. The harder I pushed myself, the longer it took me to recover from the exertion, but with my teachers' efforts I was able to graduate from Salem and—more important—to be confirmed with my class.

In our church, confirmation is a public ceremony following a very specific series of instruction in the basics of the Christian faith. It is the time when those who were baptized as babies or as children "confirm" their understanding and proclaim their decision to live as followers of Christ. This instruction was carefully led by the pastors of our church.

Honorable and integrity-filled, Pastor Mueller is one of the wisest and gentlest men I've ever known. The world would be a much better place if every child had the benefit of growing up under the guidance and instruction of such a man. Of all the places God could have led us, I am eternally grateful that he saw fit to deposit Mom and me into Pastor Mueller's care. He knew each student well, and after much prayerful consideration he selected a confirmation passage for each of us.

Eight years earlier Pastor Mueller had given Mom Bible instruction, and when the time came for her to be confirmed as a member of our church he had given her the verse, "If God is for us, who can be against us?" (Romans 8:31). Every time her passage was read in church or mentioned in a sermon or brought up in conversation, Mom would nudge me with a smile and remind me that was her confirmation passage.

For me he chose Ephesians 2:8–9: "For it is by grace you have been saved, through faith—and this not from yourselves, it is the gift of God—not by works, so that no one can boast."

That verse was true of my life in so many ways. God had saved me from my father. He had saved me from the war between Iran and Iraq. During our escape, it had been God who delivered us safely home. Through my baptism, he had saved me from my sins. And whether I recovered or whether lupus took my life, I would be eternally saved because of God's grace.

After our confirmation service, I sat in the church basement and sobbed uncontrollably. Since I had returned from Iran, Salem had been a source of unwavering consistency in my life. The teachers had guided me through traumatic times and, in the process, taught me how to love and forgive. Cutting ties with the school and my classmates left me feeling lost and disoriented.

This was a very dark time for me. As usual, though, my family rallied around me, doing their best to lift my spirits. While John kept me laughing, Joe and his family made a point of increasing their visits.

Joe's wife, Peggy, had a son named TJ from her first marriage, and together Joe and Peggy had a son named Brandon. From the time he was born, Brandon and I had shared a deep connection. When he was at "Grandma Betty's" house, everything was "Mah-Bob" this and "Mah-Bob" that.

It was hard for Brandon to understand why I started sleeping through his visits. I would drag myself from bed to the couch, but even there, I wasn't strong enough to hold my eyes open. Brandon would tiptoe to my side and gently place his tiny hand on my face. "Mah-Bob," he'd whisper, "Mah-Bob no nap."

I wanted to jump up and play with him, but my body was just too heavy with fatigue. I couldn't even open my eyes or manage a faint smile. "Mah-Bob," he persisted, patting my cheek, "no nap." I heard his voice, but it sounded as if it were coming from miles away. My heart ached.

He implored me to wake up until Mom came to usher him away saying, "Shh, Mahtob's tired. We need to let her sleep right now."

Even as he was being led out of the room, he pleaded, "Mah-Bob no nap!"

I was losing my battle with lupus. Mom tried to shield me from this reality, but I could feel it. First my body failed me and then my will to live. I had accepted the fact that I was dying. In truth, I was too exhausted to care.

Eventually Dr. Beals declared we had nothing left to lose. I was just getting sicker. Nothing seemed to be stalling the progression of the disease. If we were going to try Dr. Franke's experimental DSG treatment, it was time. Mom immediately made the arrangements for us to fly to Germany.

The trek to Munich was exhausting. When Mom and I met Dr. Franke, my body was scarcely strong enough to support the weight of my head. We were in the opulent lobby of Hotel Vier Jahreszeiten, surrounded by dark wood, marble, and stained glass. Too weak to scoot the heavy chair up to the table, I sat on the edge of the seat and leaned forward to rest my head wearily on the cool wood. I knew it was rude, but I was so drained I just couldn't help it.

Dr. Franke wasn't what I had expected. He looked like a Disney villain, with long, knobby fingers that curled over the end of a gnarled wooden cane. His hollow eyes were sunk deep into his skull, creating dark circles in his chalky skin. Only one corner of his wrinkled Oxford shirt managed to remain tucked into his pants. He was a disheveled mess, a mad scientist in form and function.

There was a jerkiness to the man's movements, and he waged a never-ending battle against the hair that fell unkempt in his eyes. When he wasn't laboriously pushing it aside with the palm of his hand, he was grotesquely cracking his wrists. A half turn down and to the right, then a quick flip up and out . . . *pop*. His body was creaky, and I wondered whether this was a side effect of the treatment. He had promised there would be no negative side effects, but he didn't seem to be aware of his creakiness. Would the same thing happen to me?

Dr. Franke had brought along his business partner. Dr. Regensberger, who wore jeans, riding boots, and a black leather jacket. We learned he was a motorcycle enthusiast with a Route 66 obsession.

Anja had come for moral support. Her translation skills weren't necessary because everyone at the table spoke perfect English.

Dr. Franke, surprised by the advanced state of my illness and fearing that the disease had already done too much damage, was reluctant to treat me. After Mom's and Anja's pleas he capitulated, but not without issuing a sober reality check. He told us not to have high hopes—not to have any hopes at all.

The next morning Mom, Anja, and I reported to Dr. Franke's small and sterile clinic. I felt like Goldilocks sitting in Papa Bear's seat as I half-reclined in the massive vinyl-upholstered clinic chair. *New Kids on the Block* was singing "step by step, oh, baby . . ." into my ears, courtesy of my new Walkman cassette player, and the latest *Babysitters-Club* paperback rested unopened on my lap. My right arm was outstretched on the armrest, the IV needle disappearing into the plumpest vein in the crook of my elbow. Even my best vein was pitifully shriveled by disease. The nurse had been forced to use a butterfly, a tiny needle I knew well by now.

It was a warm day, and Mom and I watched in amazement as the children from the preschool next door stripped down to their birthday suits and splashed around in a kiddie pool. A woman held her thumb over the end of a hose, fanning the water and creating a rainbow for the children to run through. Such a thing would never be permitted in an American preschool. With concern, Mom drew Anja's attention to the scene.

"What's the matter with it?" Anja asked. "Look at them. They're having fun." They were also providing a welcome distraction as we nervously waited on my reaction to the medication. Knowing Anja's playfulness, I'm surprised she didn't run out to join them.

About forty-five minutes into the treatment, a crowd from the clinic started to gather around me. The nurse, the receptionist, and the two doctors scrutinized my face and then huddled together, whispering in German. I couldn't tell if this was a bad sign or a horrible one. I silently took stock of my body and didn't feel anything unusual. Remembering the book on my lap and happy to have a distraction, I opened it and started to read. It was hard to concentrate because the clinic staff kept coming to ask how I felt. Each time they closely examined my face, and each time they seemed to have to fight harder to keep the corners of their mouths from revealing their surprise.

Mom was finally bold enough to say what everyone was thinking. "Look at her skin!" she exclaimed in disbelief. "Her rash is disappearing." With the ice broken, the team began to express their joy.

When the last drop of medication drained into my vein an hour and a half after the IV was hung, I felt renewed, alive for the first time in months. I wanted to go for a walk, but Dr. Franke was quick to caution us.

"You should go back to the hotel," he told Mom. "She'll be tired, so just let her rest."

But I wasn't tired. I was bursting with energy, and I was not going to waste that beautiful day. "Let's just go for a short walk," I begged Mom. "If it's too much, I'll tell you."

Reluctantly she gave in. Anja led the way. We walked past the Hofbräuhaus to the city square filled with café tables and tourists. We saw the glockenspiel and the massive bookstore that sold books in English. Every few steps they asked, "Aren't you tired? Wouldn't you like to sit and rest?"

"No," I shouted back at them with a smile. "Let's keep walking." Soon they grew weary and lagged behind.

I felt as if I were seeing the world for the first time. I was charmed by the quaint narrow streets lined with buildings of varying architectural styles that all butted up against one another. There were no gardens, yet somehow beautiful flowers were everywhere. For the first time I noticed pulleys hanging above some of the windows of the upper levels of the buildings.

"Anja, why are those there?" I asked, pointing.

"These are old buildings. Their staircases are too steep and narrow for moving furniture in and out, so they use the pulleys to lift the big pieces through the window."

We rounded a corner, and Anja stopped dead in her tracks. Her eyes took on a crestfallen expression. "This is a significant place," she said, motioning to the nearly empty square. "This is where Hitler declared war on the Jews." She shivered at the mention of Hitler's name. That was the only time she ever mentioned Hitler or the war to me.

Altogether I had four days of infusions, took three days off, and then had four more. My astounding recovery continued. With each treatment we feared I might relapse, but it was a steady uphill climb. By the end of the two weeks, I was off all my medication except for the steroids, and I was being weaned off them.

We hoped for the best, but when we went to see Dr. Beals back in Michigan we prepared for the worst. Was it possible this was nothing more than a phenomenal placebo effect? Had we wanted so badly for this to be the answer that somehow my body had tricked itself into believing it was? Would I wake up tomorrow once again unable to pull myself out of bed?

Dr. Beals, being a true scientist whose hope was tempered with reason, ran a comprehensive panel of lab tests. We watched and waited, and our prayers were answered: my lupus was under control. It wasn't in remission, but in a span of just two short weeks I had been brought back from the brink of death.

CHAPTER 20

Miraculously, by August 1994 I was healthy enough not only to go to school, but to attend boarding school. Fourteen and terrified, I moved into the dorms at Michigan Lutheran Seminary. This move had been my choice, but I wasn't exactly happy about it.

Mom drove me to my new home on a Sunday afternoon. My life at Michigan Lutheran Seminary began just like every day thereafter would begin and end—with worship. As the pastor announced the closing hymn, I glanced down at the worship folder and saw that after the song finished the students would meet with their advisors and the parents would head home. My throat tightened. I didn't want Mom to leave. I had changed my mind. Maybe it wouldn't be so bad to move to Alpena.

Earlier that morning, when Mom and I attended church at Salem, Pastor Mueller had announced that Mrs. Hatzung had died. Her battle with breast cancer had ended. She had been called home to be with her Savior—a true blessing for her, but a painful loss for those of us who loved her. I couldn't believe she was gone.

Mrs. Hatzung hadn't just taught me; she had nurtured me. Her love, kindness, and gentleness had made it possible for me to feel safe when apart from Mom following our escape. Mrs. Hatzung had helped me break down the wall I'd built around my heart. She had even given me back Mr. Bunny. Knowing how much I missed him, she'd had her daughter replicate my lanky green friend from a photo. The new Mr. Bunny was as good as the old, and what's more, in his absence I had been given an even better source of security that could never be taken from me—God's Word.

It was certainly not coincidence that had placed me in Mrs. Hatzung's care. God had always put just the right people in my life at just the right times.

The chapel swelled with the melody of hymn 332, "Go, My Children, with My Blessing." Tears flowed silently down my cheeks as the familiar hymn took on a new meaning. I didn't want to "go." I wanted to cling—to Mrs. Hatzung, to Salem, and most of all to Mom, who sat beside me crying even harder than I was. Feeling responsible for her tears, I was unable to look at her.

Even as I hugged Mom good-bye after the service, neither of us could speak. Turning quickly, I left her alone in a crowd of strangers. My heart ached. We were a team. She had proven beyond a shadow of a doubt that she would never abandon me. How could I abandon her?

My guilt and sadness intensified when I learned what had happened later that day. A couple of compassionate parents invited Mom to coffee. Tears streaming down her face, she shook her head and left. After driving a few miles, she pulled into a grocery store parking lot, where she sat in her car and wept. While there, she experienced shooting pains in her stomach that she thought were manifestations of her grief. But the pains didn't abate, and by evening she had to be admitted to Carson City Hospital. Tests revealed the severity of her health issues. She was transferred to a larger hospital and scheduled for emergency surgery.

I had promised that if I got homesick at MLS, I would return home. Under normal circumstances, my pride would have prevented me from admitting such weakness, however I was insufferably homesick. I cried every day and would have gone home in an instant if I could. But Mom's illness took that option away. She was in the hospital hours away, fighting for her life. She had undergone extensive surgery and was being kept sedated. For weeks she remained hospitalized, which meant I was forced to stay at school.

Every day of that semester, I longed for the familiarity of home. Most nights I silently cried myself to sleep, and by Thanksgiving break when Mom recovered enough to pick me up from school I was convinced I wasn't going back. After much deliberation, I decided I would return to school, but only to finish the semester—no longer.

Remarkably, the next few weeks changed my attitude. By Christmas I was wholeheartedly committed to staying at MLS.

It helped that I had been blessed with two wonderfully social room-mates. I remained very shy, but through those roommates my circle of friends steadily expanded. I grew to love dorm life and didn't even mind sharing a bathroom with an entire floor of girls. And to our surprise, my new independence helped repair the strain Mom and I had experienced in our relationship since she had announced we were moving to Alpena. When we were together, we appreciated the time we shared.

Everyone at MLS knew my story, but it didn't seem to faze any of them. What they didn't know, however, was the name I had gone by in grade school, Amanda Smith.

At my confirmation, I had officially resumed the use of my birth name. Things with my dad had been quiet for some time, and I was embarking on a new phase in my life. I wanted to move forward using my true identity, but it was an adjustment. My new classmates and teach-ers only knew me as Mahtob—or Maht, as my friends had begun to call me. The trouble was that sometimes I still thought of myself as Mandy.

Just days after school started, I had written letters to my grade school friends and forgotten the stamps. An announcement was made to the entire MLS student body that several letters had been found in the mail bin that morning with no postage and the name Amanda Smith on the return address. The conundrum was that there was no Amanda Smith enrolled at the school. "Could the owner of the letters please stop by the office and pay for the stamps?" Mortified, I headed to the office.

By sophomore year I was wearing my given name more gracefully, though there were moments when I slipped into old habits. Once I answered a page for "Amanda Smith" that was meant for an incoming freshman of that name. Another time my roommate picked up the Bible that sat atop a stack of books in our room and asked, "Maht, why do we have Amanda Smith's Bible?"

It was my Bible, of course—the one I had used all through grade school. Its binding was torn and taped, its cover tattered, its pages soiled along the edges from years of study. Its text was littered with my underlines, my notes decorated its margins, and the pages naturally flipped open to my most commonly referenced readings. This book, now filled with the lessons that shaped my character, had helped me to feel safe after our escape. Inside its front cover, in surprisingly petite letters, Mom had printed, "Mandy Smith."

The summer of 1996 brought the world to Atlanta, Georgia, for the centennial Olympic Games. Mom and I attended at the invitation of a Belgian parliamentarian named Anne-Marie Lizin. Ms. Lizin was active in a women's rights organization called Atlanta Plus, which was protesting the Muslim world's exclusion of women from the Olympic Games. Chief among the offenders was Iran, who forbade women from participating in any event that didn't permit them to remain fully covered in hijab. Atlanta Plus took the stance that any nation that didn't allow women to participate as freely as men in the Olympics should be banned from the games altogether.

Mom and I are not anti-Muslim or anti-Iranian. We are, however, pro-freedom, so we accepted the invitation. In Atlanta we joined forces with prominent women from Belgium, France, Germany, Sweden, and other countries. We marched down the street in matching T-shirts, carrying banners and chanting feminist slogans. I had been snapping pictures as we went, but when the police gathered I put the camera down.

Anne-Marie Lizin encouraged me to continue taking pictures. "You're the youngest one here," she reasoned. "The police won't bother you. You can be our official photographer."

Having lived in a society where the free expression of ideas was forbidden, I found it exhilarating to exercise my right to free speech in such an overt way. We marched, chanted, and waved our banners—and I took pictures—as the police watched. To me it was a display of democracy at its finest.

A meeting had been arranged with the president of the International Olympic Committee. When I was introduced to him, he gently cradled my hand between both of his and said, "Well now, it certainly is a pleasure to meet the most famous daughter in the world."

What a bizarre notion. The whole experience seemed wonderfully absurd. To march in a protest at the age of sixteen was strange enough, and doing so at the request of a European government official added to the peculiarity. But to be called "the most famous daughter in the world" by the IOC president felt like an outlandish dream. Most of the time my life was so ordinary, and then there were moments like this.

Following my initial DSG treatment, my lupus continued to remain fairly stable with the help of regular infusions. Every few months, Mom and I flew to Munich for another ten-day treatment. My teachers helped me through the lessons I missed while I was away, as did my friends. Even so, I was upset at having to tear myself away from school shortly after the start of my junior year.

The beginning of the school year was always full of excitement. I relished the joyful reunions with friends I'd missed all summer and the fun of nesting in the dorms. All the important decisions had to be made—where to hang which posters and how to configure our furniture to maximize the hominess of our rooms. Then, as we began to settle into our routine, came the excitement of homecoming week. A theme was picked, halftime entertainment was planned, and the homecoming court was chosen. I felt cheated to be spending those moments sitting in a clinic in Germany.

The evening I returned to school, my friends had been watching out their windows for me. My roommate ran downstairs to welcome me back and help carry my bags. Our chipper voices echoed through the stairwell as we raced to cram two weeks' worth of updates into four flights worth of stairs. Reaching our floor, she opened the door, and I stepped into the hallway where my friends had gathered. At the first sight of me, they cheered in unison, "Congratulations, Maht!" They engulfed me in hugs and laughter. Above their heads hung a hand-drawn banner that read, "Maht Congrats Rep '98!"

While I was away, my roommates had led a campaign to get me elected as a representative to our homecoming court. My mind was reeling. How could this be? My classmates had really voted for me—the quiet girl who scurried through school staring at her watch, hoping to remain invisible? As the news sank in, I felt humbled and exhilarated.

Almost immediately the question came. "Who's going to escort you onto the football field?" The rep's dad usually locked arms with his daughter and proudly walked her onto the field at the big homecoming football game. That was clearly not an option for me.

My friends generously offered up their fathers to stand in for mine. But for me there was never a question of who would escort me. Mom was my universal parent and she would do it. The question kept coming, however, and when it finally came from the dean, I realized this could become an issue. So I went to see the school president.

He greeted me with a warm smile and his congratulations. "So," he said cheerfully, "what's on your mind?"

"I want to talk with you about homecoming. Everyone keeps asking me who will walk me onto the field."

He interrupted me before I had finished my rehearsed argument. "Your mom, naturally," he said with a sly grin.

"Oh, okay, right," I stammered, breathing a sigh of relief.

"It'll be nice to see her. She must be quite happy to hear that you were chosen to represent your class."

"Yes, she is. Thank you." I left his office with a spring in my step. I didn't have to disappoint Mom.

When the night came, Mom and I stood arm in arm behind the bleachers, waiting to be introduced. I wore a sleeveless emerald-green gown with a matching shawl. When it was our turn, we strolled out onto the football field and turned to face the stands. We were met with thunderous applause: "One-nine-nine-eight—we're the class of ninety-eight. Wahoo!" "We love you Maht!" "And Mrs. Mahmoody," someone added. I stood, arm hooked with Mom's, gazing back at the most beautiful site . . . my MLS family.

All I could think was, *My cup runneth over.* In that moment, my heart was bursting with gratitude for the chaos of my youth. Had it not been for the evil acts of my father, I never would have ended up at Salem. If not for Salem, I wouldn't have known about MLS. If not for Mom's plan to move to Alpena and my stubborn insistence on stability, I wouldn't have had the courage to take the plunge. That one surreal and wonderful moment was the culmination of a lifetime of decisions forced by difficult situations. In that moment, there was nothing in my heart but gratitude.

It was this same attitude of gratitude that had captured the attention of a documentary film crew from Germany. After learning of my battle with lupus and the experimental treatment that saved my life, they came to do a piece on me. What intrigued them most was what they saw as my sunny outlook in the face of such a seemingly overwhelming obstacle.

The producers thought mine was a story that needed to be told, that other teenagers needed this type of positive example. But I didn't see myself as a role model, nor did I see myself as extraordinary in any way. I was simply coping with lupus the way I had coped with my dad's brutality—by finding the good in the bad and trusting that God had a bigger plan than I could see from my vantage point. I couldn't take any credit for that. I was simply living as I had been taught by the optimistic people God had placed in my life.

Several days into the filming, the crew and I headed to the park across the street from our house for an interview. The producer and I chatted as we strolled on the gravel path that wound its way through the trees along the river's edge. A cameraman walked backward in front of us, capturing the scene, while a still photographer snapped away from just outside of the shot. Another man kept pace while holding a boom mic above our heads. As he walked he constantly glanced back and forth between us and the block of audio-monitoring gadgetry that hung over his shoulder.

It dawned on me as we walked and talked that maybe this was why God had allowed me to have lupus. Because of the success of Mom's books, I had a voice that people were willing to listen to, whether I felt the need to talk or not. In that moment I was overcome by a surreal and comforting sense that God was unrolling a tiny corner of the canvas and giving me just the slightest glimpse of his purpose in my life.

DSG had saved my life. There was absolutely no question in my mind about that. There was also no question in my mind that countless others could benefit from this drug. Maybe I had been given a voice so that I could use it in that very moment to shine a light on a treatment that could possibly eradicate autoimmune disease.

About that time, Mom had been asked to do an interview on a Turkish television program. She agreed, but because Turkey had an extradition agreement with Iran, the interview was shot in Paris. After filming, the crew flew back to Turkey to air the piece while Mom remained in Paris to do a live Q&A. During the interview, Mom was told that the Iranian government, after learning she would be interviewed, had demanded that a statement from my father also be included.

I was at our house alone except for one of my roommates. It was my first time to spend a weekend without an adult. It seemed that every time Mom and I began to get complacent, something would happen to remind us that my dad still posed a threat.

Mom made the dreaded phone call. "Mahtob, I don't want to worry you, but . . ." I knew anything that started out with that phrase meant it was indeed time to worry.

"Everything is going to be fine," she assured me. "We just need to be on our guard. Check the doors and windows. Close the blinds. Set the alarm, and don't answer the door for anyone. If you're the least bit uneasy, call the police. It's better to be safe than sorry."

"Got it. Don't worry about me. I know the drill. Call me as soon as the interview is finished so I know you're safe."

I knew that Mom was staying at the Hôtel Balzac, which was about as safe a place as any for her given the circumstances. The staff of the hotel knew us well and had always taken superb care of us.

Once we had been there when someone threw a canister of tear gas into the lobby. It quickly wafted through the entire hotel, sending everyone for the exits. Mom and I knew we needed to evacuate but didn't know if the incident was aimed at us or not. If we left our room, we might be walking straight into a trap. The hotel staff, anticipating our concern, escorted us through the narrow corridors used only by employees and out a side door to a waiting car. My eyes burned and my chest ached as I gasped for air. Mom and I sat in the car coughing as we watched other guests pour out the front door.

In retrospect, I didn't think that incident had anything to do with us, and I was glad the hotel staff had reacted so quickly and resourcefully. But still I couldn't help worrying. Often we traveled with bodyguards, but on this trip Mom was alone.

I jumped when the phone rang. A man asked, "Is this Betty Mahmoody?" He had an accent, but I couldn't place it.

"Who's calling, please?" I had been trained never to identify myself over the phone for a stranger and never to admit that Mom wasn't home. Until I knew who was on the other end of the line, my mission was to gather information while giving away none myself.

Demanding to speak with Mom, the man told me his name, which I didn't recognize. He claimed he was calling from Australia, that his children had been kidnapped by their mother, and that Mom was working on his case. There was something off-putting about him, but I couldn't quite put my finger on what was bothering me. Was it simply his sense of entitlement, or was there something more sinister at play?

"I'd be happy to take down your number," I offered.

"She's got my number, and I've got yours," he hissed threateningly and hung up. His response shook me, but I also knew the strain experienced by left-behind parents. It could simply be that he had reached his breaking point and that his call just happened to coincide with the Iranian government's intrusion in my life.

A few minutes later the phone rang again. This was the era before caller ID. Again I ran to the phone, praying to hear Mom's voice on the line. "Hello," I said tentatively.

"Put Betty Mahmoody on the line."

"Sir, I am happy to take a messa—" He hung up before I had finished.

Right away the phone rang again. This time it was Mom.

"What happened?" I demanded. "Are you okay?"

"I'm fine. Is everything all right there?" Her voice sounded tense. Something was clearly going on, but she didn't want to worry me.

"Everything's fine here. Are you working with a man on an Australian case?"

"Yes, why?"

"Good," I laughed. "That's a relief. He keeps calling, and there's something strange about him. I didn't want to be paranoid, but given everything else that's going on, I was starting to get a little worried. His accent isn't Australian. Where's he from?"

"He's Scandinavian. There *is* something off about him, but he's legitimate, and I'm sure he doesn't have anything to do with your dad or the Iranian government."

"So what's going on there? How did the interview go? What was the statement?"

"He said that you are Iranian and that you have the blood of Fatimah. You are Muslim, and he's not going to allow you to be anything but Muslim."

"Well, that's nice," I said sarcastically. "Here I thought he might say he misses me and he hopes I'm happy. Guess I should have known better."

"Mahtob, I don't want you to worry, but I think we need to be really careful right now."

Only later would I learn the rest of the story of that night. Mom had been doing the Q&A by phone from the Hôtel Balzac. Someone who identified himself as my dad's nephew Reza called in, alleging that my dad was in Paris looking for her. It was in the middle of the night, and people from the Turkish program advised Mom to move to a different hotel immediately. She frantically began to pack, then realized my dad could be waiting just outside the hotel. She pushed furniture in front of the door and told the desk clerk not to let anyone in to see her. Then she called the American embassy, which refused to let her in until morning. Having no other options, she waited out the night.

At six the next morning she called Antoine, one of her French publishers. She was embarrassed to admit she was in Paris. Because she would be there only long enough to do the interview, she hadn't told Antoine she was coming. But when she explained the situation, he immediately came to the hotel with a car, driver, and security personnel. He made flight arrangements, took her to the airport, and waited with her to be sure she made it safely out of the country.

This was the first direct message we had received from my dad since our escape. It left me feeling defiant. I found some sort of perverse satisfaction in knowing that while he was in Iran ranting about my being Muslim, I was, of my own choosing, attending a Lutheran boarding school. I had surrounded myself with other Christians. I studied the

Bible. I didn't cover. I wore makeup. I attended school dances, where I danced with boys. After high school, I planned to attend a Lutheran college, and I hoped to someday be a Lutheran elementary school teacher.

It was empowering to see how pathetic his attempt was at exerting control over me. At the same time I trembled with the knowledge that even just one of my many egregious offenses could, in his mind, justify extreme action. Nevertheless, I pushed the thought from my head and carried on with life as usual.

One evening during my senior year, my roommate dragged me to "the commons" to watch TV. The commons weren't nearly as frightening to me now as they had been in my early days at MLS. That night it was packed with students lounging sideways in chairs with legs dangling over the armrests, sitting atop the brick ledge that lined the room, or even sprawling on the floor—all staring up at the TV that was suspended from the ceiling. I grimaced as one show finished and an episode of *South Park* started. It was a crude cartoon with a sense of humor I didn't appreciate.

Turning my attention away from the TV, I joined a conversation with some friends. We were chattering away when all of a sudden I realized that the room had fallen unusually silent. The only sounds were the whiny, high-pitched voices of the characters bouncing around the screen. No one moved. Every eye was focused on the television. My face reddened with embarrassment as I realized what was happening.

It took one of the jocks to say it out loud. "Whoa, Maht, they're talking about you!" he blurted.

I almost never watched TV in the commons, and I never watched *South Park*. What were the chances I would be sitting there at precisely the moment they did a vulgar parody of my story? I was mortified.

Finally, someone said what they were all thinking. "Come on, Maht. You've got to see the humor in it. Sure, it's sick and wrong, but *South Park* is doing a parody of *you*. That's pretty stinkin' amazing."

I had to give them that. It wasn't a distinction I prized, but I supposed, in some circles, it could be seen as an honor. The guys on the football team sure seemed to think it was "awesome."

My years at MLS were virtually carefree. I was relatively healthy, conflict was scarce, and security concerns were at a minimum. Mom's health challenges had endured just long enough to solidify my resolve to stay at MLS, and her recovery period had given her ample time to assess her life. The years of intense travel coupled with the emotional stress of her constant battle against child abduction had taken their toll on her body. She decided it was time to slow down. After I moved to MLS, she couldn't bring herself to move to Alpena full time. It was too far away from me. So she divided her time between our old house and the house in Alpena.

Many of my classmates lived quite far away. Some were from other states, even other countries. Since Mom lived only forty-five minutes from school, my house became their home away from home. On Fridays Mom would collect a carload of girls and laundry. The consummate hostess, she was in her element with a houseful of eager mouths to feed. The cafeteria food at MLS was actually good, but after a week of eating off a buffet, nothing tasted as amazing as a home-cooked meal. Weekends at my house became such a pivotal part of our high school experience that much of my graduating class listed "weekends at Maht's" or "Maht's mom's cooking" in our senior yearbook as one of their favorite MLS memories.

Our days, whether spent in the dorms or visiting someone's family home on a weekend, were filled with laughter. The intensity of our high school years added to the strength of the friendships we forged—more than friends, we became family, bonded by Christ and the experiences we shared.

As a homesick freshman, I wouldn't have believed that leaving MLS would be one of the most difficult hurdles I would ever face. But my teachers and friends and the consistency of the lessons taught from a Christian worldview had restored the stability lost with my graduation from Salem.

CHAPTER 21

Some days in life are sad; others are heartbreaking. To me, my graduation from Michigan Lutheran Seminary fell in the latter category. As graduation approached, my friends and I dreaded the fateful milestone. For us it marked the end of a utopian era. Even the word *commencement* irked me. It did not feel like a beginning.

My friends Hannah and Mollie set a reverential tone for the ceremony with a piano and organ duet of Bach's "Sheep May Safely Graze." Engulfed in the doleful melody, the rest of my classmates and I filed into the auditorium in pairs arranged by height. Being one of the shortest, I was among the last to enter. When we stood and turned to sing our class hymn, I was front and center.

"Lord, I stretch my hands to you," we sang in harmony, and then it struck me that this would be the last time all seventy of us would raise our voices together in worship. Hannah, now standing beside me, must have been sharing the thought. We stood hand in hand before the crowded auditorium, weeping, unable to sing another note. Amoo Kombiz, my dad's former best friend who had become my adopted Persian uncle, sat with Mom a few rows back, videotaping the tearful spectacle.

Hannah's and Mollie's dad, Pastor Stern, gave the sermon that day. Building on the theme of our class song, he spoke of the role his hand had played in the rearing of his twin daughters. Holding it out for all to see, he described how his hand had caught them when they stumbled, corrected them, and encouraged them.

"Graduates" Pastor Stern continued, "behind each of you there has been such a loving and giving hand. A hand that belongs to your parents, your grandparents; a hand that belongs to your teachers, your pastors. . . . Those hands, individually and collectively, have played an important part in making this day possible."

"However," he cautioned, "there's one thing you need to realize about all these hands. They're all like mine. . . . More often than I care to admit, these hands have failed. They have broken their promises. . . . They haven't always been there when others needed them. And they won't always be there. So as you journey through life, don't reach out to these hands. Rather, reach out to the Hand that's always been there for you, the Hand behind all the other hands in your life. The Hand that will always be there for you. The Hand that will never fail you. The Hand that loves you more than all the hands gathered here today, and the Hand that will guide you safely through all the tomorrows of your life."

His words rang true to me. Many of those whose hands had guided me to this day were scattered about the gymnasium. Each had in some way shared in my upbringing. All had taken it upon themselves to enrich my life with their encouragement and love.

Pastor Stern pointed to our class verse on the banner that hung behind him: "In his heart a man plans his course, but the LORD determines his steps" (Proverbs 16:9).

"In other words, graduates, as human beings we can plan, plan, and plan, but the Lord ultimately has the final say-so on whether or not our plans ever take shape."

Sitting with my classmates, about to receive my diploma, I felt very uncertain about the course I had chosen. Many of my closest friends—in fact, half of our graduating class, had chosen to go Martin Luther College in Minnesota to pursue careers in the preaching or teaching ministry. I, along with just one other graduate, was headed to Michigan State University in East Lansing. My heart broke at the thought of going from living with my MLS family to being separated from them by the span of several states.

Mrs. Hatzung had introduced me to the idea of being a missionary. When we studied the Great Commission in the book of Matthew, she'd told us this was God's command for every Christian, including us. As a child I had been ready to "go and make disciples of all nations," and I wanted to start with Iran. I wanted my fellow Iranians to know that Jesus had died to save them, too, and that they would go to heaven simply by believing in him. There was no need to pray five times a day facing Mecca or to beat oneself or to make pilgrimages or to die as a martyr in a holy war.

By the end of first grade, however, I had decided that instead of being a missionary, I would rather be a teacher like Mrs. Hatzung. It wasn't until the end of my junior year in high school that I contemplated a different field of study. I had picked up a psychological thriller called *Primal Fear*, and by the time I read the last words, I knew I would study psychology.

If only I hadn't read that book, I thought, watching my classmates walk across the stage to accept their diplomas. *Then I could go to MLC with my friends, become a teacher, and live happily ever after.* Even then I knew I would not have been content with that path. In the years since our escape, I had remained consistently driven to discover the secrets of resilience. That quest was what had ultimately drawn me to Michigan State University.

I had a gnawing need to know everything I could about the workings of the human mind. *Why did people do the things they did and how was it that certain life experiences affected individuals so differently?* I wondered. *What distinguished the person who crumbled in the face of adversity from the one who thrived?* And—more to the point—*how could I ensure that I never became the one who crumbled?* For years, I had been burdened with a deep sense of foreboding that I was just one hurdle away from becoming bitter and cynical, and I couldn't allow that to happen.

I managed to dry my tears long enough to accept my diploma. When the ceremony ended, we filed out two by two, just as we had entered, only this time the familiar corridors that led out the front door no longer belonged to us.

My classmates and I stood shoulder to shoulder on the front lawn of the school, our graduation gowns flowing in the breeze, as our professors led the long procession of well-wishers. These farewells were not easy for them either. It was unusually warm and sunny for early May. The sky was blue, and the grass was thick and green beneath our feet.

The school president paused when he reached me. "Mahtob," he said, shaking my hand, "I owe you and your mom an apology."

"For what?" I asked, waiting for the punch line. President Prange was known for his sense of humor.

"Four years ago, on orientation day, I manned one of the registration tables. I was aware of your background, and I knew you were one of the incoming freshmen. As parents made their way to my station, I handed them a stack of consent forms and joked, 'Sign here and I'll make your child disappear.' It wasn't until I saw your mom's signature that I realized who you were. I felt horrible. I hadn't thought about what such a statement would mean to you. What an insensitive thing to say! I'm sorry. I just needed to get that off my chest."

By the time he finished explaining I could barely breathe. Under different circumstances, it probably wouldn't have struck me so funny, but the physical and emotional exhaustion of the occasion had taken its toll, and I couldn't stop laughing. It was a much-needed reprieve from my sadness.

Late in the evening, emotionally and physically exhausted, I faced one more excruciating round of good-byes and collapsed behind the wheel of my car, thankful not to be making the hour-long drive on my own. Hannah had decided to go back with me to Mom's house for the night. We were a pathetic pair, sobbing uncontrollably most of the way.

It was on a dark country road, through her tears, that Hannah first taught me a poem that has stuck with me ever since. She called it "The Weaver's Poem," and I have since learned that the words she taught me were slightly different from what the author B.M. Franklin originally wrote. But the powerful meaning was the same:

My life is but a weaving
Between my Lord and me.
I cannot choose the colors
He weaves so skillfully.

Sometimes He weaveth sorrow
And I in foolish pride
Forget He sees the upper
And I the underside.

Not 'til the loom is silent
And the shuttles cease to fly
Will God unroll the canvas
And explain the reasons why

The dark threads are as needful,
In The Weaver's skillful hands
As the threads of gold and silver
In the pattern He has planned.

Those beautiful lines of poetry helped put everything into perspective for me. All the messages of the day melded together for us in that car ride—our class verse, the class hymn, and Pastor Stern's assurance that our every step is in the loving hands of our Lord and Savior.

The tears and good-byes, the intolerable grief of losing my home at MLS and, most important, my Seminary family—all that was just one very dark thread in the tapestry God was weaving of my life. God had a plan that I couldn't completely see from where I was standing.

I pictured the magnificent Persian carpets that had surrounded me my entire life. Without the dark threads, what would they be? It is the contrast of light and dark and everything in between that gives them their character, their vibrancy—their life.

Many dark threads had been woven through my life already, and with the perspective of time, I had come to cherish the blessings left in their wake. Hannah had given me a poignant reminder that in the grand scheme of things, life's hardships really do bring about God's greatest blessings. If ever there was a life that was a shining example of that truth, it was mine.

My grief, though real and intense, was shortsighted. This was simply one of the many threads in God's weaving. No doubt this thread, like all the others before it, would weave together in time to create something uniquely beautiful.

CHAPTER 22

The fall of 1998 brought with it another move. The only person I knew at Michigan State University was my roommate, Trisha. Trish and I hadn't been close friends in high school, but I'd been greatly relieved when I learned we had both been accepted to Lyman Briggs College, one of MSU's smaller and more competitive programs. This interdisciplinary "residential college" basically took one of the largest universities in the nation and broke it down into a more manageable bite-sized piece. Only a few hundred students were selected each year to begin the program. We lived, ate, and even had most of our classes all in one building.

Lyman Briggs students were a studious bunch—serious scholars of the natural sciences with an appreciation for liberal arts and the social implications of scientific advances. To say that Trish and I lived on the rowdiest of floors in Holmes Hall, while true, is a bit laughable. Our floor's collective rowdiness was exceedingly tame by MSU standards. It was a coed floor, which is how I came to know Brian. His room was just across the hall on the diagonal from ours, and the instant he spotted Mom and me lugging in my copious amount of belongings, he jumped right in to help. I didn't know it yet, but he would become a faithful friend and loyal protector.

Although I had chosen to focus on the natural sciences like biology, physics, and chemistry, my passion was the social sciences—psychology, sociology, anthropology, etc. My first psychology class only confirmed this inclination. We read books like Breggin and Cohen's *Your Drug May Be Your Problem*, Freud's *The Interpretation of Dreams*, and Modrow's *How to Become a Schizophrenic*, a tome that pinned the blame on inconsistent parenting. My professor claimed to have successfully treated people with incapacitating schizophrenia without the use of psychotropic medications.

I was hooked. I knew that my heart belonged to the social sciences. I didn't care about neurochemicals or the functions of different parts of the brain. I was driven by a hunger to understand human thought and behavior. How did our thoughts influence our behavior and vice versa? How did our life experiences affect our thoughts—or was it the other way around? Did our thoughts prompt our life experiences? How did culture, environment, family structures, and religion fit into the equation?

It struck me in that first psychology class that somewhere near the root of many mental-health conditions are the emotions of guilt and fear. In the far recesses of my mind was born a theory that a feeling of guilt was the driving force behind mental illness. I'm not arguing this as scientific fact. It's just the observations of a young person dipping her toe into the study of the human mind while guided by a professor whose philosophy, while fascinating, was extremely controversial among his peers.

Undergraduate courses in psychology teach almost nothing about treatment, but that didn't stop me from dreaming up my own treatment approaches. To me it seemed common sense that if guilt were the root of the problem, then forgiveness was the solution. And where was forgiveness found? In the Bible.

The Bible's teachings can be divided into two categories—law and gospel. The law shows us our sin and our need for a savior. Throughout time and across the various regions of the earth, a similar moral code has ruled. Murder is considered to be wrong, as are stealing and adultery. It's not just Christians who ascribe to these values; they're societal norms. God has written his law on our hearts. Whether or not we ever open a Bible, we know God's law. Our conscience is proof of that. What we don't inherently know is the gospel, the good news that tells us Jesus is our savior.

The root of the problem, as I saw it, was that we often fail to forgive ourselves and instead hold on to our guilt and the fear of punishment that it breeds. My theory was that a treatment approach built on these law and gospel messages, with an emphasis on the "good news," could go a long way toward improving a person's mental health.

Like many people who enter the field of psychology, I was on a mission to form a better understanding of myself. The concept of forgiveness as a solution to guilt was a lesson learned since first grade. Could it be that this was at the heart of my resilience?

I didn't dare speak of these things with my professors. For one, I was too shy to approach them. In addition, I found MSU, especially where the sciences were concerned, to be extremely secular—at times even crossing into anti-Christian.

On two different occasions I was called on to give a public confession of my faith in class. Both were difficult experiences. The first came in a biology class, which featured what I thought to be an overemphasis on evolution.

The instructor intrigued me. I had imagined a high-ranking professor to look polished and professional, wearing a suit and heels. Instead she had long, stringy, gray hair and wore hippie clothes and Birkenstocks when she lectured. I admired her nonconformity. She proved it was possible to excel academically and professionally while still maintaining one's individuality. She encouraged her students to think and speak freely, believing that active engagement in the subject matter was a valuable part of the learning process. If a student answered a question incorrectly, the instructor was prone to say something like, "Hmm, interesting thought. I can see where you might get that impression. Does anyone else see it differently?"

Even in this atmosphere of openness, I still hid bashfully toward the back of the lecture hall. Then one day she asked the question, "How did the universe come to be?" She scanned the students, who sat at tables in an arc around her, each curved row slightly higher than the previous.

I tried my usual evasive tactic. I stared at my notebook and pretended the notes I was scribbling were of vital importance. But I could feel her looking at me. "Go ahead," she said.

I glanced at the students seated beside me, hoping one of them would answer. When they didn't, I pointed at myself and gave the professor a sheepish look that said, "Who, me?"

"Yes, you," she answered. "Please tell us how the universe came to be."

My mind raced. I knew the answer she wanted me to give. I also knew that I didn't believe it. I quickly weighed my options and ultimately decided that this wasn't an Iranian classroom where I was required to give the teacher the answer she demanded. This was America. Here I was free to think and to say what I believed.

Clearing my throat, I very quietly quoted Genesis 1:1, the very first words of the Bible: "In the beginning God created the heavens and the earth."

Though I knew it wasn't what she wanted to hear, I still presumed she would react with her usual tact. Instead she berated me. I was humiliated. After class, students I had never met approached me to apologize on her behalf. They didn't all agree with what I said, but they felt bad that I had been so cruelly rebuked. Some did agree, and one even went so far as to thank me for speaking up. "I wish I had your courage," she said, patting me on the shoulder.

The second such experience came in a different class not long after the murder conviction of Jack Kevorkian, the doctor who championed the cause of physician-assisted suicide. This lecture hall was narrow and deep. I had learned that the best place to hide was in the middle of the front row, directly in front of the professor. She naturally looked well above me, into the center of the mass of students.

"As I'm sure you've all heard by now, Jack Kevorkian, 'Dr. Death,' was convicted of murder. I want to hear from you. Should he have been convicted? Was what he did really murder, or was it mercy?"

I sat calmly, waiting for the professor to call on someone in the middle of the room. Instead, she stopped in front of me and asked, "What do you think?"

"I think the jury was right to convict him."

"Okay. Why?" she prodded.

"I believe God gives life, and he's the only one who is justified in taking it."

The class exploded at the mention of God. Suddenly everyone, it seemed, had something to say. Tempers flared. Most of the comments did not center on whether euthanasia was right or wrong. Instead they focused on speaking out against me and my statement. Some asserted there is no God. Others held that it's not God who gives and takes life. Still others insisted there is no room in modern society for what they perceived to be antiquated, ignorant, and prejudicial religiously based ideologies.

I was shocked and infuriated. Who was being prejudiced? Not me, but the ones who were lambasting me for my beliefs. I had been asked for my opinion and I had given it. Why was all this anger being directed at me? Why the shouting? Why the hostility? Why was I coming under personal attack? I wasn't telling them they had to think the way I did. I wasn't yelling and pointing my finger because we had different opinions.

Again I sat there thinking, *This is America. What is happening? As an American, am I not guaranteed the right to freedom of religion? Am I not guaranteed the right to freedom of speech? That's what makes this country so great. We are free to disagree.*

When I was younger, Mom had taped a newspaper clipping to the edge of her computer monitor. The words were attributed to the French philosopher Voltaire: "I may disagree with what you say, but I will defend to the death your right to say it." It became frighteningly clear to me that day that where religion was concerned on my campus, that philosophy did not apply. In the name of political correctness, religion and specifically Christianity had become taboo.

I vowed never to open my mouth in class again. My resolve to keep my mouth shut was seriously tested, however, in a sociology class where the professor asserted that one person cannot make a difference in society. She said the world is full of injustice and we, as members of society, have to accept that because society is more powerful than the individual.

I thought I had misunderstood her. How could she possibly believe that? And why did no one else in the room seem the least bit alarmed that she had stood before us in a position of authority and uttered such nonsense? I sat listening in disbelief, wanting so badly to stand up and tell everyone that she was wrong, that one person *could* make a difference. My mom was proof of that.

When Mom was told by the courts that in order to get a divorce she would have to serve notice to my dad, thus alerting him to where we were, she didn't just say, "Oh, okay. I guess there's nothing I can do." No. She threw herself headlong into a battle to reform our legal system to make it possible for her and others to get a divorce in a way that upholds due process and yet offers protection to those who need it. She spoke out about the injustice and garnered support from citizens and politicians alike.

Together they lobbied, working within the system to change the system. And the wheels of democracy turned. Michigan became the first state in the nation to allow someone to file for divorce in a county other than their county of residence. Five and a half years after our escape, she was able to obtain a divorce in a way that respected my father's right to defend himself in court and still afforded us protection. One person *can* make a difference.

Mom didn't stop there. There was a federal law that rendered it a crime for a parent to kidnap a child over state lines, but that law did not apply to international borders. Legally speaking, wrongful retention constitutes kidnapping. Had my father held us in Kansas, he would have committed a crime. But he didn't hold us hostage in Kansas, he held us hostage in Iran, and because of a loophole in the American legal system, he was considered an innocent man.

At the same time Mom was lobbying for state reform, she lobbied for federal reform. In late 1993, more than seven and a half years after our escape, President Clinton signed a federal law forbidding international parental child abduction. One person can make a difference.

By the time that class was over, I was livid. I stormed out and stomped all the way to the bus stop. By the time I got there, I had decided I had to say something. I sat on a bench, grabbed my notebook from my backpack and scribbled a heated essay on the value and social responsibility of an individual in society. My bus came and went, and I remained on the bench, clenching my pen so firmly my hand ached.

After several pages of venting, I was finally able to breathe. I took the next bus back to my dorm and called Mom the minute I got in my room. "How could she say that?" I fumed. "And everyone just sat there soaking it up. What we need to be hearing is that we *can* make a difference in the world. A democracy is only effective if its citizens play an active role in defending against injustice. How could a public university in *America* tolerate such treason?"

I was shouting, pacing around my dorm room, arms flying through the air in disgust. "It just doesn't make any sense. What about Gandhi? What about Rosa Parks? What about Hitler, for crying out loud? His contribution was horrendous, but he still influenced society. Individuals influence society all the time."

"Don't you think maybe she was saying something so outlandish just to elicit a response from the class? Maybe she was just trying to spark a conversation."

"If that's what she was doing, she carried it too far. If you use an example like that, at some point you have to set the record straight when no one takes the bait."

Ever the voice of reason, Mom cautioned me to think before giving the professor my essay. "I'm not telling you not to do it. I'm just saying to think it through. Is this the way you want to fight this battle? You're right; individuals do make a difference in the world. We both know that. And it's good that you don't blindly accept everything your professors teach you. When it comes time for your exam, you can write, 'What you taught us is . . .' That doesn't mean you have to agree with it.

"Maybe this class is just a means to an end. Maybe it's better to just keep quiet, pass the class, and move on to the next one. Or maybe not. Maybe it's worth it to you to speak your mind. If it is, you've got to be ready to live with the consequences. It may hurt your grade. Can you live with that?"

She knew I couldn't.

"Whatever you do, remember you catch more flies with honey than with vinegar."

She was right, of course. This wasn't a crucial battle. I could try to prove my point, but what would that accomplish? I knew what I believed. That professor couldn't change that. I didn't need to convince anyone in that class that I was right. I would let my actions do the talking. I would stick to my convictions and live my life according to them. That's how I would make a difference.

CHAPTER 23

From the time *Not Without My Daughter* was first published in 1987, Mom and I had received thousands of letters from people around the world. But the summer of 2000 marked the start of a new trend. Suddenly I began receiving e-mails from strangers. Their messages were the same as the lovely letters Mom and I had received for years. But receiving them on my personal computer, behind the secured walls of my home, my haven, was an unsettling turn of events for me. I tried to feel flattered, but instead the e-mails left me feeling threatened and harassed. These kindhearted gestures crossed some invisible boundary and were, to me, a disquieting invasion of privacy.

Internet use then wasn't what it is today. In my senior year of high school, a forward-thinking professor had taught our class how to perform an Internet search. It was a complicated, space-age discourse interwoven with terms like *Boolean operators* and *keywords*. My computer kept locking up, and my searches didn't return pertinent information.

I found the whole process cumbersome and immensely inefficient. So it was a completely alien experience when people I didn't know started to locate me by untangling the invisible webs that I couldn't wrap my head around, the ones that would supposedly one day connect the entire world.

How had they found me? How did I know they were who they

claimed to be? Mom and I hadn't heard anything directly from my dad since he'd sent the message saying he wouldn't allow me to be anything but Muslim. That had been nearly four years earlier, but we were still on guard.

Was this just another of his ploys? How did I know he wasn't posing as a well-wisher in order to gain access to me? Or maybe he had enlisted the help of these people to draw me into a dialogue. Even if he didn't have anything to do with these intrusions, if these people could find me, so could he.

I probably wouldn't have found the e-mails so disconcerting if there hadn't been so many at once. The first came on July 12, closely followed by messages on July 25, July 26, August 5, and August 19. Every few days, it seemed, yet another person was contacting me, telling me how much they admired Mom and me and wanting to know if I'd ever spoken with my dad again.

I methodically analyzed each message for clues, acutely aware that there were too many unknown variables for me to crack the code. At the same time, I was plagued with guilt for not responding to the e-mails. If they were genuine, then these were gracious gestures from strangers who cared enough to reach out to me.

But just as my resolve would begin to crumble and I was on the verge of hitting reply, I would get a message containing a thread of information I couldn't recall sharing publicly, and my protective impulses would again take over. Two e-mails in a row congratulated me on my decision to become a doctor, but I couldn't remember ever saying in an interview that I was pursuing premed studies. My instincts told me something was brewing, and I had learned over the years the importance of trusting my intuition.

I had decided years earlier that I would never engage my father in conversation. I didn't feel I owed him anything. Mr. Voeltz's monotone wisdom still rang through my mind: "If you abuse a privilege, you lose the privilege." Forgiving my father didn't mean I had to subject myself to any more of his abuse. I also didn't want to put him through any undue trauma. I reasoned that any word from me would feed his hope of rekindling our relationship, and I was entirely opposed to that. I also knew that nothing I had to say would be what my father wanted to hear. I feared that any communication on my part would only serve to enrage him, leading to disastrous results. Knowing firsthand how violent he became when he didn't get his way, I was petrified of what he was capable of doing.

I had spent most of my childhood just hours from Dearborn, a suburb of Detroit that was said to contain the highest concentration of Muslims outside the Muslim world. I didn't know if that was true or not. I had never checked the numbers. I did know however, that every few years news would break of another honor killing right here in Michigan. There had even been an alleged honor killing in or around East Lansing about the time I started at MSU.

I knew my father was trying to reach me, but I didn't know his motives. Did he just want to talk or did he want to see me? Did he want to take me back to Iran? Did he want to restore the family's "honor" by killing me for being Christian, for not wearing hijab, for wearing makeup, for listening to rock music, for reading books that weren't approved by the Islamic Guidance Committee? If he was planning to kidnap me, had he paused to consider the implications for me? Taking me back to Iran would literally be a death sentence because I was a Christian born to a Muslim father. Even if he wasn't interested in restoring the family's honor, who's to say the government wasn't ready to do it for him?

I hated being so cynical about the e-mails, but my dad posed a real and potent threat. As I grew older, Mom and I had slowly let down our guard at times, but that summer warning bells had begun to sound. I had a growing feeling that something was awry. The day after my twenty-first birthday, my suspicions were confirmed as I read the fateful words that flickered before me on my computer screen.

It was a message from a Finnish film producer. While in Iran on business, he had met my father, who tearfully expressed a deep desire to see me.

Wonderful, I thought, *this is just what I need. Is this guy for real?*

The Finnish producer wrote that he had heard from "several sources" that I wanted to see my dad again.

Really? Who are these sources—my dad and his evil henchmen? How about doing some research before interfering in my life?

My stance had been unwavering. Any interview the producer could have watched would have revealed my position on reuniting with my father.

This guy clearly has an agenda . . . my father's agenda.

The producer informed me that he was making a documentary about my father. He invited me to be a part of the project and, more specifically, to meet with my father.

Fantastic! Now this guy, who is sympathetic to my dad and his mission to reunite with me, has my e-mail address, which means my dad has my e-mail address. What other contact information do they have? This is bad. This is very, very bad.

My father had asked him to convey his birthday wishes to me.

My father can save his birthday wishes. It is an apology that he needs to send.

I ignored the e-mail. Nine days later, another e-mail arrived. It was identical to the last one, save the line about my birthday.

The contact from the producer left me terrified, and I retreated from the world to the only dependable escape I knew—sleep. I slept entire weekends away, nestled under the covers in my childhood bedroom at Mom's house. During the school week, back at my apartment in East Lansing, my waking hours were spent fleeing reality by reading. I immersed myself in my textbooks, and when there was no more studying to do, I read long novels. I was desperate to keep my mind so intensely absorbed that there were no free thoughts left for contemplation.

Mom tried to talk with me about how I wanted to proceed, and I refused to answer, which she took to mean that maybe I wanted to see my father. But I didn't. I didn't want to see him. I didn't want to talk to him. I didn't want to deal with his harassment. I wanted everything and everyone to just leave me alone. I didn't want to think. I didn't want to feel. I didn't want to be. All I wanted was to go to sleep and not wake up until this had all gone away.

Finally one weekend, when I was at Mom's house, curled up in a ball beneath my covers, Mom came in. Sitting on the edge of my bed, she spoke softly, "Mahtob, I know you don't want to talk about this right now, but we need to send a response. We can't put it off any longer, and I think it needs to come from you."

I didn't answer.

"Do you want to see your dad? It's okay with me if you do."

"I don't," I snapped, feeling numb. Since all this had begun, I had been in shock. Too stunned to cry, I shivered uncontrollably, even under the blankets. And though I was held down by the weight of their layers, I had the feeling that I was floating somewhere in the corner of the room, watching my world fall apart from a distance. The only emotion I felt was fear, laced with the fierce hatred I had become intimately acquainted with as a child.

"Do you want to do an interview?"

"No." I didn't like the sound of my voice. It was icy, bitter.

"Then you need to tell them that."

"No. In all these years I haven't given him any reason to hope for a reunion, and still he hasn't given up. No matter what I say, he's going to be angry. You know how he is. He doesn't need to be provoked to explode. Any statement from me would only be a provocation. If I say I don't want to do the interview, either he'll see it as a good sign that I've opened the door of communication, or he'll see it as a sign of disrespect and he'll come after us. Either way, it'll only make matters worse. I'm not adding fuel to this fire. Plus, you know how the media works. If I give a statement, they could twist and turn it to serve their agenda. I don't trust anyone involved in any of this. I am not giving them a statement."

Realizing there was nothing she could say to convince me, Mom prepared a response from both of us. She returned to her seat on the edge of my bed and read it to me. "I still think it would be better coming from you."

"You can do what you want, but I am not saying anything." I rolled over, turning my back to her.

I held out an unrealistic hope that the extent of this intrusion would be limited to a few unsettling e-mails. Even then, I knew that was naive. Already Mom had been contacted by the State Department and cautioned. Several family friends had received similar requests for interviews. Even the judge who had issued my parents' divorce had been approached. All indications pointed to this being an ugly and far-reaching campaign. Nevertheless, I hoped.

CHAPTER 24

In mid-October 2000, my worst fear became a reality. It happened on a gloriously crisp autumn afternoon.

I loved autumn in Michigan. The earthy scent of fallen leaves, their crunch beneath my feet, the refreshing blast of air brushing against my face as I walked up the path to my apartment door—it was all wonderful. Even though fall heralded Michigan's seemingly eternal winter, it was my favorite season . . . until spring hit, that is.

My junior year at MSU, I shared a cozy two-bedroom apartment—my first—with three other girls. After six years in the dorms, four in high school and two in college, apartment living felt gloriously cosmopolitan. The facts that we were on the flight path to the airport and literally next to the expressway were inconsequential. I could gladly tune out the hustle and bustle of land and air traffic in exchange for the luxury of living in my first apartment.

The moment I opened the door that October day, I was hit with an intense sense of foreboding. There on the wall directly in front of me was a sticky note that read, "Maht, call your mom. It's important!" As I followed the curve of the stairs, my eyes landed on a second note: "Maht, your mom called." Then there was a third note, and a fourth . . . and a hundredth. Well, maybe there really weren't that many, but to me it felt as if there were Post-Its everywhere, on nearly every wall, the refrigerator, even the bathroom mirror. By the time I added the note from the door of the bedroom I shared with Trish to the stack in my hand, I was absolutely certain disaster had struck. I had that feeling of panic that only seized me when the threat of my father reared its head.

This was a feeling I knew well. It had gnawed at me most of my life. I could hide from it, pretend I wasn't in danger, make believe I didn't live every day of my life with the intense dread of my world being turned on end with the flip of a switch, but there was no escaping it. The threat of my dad lurked in every shadow.

Flinging my backpack on my bed, I frantically tore through pockets in search of my phone. Not wanting to be one of "those people," I had fought the cell-phone revolution with gusto. But with all the recent suspicious activity, Mom's unceasing insistence that "a little bit of communication saves a lot of worry" had finally won me over.

The trembling that came with my dad's intrusion in my life always started deep in my core. Usually I was able to control it, hiding it from view, masking it behind a stoic smile. In that moment though, it seized my entire body. My hands shook so violently, my fingers struggled to grip the backpack's zippers. My heart pounded in my ears.

Slowly, purposefully, I forced myself to take deep breaths. Everything was going to be all right. There was no need to panic. Maybe it wasn't my dad. Maybe I was overreacting. Where was the phone?

Blindly I opened one compartment after another searching for it. Finally I reached for the small pocket on the front of the bag, the pocket where I always kept my phone. Why was that the last place I checked? That was where the phone belonged. Disoriented, I flipped the phone open and found numerous missed calls and voice-mail messages.

I willed my eyes to focus, my mind to concentrate. Pressing the walkie-talkie button on the side, I mentally rehearsed my casual sounding voice.

"Hi, Mom. What's up? I see you called." Ugh, it came out sounding too cheerleaderish, not believable at all.

"Mahtob, where are you?" Her words were clipped, breathless. I knew that tone of voice. She was frantic.

"I'm home. I just got back from class. I had my phone turned off until just now." Was she buying my calmness?

"I don't want to worry you, but . . ."

This was not good.

"Your dad has found us. I answered the phone at home today, and it was him. He asked for you."

There it was. My single greatest fear was now my reality.

Since childhood, the words *your dad* had angered me. He wasn't anything to anyone else in my family. People didn't say to Mom, "your ex-husband." No, they said, "Mahtob's dad." They didn't say to my brothers, "your ex-stepdad," or to my grandma, "your ex-son-in-law." It was always, "Mahtob's dad." He was mine, no matter how badly I didn't want him. And no matter how badly I wanted to be my own, I was his.

"Did anyone follow you?" Mom said.

"No, I don't think so. I paid close attention and I didn't see anything suspicious."

"Go check to make sure your door's locked," she ordered.

"It's locked. I always lock it."

"Is anyone else there?"

"No, it's just me." My calm facade had crumbled. I could hear the tremor taking hold of my voice.

"We already knew he had your e-mail address. Now we know he's got our home phone number, which means he has the address. He may know about your apartment too. We can't be too careful. Don't let anyone in. I'm almost there," she continued. "Pack a bag. I don't know where we'll go or how long we'll be gone. We can always find a place to do laundry."

Her words continued, but my mind was adrift in a violently churning sea of recent events. Waves of realization crashed over me. A myriad of independent dots simultaneously connected, revealing a sickening scene—hang-up calls at Mom's house, the flood of e-mails from random strangers, the message from the State Department to be on alert, the persistent film producer from Finland . . . *The producer from Finland. This is his fault.*

For years Mom had stood before audiences and said that one of the strongest factors we had working in our favor was my father's laziness. In Iran, Mom had used his weakness to our advantage. After her bout with dysentery, which nearly ended her life, she'd decided our best hope of escape lay in outworking my father.

Her plan had worked. It was my father's laziness that had helped us escape, and it was his laziness that had kept us safe since. He lacked motivation. Sure, he wanted to see me again, but on his own, he was exceedingly unlikely to take any action—unless he was provoked or he had someone to do the work for him.

Enter the producer from Finland.

I had come to know my share of producers over the years. They were tenacious people. A producer must be driven, resourceful, creative, and above all persistent. And my father was masterful at reading people and discerning how best to utilize their assets for his gain. That was, I believe, one reason he and my mom had done so well together in the years before we went to Iran. Mom is an untiringly hard worker. My dad had never needed to lift a finger because before he could think of what it was he wanted, Mom would already have it waiting for him. Now he had roped in a producer.

I raced about my room opening and closing dresser drawers and closet doors, throwing clothes in a duffle bag without bothering to fold them. There was no time to waste with neatness. I raced around the corner into the bathroom, open bag in hand. I tossed in a toothbrush, toothpaste, my makeup bag.

What was I forgetting? What else did I need? I couldn't think. My head was swimming.

My phone chirped, and then Mom's voice came over the speaker. "I'm walking up to the door. Come let me in."

I ran down the stairs and opened the door just wide enough for her to squeeze through. The instant she was in, I slammed it shut and locked the dead bolt. She looked pale and disheveled.

"What are we going to do?" I asked, following her up the stairs. As we passed through the living room I drew the curtains.

"Before I left home I grabbed our passports, just in case we need to leave the country. Yours is expired. The first thing we need to do is go to Chicago and get that renewed. We shouldn't be around here anyway. Your dad may be here."

I scribbled a note for my roommates explaining the situation and asking them to be careful. Then I grabbed my backpack and duffle bag from the bedroom and headed for the door. We paused at the top of the stairs. Was it safe to go outside? Turning back, I peeked through the closed curtains. The only movement in the parking lot below us was the blowing of the fall leaves across the pavement. Deciding the coast was clear, we hustled for the door.

Mom was barreling out of the parking space before I had my seatbelt buckled. "I have to go to campus," I declared with urgency.

"What? Right now? That's not a good idea."

Mom's priority was to get out of town and out of the path of the storm that was following us. "I'm scheduled to work on the mother infant study tonight. I can't just not show up. They'll worry, and if they call me I won't be able to explain." We had already decided that we should be extremely cautious about what we said over the phone. There was no guarantee our lines were secure.

"You're right." Mom turned the car toward campus. "We'll have to make it quick and hope no one spots us."

I had been an undergraduate research assistant on the Mother Infant Study at MSU since my sophomore year and felt as if I were part of a groundbreaking historical work. I wasn't aware of any other piece of research that had explored so comprehensively the implications of domestic violence in the lives of mothers and their children. It was work I found challenging and immensely rewarding.

Mom dropped me at the back of the old brick building. Nervously, looking all around, I scurried to the door, down the stairs, and into the office, where I found three of the graduate assistants who ran the project. My voice sounded distant as I explained. "I'm really sorry, but I can't work tonight, and I don't know when I'll be able to work again. I'm *so* sorry. I know that puts you in a bind."

I leaned back against a desk for support and stared mostly at my feet, unable to look any of them in the eye. When I did glance up, it was clear by their matching expressions of concern that I was failing miserably at maintaining my calm. I could feel my body and my voice trembling.

"What's the matter?" one of them asked. "Is everything all right?"

I felt like all the air had been sucked out of the room. Sweat beaded on my forehead and atop my lip. I didn't want to say it out loud. I didn't want it to be true, but I couldn't just abandon my fellow researchers without an explanation. They deserved at least that much. "My dad found us," I whispered breathlessly.

With those words the floodgates broke open, and I began to sob uncontrollably. Until that moment I hadn't shed a single tear since the e-mail announcing my father's intention to stage a reunion. But there, in that tiny office, forced to give voice to the reality of our situation, I was overcome by emotion.

The spoken word possesses a mysterious power. In silence, truths can be denied, but once they're paired with words and uttered aloud, they are transformed into tangible, salient entities from which there is no hiding.

In that instant, the weight of my new reality was heavy upon me. My dad had found us. Mom and I had taken every precaution, and yet he had found us. It had been nearly fifteen years since Mom and I had escaped, and still we were not free.

That was a pivotal day for me. For the first time since our escape, Mom and I had chosen to run. Every other time my dad posed a threat, we had stood our ground and fought, but not that day. One phone call from my dad and we had pulled up stakes and left our lives behind.

I sat silently in the passenger seat, arms folded across my chest, as Mom drove us out of East Lansing. My anger swelled as the distance between me and my life grew. Who did my dad think he was to interfere like this? What right did this producer have to meddle in my business? For him it was just another story, but this was my life.

How had they found us? Why now? If my dad was going to resurface, why had he waited until I finally dared to let myself believe Mom and

I were safe? Was it his aim to deal the greatest possible psychological blow? Where was he? He had been put on a government watch list and couldn't legally enter the United States, but I knew that wouldn't stop him. If he wanted to get in, he would. Was the Iranian government somehow behind this as they had been behind the Turkish interview fiasco? My mind raced with questions for which I had no answers.

Evening descended shortly after Mom and I took flight. In my rage, I refused to recognize the beauty of the Chicago skyline as we drew near. I'd always loved the way the lights of a city twinkle from afar in the darkness. Even in Tehran, an evening drive along the curvy mountain road that overlooked the city had filled me with joy. This night, however, I felt no joy—only intense bitterness mingled with overpowering exhaustion.

Mom and I were both weary by the time we drove into the heart of the city. In a daze, we wandered into the luxurious Westin Hotel on Michigan Avenue in the Magnificent Mile shopping district. Mom paid an exorbitant amount of money so that we could spend a few brief hours sleeping in a place that felt safe.

The bed, as promised, was heavenly—layer upon layer of fluffy pillows, crisp sheets, and the most luxurious down duvet—all in white. I sank into the comforting embrace of that bed and enjoyed an inexplicably peaceful night's rest. Those few hours of reprieve were a beautiful and gracious gift from God.

In the morning I awoke, and for a split second I felt nothing but the complete relaxation of floating in clouds of down feathers. I was wholly at peace. Then I opened my eyes to the light, realized where I was, and was jarred back into my terrifying reality.

CHAPTER 25

Not knowing how far we would have to run to evade my dad, we first needed to renew my passport. We headed to the federal building in downtown Chicago. On the outside it looked like a modern skyscraper, but inside, where Mom and I sat waiting for hours for my paperwork to be processed, it was dimly lit and drab. Dozens of other people sat in chairs lining the room, all waiting for their five minutes with one of the officials seated behind the glass divider.

Hours passed, and my mind raced. The implications of my father's intrusion were settling in, and the more I thought about the situation, the angrier I became. Eventually I would be called to the window to sign the forms. I would be given a new passport, and then what? Where would we go? How long would we run? What about my life—my family, my friends, my apartment, my research, my job, my classes?

On top of everything else, this was midterm. I had three exams and a paper due. It was one thing to miss a day or two of classes, but I couldn't miss my exams. I couldn't refuse to turn in my paper. If I did that I would fail not just my classes, but my ongoing battle to live a normal life.

Sitting there in the dreary passport office surrounded by immigrants, most of whom it seemed didn't speak English, my stubborn streak kicked in. I wasn't willing to walk away from my life. I wasn't willing to let my dad take away everything we had worked so hard to accomplish. We would go back, and we would fight!

Mom was more reluctant than I was. Answering the phone and hearing my dad's voice had been traumatic for her. Later I would learn she had hung up and vomited. Just the sound of his voice still terrorized her even after nearly fifteen years. He probably would have found some sick satisfaction in knowing that.

Striking a compromise, Mom and I agreed to go back to Michigan, but to keep away from her house and my apartment. We stayed on the move and on guard. Each night, as late as we could manage, we checked into a different hotel, where we did our best to sleep for a few hours. By dawn we were showered, dressed, and back on the road.

We knew it was taking a huge risk to maintain a routine of any sort, but I was determined to finish out the semester. So Mom drove me to my classes and watched to make sure no one followed me into the building. Sometimes she parked and watched the area while I was inside. Other times she drove around aimlessly, trying to avoid detection.

We didn't know if we were being followed. We didn't know if my dad was in the country. We didn't know if the Finnish producer was in the country, if others were working with them , or to what lengths they would go to stage a reunion.

When class finished I would call Mom. If the coast was clear, she would drive as close as possible to the door and pick me up. If it wasn't, I would hide out in the building, trying to look as calm as possible, until she sounded the all clear. We were suspicious of everyone and everything.

I was especially concerned for my roommates' safety and found it particularly frustrating that they might be in danger simply by virtue of our association. Trish was the only one with whom I kept in contact. Our conversations were clipped, and we spoke in coded messages rendered decipherable only by years of genuine friendship. I found it ironic that as a child some of the adult members of our church had tried to petition to have me removed from their school because they were afraid of the danger my presence would bring, and yet, Trish, who weighed maybe a hundred pounds soaking wet, didn't think twice about jumping in her 1986 station wagon, the kind with the faux wood paneling, and meeting me. She brought me clean clothes and textbooks, but most of all she brought me a much-needed dose of encouragement.

Law enforcement agencies became involved. The FBI, the Michigan State Police, the MSU Campus Police, and even the Canadian authorities worked to ensure our safety. Trisha's parents were alerted to the situation, so Scott, Trish's fiancé, started driving her to class and keeping a protective watch over her. No one told me then that their biggest fear was that if someone came to kidnap me, they would take Trish instead, mistaking her dark hair and olive complexion for a sign of Iranian and not Italian ancestry.

Eventually, Mom and I had to go back to her house. This was the only way to get the calls traced and to try to establish my dad's whereabouts. We were never alone in the house. The men in our family took turns pulling guard duty. The curtains were kept drawn at all times.

Everyone was on edge. Tempers ran hot. Mysterious things kept happening—subtle, doubt-inducing incidents that made us all feel as if we were losing our minds. An uncle, armed with a gun, would walk the perimeter of the fenced-in backyard, stopping to ensure the gates on either end of the house were securely locked. Fifteen minutes later they would repeat their surveillance, only to find the gates unlocked. These little inconsistencies, coupled with our intense fear, left us feeling paranoid even to the point of not trusting our paranoia.

At the same time, the phone didn't stop ringing. We had to answer in order to trace the calls. We could hear someone breathing on the other end, but no one spoke. They would hang up, and immediately the phone would ring again. These calls came every ninety seconds, sometimes every minute or every thirty seconds. On the good days they came every fifteen minutes. It was clearly a game, and it was driving me insane.

Because the calls were international, we weren't able to trace them to their point of origin. The only thing that could be determined was that they were coming into the United States from Montreal. My dad had relatives in Canada, and in those days we knew that if he had made it that close, he could quite easily drive through the border into Michigan. A passport wasn't needed to travel between the two countries.

After we returned to Mom's house, she played my dad's message for me to hear. The answering machine was on a shelf at the top of the stairs that led to the basement. I sat on the cold gray tile, my feet resting on the second step down, as Mom hit the play button. I only listened to the recording once.

I was surprised to learn that I didn't remember his voice. When I'm frightened, my heart still echoes the deep pounding of his footsteps, but time had erased his voice from my memory. He had a heavy British accent. If his words hadn't been so infuriating, I may have even found it charming.

Like all the other events surrounding his intrusion, I kept no log of day or time or manner of attack. It was too painful to physically document these things. I didn't want them to be real. I didn't want them to be part of my life, and so for more than a decade I've left them as intangible fragments carefully locked somewhere deep in the furthest recesses of my mind.

His message, as I recall it now, went something like this: "This is Dr. Mahmoody calling." *Dr. Mahmoody! He was addressing me, his daughter, and he had the gall to refer to himself as Dr. Mahmoody.* He said he wanted to talk to me, to tell me the truth.

"You're twenty-one. Now you can think for yourself." He clearly didn't know the first thing about me. I may have been quiet, but since childhood I had been an extremely strong-willed, free-thinking individual. No one told me what to think.

"I want to tell you the truth because what you've been told all these years is a lie." Hearing that, I had literally laughed out loud. I turned to Mom with a hate-filled smirk and quipped sarcastically, "What? Did he forget that I was there?"

What an arrogant con artist, I thought. *What an absolute narcissist.* He actually believed he could just show up and rewrite our family history. He would feed me a tale, and I would believe him. Just because he said so, I would discount everything I knew to be factual and take his lies to be truth. How sad and pathetic . . . and terrifying.

I wondered if he actually believed his own lies. Had he been telling his fabricated stories for so long that he had forgotten what had really happened, or was there a tiny sliver of his soul that couldn't be deceived? I still don't know the answer to that question. I would like to believe that his conscience wasn't completely dead.

He claimed to have found my contact information on the online MSU student directory. I didn't know if that was true or not, but when I checked, it was listed there. The age of the Internet had brought with it a whole host of new security considerations.

Not long after that first phone call, he started sending me e-cards. I rarely opened them and never responded. I just wanted him to go away.

On campus, I was on high alert. When I drove, I looked intently at every person in every car I passed. I tried to memorize every detail that surrounded me—makes and models of vehicles, license plate numbers, street names that I hadn't bothered to learn before. If I had to call for help, I would need those details. I varied my routes to and from class to try to throw off any would-be stalkers. The problem was that I had a set schedule. Still, I wouldn't make it any easier for "them" than I had to.

All these measures took time and an incredible amount of mental and physical energy. I desperately needed sleep, but I was too scared to let my guard down enough to rest. What if the attack came in the night while I was asleep? I survived on around three hours of sleep a night, and the sleep deprivation left me manic and jittery.

Over the years Mom and I had put great effort into balancing normalcy with safety. I had become accustomed to taking extensive security precautions while managing to engage in most of the activities I had desired. Up until now, my life had moved on rather smoothly in spite of my dad. This was the first time he had proven so disruptive to my daily functioning.

I felt selfish for wanting to go back to my normal life. I didn't want to abandon Mom, and I didn't want to endanger my roommates, but the drive from Mom's to East Lansing was brutal, and I missed my friends and my apartment. One evening, just before Christmas, I decided to go back to the apartment just long enough to celebrate and exchange gifts with my roommates. Once I was there, it felt so good to have a taste of my real life again that I decided I would spend just one night. It was already late, and we were having such a joyful time. And then the call came from Mom.

Someone had just fired a gun outside John's house. Earlier in the week, Joe's dog, who never left the yard, had disappeared without a trace. I didn't want to believe it had anything to do with me, but now that both of my brothers had been affected, I couldn't deny the likelihood that these mysterious happenings were all connected.

Just like that, the party came to an end. I scurried around the living room throwing my gifts in a bag and sprinted down the stairs. I had to go home. I couldn't handle being the one to lead "them" to my friends as I had to my family. My three roommates followed me to the door, offering their encouragement as I put on my boots. Unable to find words to comfort me, they wrapped me in an embrace. "This is never going to end," I sobbed, feeling utterly defeated.

For reasons beyond my understanding, my family's struggle had become so much bigger than my family. Governments were involved; readers and viewers were involved; a documentary producer was involved, and in recent days I had learned that even an MSU student had become involved, working as an intern on the film project. In that moment, I knew that even if my dad were dead, I would never be free of this curse.

Around that time my niece, Kelsey, was pulled from school. She had just started preschool when my dad found me. How do you explain to a four-year-old that even though she loves school and all her friends get to go to school and play with each other, she has to stay at home just in case her aunt's daddy tries to steal her? She looked so much like I had at four that we were afraid my dad would try to kidnap her in an attempt to relive the years he had lost with me.

John, Dianne, and Kelsey lived in a small town nearly an hour from Mom's house, yet they had experienced a number of mysterious incidents that we feared were not coincidental. On several occasions my brother and sister-in-law had had a strange feeling that someone had been in their home while they were away. The gunshot near their home seemed to confirm that we all had valid cause for concern. We weren't just collectively imagining these things.

The weather forecasters were calling for a blizzard the night before my last final of the semester. The state police had issued a statement asking people to stay off the roads, so I had no choice but to stay at my apartment. In the morning there were mountains of snow everywhere. Every school except MSU was closed, many businesses were closed, and public transportation had shut down.

When I arrived on campus and saw that the parking lots had not been plowed, I grew nervous. I would have to park in the parking garage, which was against my policy. It was just too much of a risk. Entry and exit points were far too limited, and there were virtually limitless places for an attacker to hide. I circled around in the hope of finding a lot somewhere on campus that had been cleared. Even if it meant walking farther, it would be better than parking in a ramp. Finding no other alternative, I returned to the closest ramp and parked.

There's something exhilarating about breathing deeply on a snowy day, and everyone in the lecture hall seemed to feel it. The mood was light and jovial, something I hadn't experienced with any exam I had ever taken. The students were laughing and smiling, swapping stories of their adventures of getting to class that day. We only quieted down when the exam was passed around.

I quickly lost myself in the multiple-choice questions. I couldn't fill in the corresponding bubbles fast enough. I knew this material. I reached the end with a smile, feeling absolutely confident that I had answered each question correctly. With a satisfied sigh, I lifted my head and realized that I was the first one done. This was really unusual for me. I'm a slow reader and a slow test taker, more likely to be the last to finish than the first.

Perplexed, I looked back over my answers. Still, no one else was finished. I read through the entire exam a third time and decided I had waited long enough. Quietly I walked to the front of the lecture hall and, with a shrug, handed the paper to the professor.

Out in the main corridor, students filled the halls. I squeezed my way through the crowd, pausing at the door and taking a mental inventory of the surroundings. Everything seemed fine, so I gave the door a push and stepped out onto the sidewalk. Already, I was dreading going back to my car in the parking garage.

Other students were headed the same way I was, but their numbers dropped off one by one as I made my way toward the ramp. Soon there were just two male students a short distance behind me. Across the street there was a lone vehicle in the parking lot of the planetarium. Something about it made me uneasy. It was a van, the kind with no windows on the back, and it was parked perpendicular to the parking spots. As far as I could see, there were no other people around except for the two young men behind me. I could hear them quickening their pace.

My mind raced, trying to put the pieces together. All I could think of was that my dad and the film crew were inside that van. What was their plan? Were they going to jump out and force me into an interview or a reunion, or were they just going to grab me, throw me into the van, and drive off?

The footsteps were right behind me. Then came the tap on my shoulder.

I knew there was a student working as an intern on the documentary. I knew his name. I knew his hometown. I knew which dorm he lived in. I even knew his major. The only thing I didn't know until that very moment was what he looked like.

I stopped dead in my tracks. If there was going to be a confrontation, it was going to be out here in the open and not under the cover of the parking garage.

"Are you Mahtob Mahmoody?" he asked. His friend didn't say a word.

"No," I lied.

"You're not Mahtob Mahmoody?"

"No. What do you want with her anyway?" I was shaking and cursing my ridiculous hat, which had slid down and was partially obstructing my view of the van parked across the street.

"I'm trying to deliver a package to her. It's from her dad."

"Well, good luck with that. I don't know who she is." Trying with every ounce of my being to sound confident, I turned and walked calmly away from them, all the while praying that they wouldn't follow me, that the doors of the van wouldn't fly open to swallow me up, that the film crew wouldn't emerge from the shadows. With great effort I steadied my breathing and straightened my shoulders. I glanced behind me once, and they were standing still where I had left them as if deciding what to do. Then they turned, and I heard their footsteps retreat.

That's when my bravado crumbled. Running to the parking garage, gasping for air, tears streaming down my face, I hurtled myself up the stairs and darted for the safety of my car. There I locked myself inside and sat frozen with fear behind the wheel. I didn't know what to do or where to go. "Dear God, please help me," I begged aloud.

I hadn't asked the young man's name. Why hadn't I asked them to identify themselves? I needed to give the police something to work with. I pulled out of the parking structure and turned toward the dorm where I knew the intern lived. As suspected, I spotted the two of them along the route. I turned off before I reached them and circled around just in time to see them walking up the steps of the building where the intern lived.

That was all the proof I needed to race to the police station, where I filed a tearful report with the detective who was working my case. The package, I would later learn, was a video from my father. The detective offered to try to get it for me, but I told her I didn't want it. I wasn't interested in anything my dad had to say.

Of all the law enforcement agents who helped us, that detective stood out. She wanted so badly to help me. She gave me a parking pass that would get me into the faculty lots so I could park as close to my classes as possible. She followed up on every lead, ran patrols by my classes, and encouraged me to report anything that made me the least bit uncomfortable. She assured me it didn't matter if it ended up being nothing. No suspicion was too trivial.

At one point I even sat with a sketch artist and described a middle-aged man who had smiled at me in passing. It hadn't been a flirtatious smile, just a smile of acknowledgement. But it was midsemester, and I had only recently begun to see him as I made my way between classes. That was the first red flag. The second was that he made eye contact and smiled one day as we met on the sidewalk. People just didn't do that on our campus. We kept our heads down and walked with purpose from one building to the next. But this man walked amiably with his head up, smiling at students as he went. On top of all that, he bore a slight resemblance to my dad. They had the same slouchy jowls.

I knew it was probably nothing, but I was afraid to leave any stone unturned, so I mentioned the man to the detective. She had the sketch artist make a rendering of the man I had seen, and she went and talked with him. As it turned out, he was simply a friendly professor who taught a class in a nearby building. It really was nothing, but in those days, as far as Mom and I were concerned, everything was something.

The following spring I took Kelsey to Mom's house for a sleepover. John and Dianne were out visiting some friends when I took her home the next evening. They'd left the door unlocked for me and said to call when we got there. Before I could pull into the driveway, their dog, an extremely intelligent and mild-mannered chocolate lab, ran into the road. She paced back and forth in front of my car, barking and growling.

I'd never seen Cocoa behave like this. She tried with all her might to caution me to keep away, but I didn't heed her warning. I inched my way into the driveway and parked. She ran circles around the car, begging me to stay in the shelter of the locked vehicle. Still I didn't listen. Kelsey and I got out, walked around to the trunk, and loaded our arms with her sleepover paraphernalia. All the while, the dog continued her frenetic pleas.

"Cocoa, it's just us. You know us." I said, holding my hands out for her to sniff. When reasoning didn't work, I turned to commanding her to be quiet. Kelsey, even then independent and fearless beyond her years, headed through the darkness toward the house. The gravel of the driveway crunched beneath the wheels of the tiny pink suitcase she dragged as I slammed the trunk and locked the doors.

Cocoa carried on pacing nervously in our path, begrudgingly letting us force her backward as we approached the front door. When we climbed the porch steps, she growled and bared her teeth, something I'd never known her to do.

"What on earth has gotten into you? Move out of the way," I ordered, but she didn't. Even as I reached for the door handle, she wedged her body in between us and the danger she knew lurked inside.

The door didn't budge. I pulled again and nothing. It was locked. Finally, comprehending Cocoa's distress, I calmly turned Kelsey around and said, "Come on, sweetie, back to the car. The door's locked. It looks like we'll have to wait for Mommy and Daddy to get home to let us in."

She didn't argue. "Quickly now," I urged her, trying not to sound alarmed. "Let's see how fast we can make it to the car. Hurry."

"I'll beat you," she giggled, moving her little feet as fast as they would go.

"Go to the driver's door. You can climb over the seat and into the back, like an obstacle course," I instructed as if we were playing a game. She didn't see me looking over my shoulder to make sure the intruder wasn't coming after us. Cocoa, ever faithful, continued to stand guard.

I opened the door, and Kelsey jumped in. In one fell swoop I threw the suitcase into the front passenger seat and squeezed myself and my armload of stuff behind the steering wheel, slamming the door and locking us inside. I was buried in the pink and purple makings of a slumber party—a pillow, a blanket, a stuffed animal, and a Tupperware container filled with the homemade cookies Kelsey and I had baked together with Grandma Betty—the ones that were her daddy's favorite. Shoving it all on top of the suitcase, I eyed the house, my gaze darting from window to window, searching for any movement. I saw nothing but darkness.

"Wow, good job," I said to my niece. "You were speedy! I almost couldn't keep up with you. How fast can you get yourself buckled?" I fastened my own seatbelt and reaching for my cell to call my brother. I was backing out when she announced her success.

John answered in his normal jovial way, "Heeeh-lo," he said, putting the accent on the first syllable and drawing it out. "What's up?"

"You're not home, are you?"

"No, haven't left our friends' house yet. We'll be there shortly. Make yourself at home. Cocoa's outside. You can let her in. She'll just sit on her mat by the door."

"The door's locked."

"No it's not. I left it open for you."

"The door is locked. Cocoa was going crazy, trying to keep us away from the house, and when I tried to open the door it was locked. We're fine. We're back in the car and driving. No one seems to be following us."

"Keep driving. Don't come back until I give you the all clear. I'm on my way."

"Don't go in alone," I pleaded.

John arrived home in a matter of minutes to find the house just as he'd left it. The door was unlocked. Nothing was missing, and nothing out of place. Whoever had been inside had vanished.

It was infuriating—one more incident that could easily have been imagined, only it wasn't. Who was behind it? Was it my dad? I doubted it was him personally. Had he hired someone? What kind of person accepts such a job? What else are they capable of? What was my dad trying to accomplish?

How could I make this end?

CHAPTER 26

In the fall, when my senior year began, I moved into an apartment with Trish and Brian. Mom had agreed to let me move back to East Lansing only if I had a male roommate, and Brian had been a faithful friend since my first day on campus. Things had quieted somewhat with my dad, but the intrusions had not completely gone away, and we were all still on high alert.

One evening I sat at a small table in the university library café, surrounded by a sea of students. Beside me was a boy, sitting alone. His table matched mine—a mess of books and papers. He looked to be of Asian descent. I wondered about his story. Was he like me, a mix of two cultures? Had he been born here or there—wherever there was? Did he grow up afraid of being taken back by a parent?

To my left, a group of coeds interrupted their flirting with an occasional round of questions from their study guides. A steady stream of hungry, caffeine-addicted students filtered through the line at the coffee bar just behind me.

I preferred to sit along a wall, not just so I could more easily maintain my illusion of invisibility, but because along the wall there were fewer directions to monitor—it was safer. In my four years at MSU, I had come to know the library well and could easily and inconspicuously navigate the stacks to several exits on various sides of the building. This had become second nature. My cell phone was always within reach, as was a can of mace and a massive tangle of keys studded with a chain of carabiners, extra key chains and a whistle. If no one heard me blow the whistle, the mace and my makeshift metal whip could be used as weapons.

Not long into my cramming session, I noticed some movement out of the corner of my eye. Without raising my head, I watched three Asian teens approach the boy at the next table. I wasn't listening to their hushed whispers. My mind was back on my notes when I heard it. The sound cut through the cacophony and startled me to attention.

How many years had it been since I'd heard that terrible sound? Later I would do the math: 2002 minus 1986 equals 16 years. How differently I had reacted to it as a child. Somewhere along the road of life I had lost my courage. I wondered when that had happened.

As a twenty-two-year-old, the sound of angry fists slamming into human flesh left me frozen with terror. It's strange the way a body absorbs the sound of a punch. If that same force hit a table, plates would jump, silverware would tremble, water would ripple in the glasses. But a body quiets the blow to a grotesque dull thunk.

The scene played out before me in slow motion. The boy whose table matched mine was badly outnumbered, and I watched silently as the three ruffians beat him up. They knocked him out of his chair, punched him, kicked him, and cursed him. I looked around the room at all the other students, my eyes pleading with them to do something to protect this boy who wasn't able to protect himself. No one moved. In my head I was screaming for someone, anyone, to make it all stop. How could it be that not one person would take action? How could it be that I, of all people, could be one of them?

Just as quickly as they'd come, the attackers fled, leaving the boy alone and gasping for air on the floor, writhing in agony. My fear had been replaced by bitter anguish. I wanted to cry, but I didn't. I wanted to go to him, to help him up, to comfort him, and yet I remained frozen.

The whole room was filled with an oppressive silence. All the sounds of a few minutes earlier—the hissing of the espresso machine, the din of students conversing, the scraping of chairs on the floor, the thud of books landing on tables, the squeak of tennis shoes on linoleum—had come to a halt with the sound of fists pounding into a body.

Shame is hard to hide. It reveals itself in our expressions, in our body language. Shame averts the eyes, bends the head toward the ground, and stoops the shoulders. It was a feeling I knew well.

It was with shame that the boy collected his belongings, his sounds echoing in the still room. He shuffled his papers, tapping them on the table to straighten their edges. He stacked his books one atop the other and stuffed them into his backpack and zipped it. The swoosh of his bag brushing across his shoulder was followed by his barely audible groan as its weight landed on his back.

It was with shame that I listened to his uneven gait as he limped toward the main door. I still couldn't move. The sound of fist pounding flesh had transported me back to Iran.

I don't know what set my father off that time. He was screaming as his fists pounded into Mom, calling her a *saag*, a dog, a most detested and filthy creature in the Persian culture. "I'll kill you," he seethed. "Do you understand me? I'll kill you, and you'll never see Mahtob again."

Her arms were up, shielding her face in an unsuccessful attempt to deflect his blows. I ran to her and wedged my body between theirs, begging my dad to stop hitting her as I tried to push him away. He brushed me aside.

Undaunted I jumped back into the fray. This time he picked me up and threw me across the room. I crashed into the wall and slid to the floor.

Still undeterred, I started screaming, "I have to go to the bathroom! I have to go to the bathroom!" That had worked in the past. He knew I was afraid of the bathroom. I never went into a bathroom alone. Mom always went with me. The bathroom was our safe place, the place where we whispered our prayers. But he didn't know that. It was our secret.

That night, though, not even the bathroom would save us. Out of the corner of his eye he caught me sticking my fingers down my throat to make myself vomit, just as Mom and I had rehearsed. It was our absolute last resort, to be used only in the direst emergency. He turned to come after me, and Mom yelled for me to run for help.

I didn't want to leave her, but she was begging me. "Mahtob, run! Go get help. Hide. Don't let him find you. I'll be okay. Run!"

I ran down the stairs to where Reza and Essie lived. Desperately I banged on their door. "Help! Please, help," I shouted, but I'm not sure the words actually escaped my mouth. There was no answer.

I could hear my dad coming for me. Mom was begging, "No, please, Moody. Don't do this." He slammed the door, and her protests were silenced. "You'll never see Mahtob again," he growled again.

I continued to pound on Reza and Essie's door. Still no answer. My heart raced. I heard my dad slide the key into the lock, and the bolt slid into place. Mom was trapped inside our apartment. Was she okay? *Hide*, I thought, *I've got to hide*.

The footsteps grew louder with every step as he pounded down the stairs. They echoed in the stairwell. I ran around the corner. There was a baby crib stored in the hallway. I crawled into the darkness beneath the crib and prayed he wouldn't find me. He did, of course, because I was five and five-year-olds hide in predictable places.

The next two weeks were a blur. He took me away from Mom and told me I'd never see her again. My only hope was that God would keep her safe in my absence. Every night I gazed out at the moon and knew that no matter where we were, Mom and I were seeing the same moon and thinking of each other. She had promised me that.

Mom had prepared me for separation. She had coached me and had given me songs to sing. They were our secret code. It was her way of giving me her words of comfort for the times she couldn't be there to soothe me in person.

They say the body attacks at its weakest point. If that's true, my weakest point in those days was my stomach. I had a bad case of diarrhea during those two weeks. Thankfully the apartment he had taken me to had a toilet instead of the standard hole in the floor. Day after day I sat on the toilet for what felt like an eternity while he paced back and forth, interrogating me.

"Mahtob, tell me what you and your mom are up to," he demanded. "Who do you talk to? Where did you go when you were late for school?"

"We're not up to anything. We don't talk to anyone. We got lost."

"You didn't get lost. You know the way to school."

"Yes, we did. We got lost." It's what Mom had coached me to say if he asked.

"You're lying to me."

Sometimes his nephew would sit on the floor between us and urge him to calm down. It was an exercise in futility—for the nephew and for my father. "What is your mom up to? Where do you go? Who do you see?"

The questions were incessant, but I was stubborn. Sometimes I didn't answer at all. I stared at the floor and sang in my head, *God is so goooood. God is so goooood* . . . Sometimes I sang, *The sun'll come out* [inhale] *tomorrow* . . .

"Answer me," he'd bellow, "where do you go?"

Silence. *Ohhh, thuhhh sun'll come out* [inhale] *tomorrow* . . . Oh, how I hated him.

Had I known then that my dad would take me back to my mom in two weeks, the separation would have been much more bearable. I really believed him when he said I'd never see her again.

There were children who lived in my prison. I don't remember them, but there must have been children because there was a room filled with their toys. One day, sitting on the floor, I spotted a familiar hint of yellow poking from beneath a pile. Brushing the other toys aside, I unearthed a miraculous reminder of home—my real home, the one back in Michigan. It was a little doll with a cloth body filled with foam beads. It had yellow clothes sewn on and a yellow hat with white lace trim stitched to its head. Its smiling face was plastic with a few small curls sticking out where the hat and the face met. This doll's bangs were matted and tangled just like mine.

I closed my eyes and took a deep breath. *Ah, home.* I could almost imagine that it smelled like home. That doll was a gift from God. I carried it everywhere with me, taking secret comfort in its familiarity.

Worse than my dad's rages and incessant questions during those two weeks were the air raids. During the bombings I was inconsolable. I kept thinking of Mom alone in the apartment, locked in so she couldn't take shelter in the hallway with the others who lived in the building. What if the bombs got her and I wasn't there? I knew she must have been worried about me, too, and the thought of causing her distress was as painful for me as my concern for her safety.

Ameh Bozorg put her foot down at last. "Can't you see?" she scolded my father. "The child doesn't know anything. Take her back to her mother."

Despite his brutality, he loved me. He couldn't stand to see me so distraught, and neither could his family. During an air raid he finally relented and took me back to Mom.

Over the years I had repeatedly been forced to come to terms with my past. But the experience in the library—and more specifically, my reaction to it—left me feeling confused.

In my psych classes I had learned that people are creatures of habit. We develop internal scripts for dealing with emotions and experiences and, generally speaking, we follow them. In other words, we tend to respond to situations in a manner similar to the way we responded to them in the past.

Why then, hadn't I intervened when the boy was being beaten? When had my script been rewritten? Was I losing my resiliency? Was I being broken, or was my memory faulty? Had I just convinced myself that I had been a scrappy little kid who wasn't afraid to intervene?

After wrestling with these questions for a few days, I called Mom and told her what happened. I asked how I used to react when my dad beat her. In her wisdom, she answered my question with a question of her own. "Well, what do you remember?"

"I was fearless," I said. "I didn't just stand on the sidelines and wait for it to be over. I jumped in front of him. I pushed him. I yelled at him, I created diversions and begged others to help."

"Mahtob, you've always had a good memory," she reassured me.

"Remember when we went to Texas to visit the Bartons right after we came home from Iran? We walked into a restaurant, and right away you told me all about being there three years earlier, when you were just four. You didn't just show me the table where we'd eaten; you actually pointed to each chair and said, 'This is where I sat, and this is where you sat, and this is where Daddy sat.' You even told me what each of us had ordered. You have an incredible memory."

Then it was true. It wasn't my memory that was failing; it was my resiliency. And that was much more terrifying.

CHAPTER 27

When my dad interfered with my life, he was never considerate enough to sound the all clear when his intrusion subsided. So I was left hanging in an ever-tenuous state of alarm. Lupus, being an opportunistic fiend, seized the occasion to reassert its destructive grip on my body.

Dr. Beals, well acquainted with the body's tenacious striving to preserve itself as long as humanly possible, knew to explore six months into the past when identifying a flare's trigger—a fact I was acutely aware of as my dad's reappearance in my life reached its six-month. To my relief, the sixth month came and went without medical incident, as did months seven, eight, nine, and ten. It was around month twelve that I finally had to face the fact that my lupus was once again out of control.

Knowing the seriousness of my health complications, I turned to my ever-faithful rheumatologist for her medical expertise.

"Tell me, what do you hear from your dad these days?" she asked as she sat down on her little stool with wheels. I sat in the teal wingback chair. Dr. Beals preferred to let her patients spend the vast majority of their time talking with her from the comfort of the cozy chairs in the exam rooms as opposed to sitting precariously on the edge of a cold exam table.

"It's basically the same," I told her. "He still sends e-mails, and I still don't respond. He hasn't given up on filming a reunion. Now he's changed up his strategy. Instead of insisting that he's my father and he won't allow me to be anything but Muslim, he's turned to saying he's dying. I think he's just hoping to create a sense of urgency. His documentary is still under production. Since I saw you last, I found out that they've arranged for an MSU student to work as their intern on the project. He's following me."

"That's a lot to deal with. How are you doing with all of it?" she asked, giving me her full attention. My chart lay unopened on her lap beneath her folded hands.

"I'm fine. I've got lots of practice at dealing with the chaos. I'm doing just fine." I gave my best attempt at making my smile reach my eyes, but I was just too exhausted.

"How are you *really* doing?" She knew me well. There was no putting on a brave face with her.

My eyes welled, and my chin quivered. "I hate it." The words caught in my throat. "I hate everything about it, and I hate him."

She reached forward and took my hands in hers. Looking me straight in the eyes, she said simply, "That's understandable."

"I don't want to hate him," I sobbed. "I don't want to live with that bitterness. I know it's not healthy—for my body or my soul. I forgave him years ago for what he did to us in Iran, but he just wouldn't let it be. He had to start causing problems again. I just want him to leave us alone. I'm so tired of being afraid all the time."

"Have you tried praying for him?" Dr. Beals asked softly.

"What?"

"Have you tried praying for him?" She sat quietly, giving me time to ponder her question.

I shook my head and took the tissue she offered. I couldn't breathe.

"Maybe it's worth a shot. I've been doing this for a lot of years, and one thing I've learned is that the body is reached through the spirit. First you have to heal the soul. Then you can work on the body."

Dr. Beals had a wisdom about her that I found to be uplifting. When I was in despair, she gave me hope. I knew she was right. If I couldn't find a way to once again make peace with the idea of my father, my health would continue to decline.

"Don't be too discouraged about this step backward in your health. This is a part of the disease," Dr. Beals reassured me. "You've done well to stay as stable as you have for as long as you have given all the stress you've been under. We've been down this road before, and we'll get through it together, just like we always have."

"I know. I just don't want to go back on meds. I can't stand the thought of being on meds the rest of my life."

"Well, let's not think about it in those terms then. We'll start out aggressively and see if we can stop this flare in its tracks. Then we'll get you off the meds as soon as your body lets us."

"What do you think?" I asked, feeling defeated. "Six months? A year?"

"You know I can't make any guarantees, but we will do everything we can to get you off everything except Plaquenil as quickly as possible. You already know I think it would be good for you to stay on that one as a maintenance measure. We'll keep a close eye on your labs and start decreasing dosages once you're stable. The only way this works, though, is if you take your medication as prescribed. Remember our deal?"

"I remember. You are going to do everything in your power to help me get better. But you can only help me if I am completely honest with you and if I follow our treatment plan to the letter."

"Precisely."

We had first established our agreement when I was just thirteen. Those were the terms on which Dr. Beals had accepted me as a patient. If I couldn't hold up my end of the bargain, then I would have to find a different doctor, because she couldn't provide effective treatment for me without my participation.

Dr. Beals had trained me well. We were a team and, even as a teenager, I'd been the one who called the shots. She'd taught me to take responsibility for the decisions I made and their impact on my health. Believing in education, Dr. Beals had instilled in me a hunger to understand the mechanisms by which my body operated so that we could better collaborate in treatment planning. She was merely a resource for me, a source of knowledge and guidance. My job, as the one living every day under the weight of my illness, was to make use of every tool at my disposal to improve the quality of my life.

I wasn't the only one who got such personalized treatment from Dr. Beals. She spent as much time with each patient as they needed. This attention to the human side of patient care was, in great part, what made Dr. Beals such an outstanding physician. Often, when I checked in for an appointment, the receptionist would hand me a packet of medical journal articles or newspaper clippings, saying Dr. Beals had asked that I read them while I waited so we could discuss the latest findings during my appointment. It wasn't unusual for me to leave her office with a stack of books and a prescription sheet with other recommended reading.

From the outset Dr. Beals had treated me as an equal, valuing the insight I brought to our process. "You're the only expert on your health," she had told me when I was scarcely more than a child. "Everyone's body is different and responds differently to different treatments. You are the only expert there is on your specific case. You're our best source of information."

I hadn't always liked her recommendations, but I had never doubted her concern for my well-being. It wasn't her fault that the standard treatment for lupus was medication. It also wasn't her fault that I had such a bad attitude about taking pills.

After today's visit, she sent me on my way with a hug, a lab slip, and a stack of prescriptions. My emotions were mixed. I felt recharged, ready to take on the battle for my health and yet frustrated to be standing once again at that all-too-familiar crossroad. Getting off medication was no small achievement in my world. Staying off medication was the ultimate victory, and having to start the meds again felt like a stinging defeat.

Mom was always eager to hear where things stood after an appointment. I tried to sound positive as I ran through the list of prescriptions. She knew the meds as well as I did. Telling her the drug name and dosage was enough to tell her the severity of the flare. These blows were perhaps more devastating for her than for me.

I knew the routine. The top of my dresser was once again lined with the ugly orange bottles with white lids, and my days were once again bookended with brutal medication regimens. Some pills were designed to counteract lupus symptoms, and some were designed to counteract side effects caused by the other pills.

As in some of my previous flares, the medication did stop the progression of the disease and eased some of my symptoms, but I still didn't feel well. Debilitating fatigue plagued me and made it a monumental task to maintain my school and work schedule. My headaches persisted. My hair continued to fall out, and my joints continued to ache. My labs continued to confirm that lupus was causing my body to attack itself. And the emotional toll of the disease was perhaps the most difficult aspect for me. It was brutal to be trapped in a body that made simple daily functioning so arduous.

Every day it got more difficult to swallow the pills. At some point, they started to literally leave a bad taste in my mouth. Finally one night I stood before my dresser in the room I shared with Trish and realized I just couldn't do it anymore. I couldn't force myself to swallow one more pill—so I stopped. I knew full well the decision to stop my medication could have disastrous effects, but I had reached my limit.

CHAPTER 28

The class started at 10:40 a.m. and met only twice a week, both reasons why I enrolled in Dr. Gershen Kaufman's Affect and Self-Esteem class. In January 2002 I was beginning the last semester of my senior year, and I was burned out—overwhelmed with life, security concerns, resurgent health challenges, and the looming identity crisis that was sure to accompany graduation. I had never done particularly well with the unknown, and the unknown was what I was facing in nearly every aspect of my world.

Just one psychology course short of earning my major, I wasn't looking for a class that would change my life. I just wanted one that I could blow off and still four-point. So when the professor began our first session by telling us outright that this would not be a blow-off class, I was ready to drop it. He told us that in order to pass, we would have to work harder than we had worked in any class before. Our reading would be intense, and we would be required to write a paper each week. On top of that, our grades would be issued on a pass/no-credit basis. There would be no letter or number associated with our efforts.

There is no way I'm staying in this class, I thought. But I decided to sit through the rest of the session as a courtesy to the professor—and because I was too self-conscious to get up and walk out. Little did I know God was using my fatigue to put me where I needed to be and using my shyness to keep me there.

I had all but stopped listening when Dr. Kaufman caught my attention with a promise. He told us that for the next fifteen weeks we would be the subjects and the experimenters of our own research study. The degree to which we applied ourselves to using the tools he taught us would directly correlate with their impact on our lives.

I was passionate about research. For most of my university career, I had worked on psychological research projects, often two or three at once. How could I turn down the opportunity to apply the lessons I had learned during the last four years?

Dr. Kaufman went on to explain the structure of the course. We would be divided into small groups. Each week we would learn a new tool, apply it to our lives, and then process our experience with that tool in our groups.

Our first assignment involved collecting happiness. It sounded simple enough. Each day we had to write a list of five specific things that had happened that day that we were happy about. That was it. I could do that.

That evening I sat at the dining-room table in my apartment and stared at the blank notebook page. Trish was curled up on the loveseat with a textbook, and Brian sat on the couch with his feet up on the coffee table and the day's newspaper opened to the crossword puzzle. I thought and I thought and I thought .

Nothing.

I wrote my name at the top of the page. Still nothing.

Beneath my name I added "PSY 325 Affect and Self-Esteem." Still nothing.

I added "Professor Gershen Kaufman," and, in the middle of the intimidating white space at the top of the paper, I inserted, "Collecting Happiness." Still nothing.

I jotted the number one along the side of the paper. There had to be something I was happy about. I replayed my day in my head. *Think. Think. Think. What made me happy today?*

I saw myself as a positive person. Grandpa had instilled in Mom a belief in the old adage, "Where there's a will, there's a way." Those words had been our mantra in Iran. It was an attitude of action, leaving no room for despair. What was needed were work and ingenuity and perseverance. Blend those together and eventually a solution could be found to any problem. Later, as we grew in our faith, that message had been put in the larger context that "with God all things are possible" (Matthew 19:26).

These were some of the seeds of resilience Mom planted in me. I had grown up listening to her advise parents engulfed in despair after failed attempts to recover their kidnapped children. She'd told them to make lists of positives, and she had counseled me to do the same whenever I was down.

On Mom's list of positives, though, I could put down any general reason for being happy. Often I included reasons that sounded good on paper but that I didn't really feel particularly excited about at that moment—like a smile that lifts the corners of the mouth but stops short of brightening the eyes. My lists of positives were filled with items like: I am alive. I have a family who loves me. I have good teachers. The weather is decent. I am free. Yada, yada, yada.

Dr. Kaufman's assignment was different. Each item on his list had to be specific to the day.

I added the numbers two through five down the side of the page and continued to agonize over my lack of happiness. I twiddled my pen between my fingers. The more frustrated I got, the faster I twiddled. Eventually I came up with two meager items, then joined Brian on the couch to work on the crossword puzzle.

Before long Trish closed her book and squeezed onto the couch too. My roommates and I ended many a day sitting shoulder to shoulder, huddled over the crossword puzzle. There were generally three items present on our coffee table: my Bible, ready and waiting for our next religious debate; Trisha's dictionary, for looking up clues; and a newspaper neatly folded just the way we liked it—to the day's crossword puzzle. More often than not, we would get caught up in reading word definitions and lose track of the puzzle.

The next day I made another attempt at collecting happiness, and the result was more of the same. I mentally replayed my day and grasped at any tiny reason to be happy. That time I came up with four items, and for number five I put, "I made my list."

After days of struggling to eke out a list, I tweaked my strategy by doing things that I knew would make me happy, just so I could write them down. I opened the vegetable drawer in the fridge and rid it of all the bags of veggies that were either soupy or growing. I washed the drawer and replaced the produce that still had some life left in it. Having it done and off my back, I felt happy. "Number one: I cleaned the vegetable drawer. . . . Number five: I made my list."

Things continued like that until one afternoon at work. At the time I was a receptionist at a photography studio. I had spent a good part of the afternoon helping a mom place an order for senior pictures. Choosing just the right combination of pictures was no small feat.

We chatted as we forged our way through the order process, then suddenly she surprised me with a compliment. The words had no sooner left her lips and landed on my ears than I realized I was happy. I couldn't help but say it aloud: "I'm happy! Your compliment makes me feel happy. I have to remember to write this down tonight. Thank you."

The woman looked at me as if I were from another planet. I was grinning from ear to ear and laughing as I explained my assignment and what a struggle collecting happiness was proving to be.

That was a turning point for me. I was finally starting to take notice of the things that made me happy as they happened.

Not long afterward I was driving from campus to my apartment less than three miles away. It was one of the first extremely beautiful days in the spring, when forty degrees feels like a heat wave. The birds were singing. The sun was shining. The sky was clear and blue, and the air smelled fresh.

I turned down one of the side streets north of campus—a street lined with houses rented by college students. Halfway down the block I could see a group of guys out in their front yard. As I drew near, I realized they had moved their living room out to the front lawn so they could soak up the beauty of the day. Some lounged in recliners with their feet up, watching a TV they had pulled out through an open window, while others tossed a football around. Their faces were bright with smiles.

Driving alone in my car, I let out an audible chuckle. Its unexpectedness startled me, which made me laugh all the more. Seeing those guys enjoying the birth of spring with such abandon made me happy. I made a mental note to write down the experience when I got home.

I came to the corner and turned to find a distinguished-looking elderly couple walking hand in hand. They, too, were smiling. There was something in the way they looked at each other that touched me. What was it, I wondered, that made it possible for them to share such glances? Was it a level of intimacy that came from years of shared heartache and joy? Was it confidence in their commitment to one another? Was it simply a mysterious affinity each harbored for the other? They talked as they strolled down the sidewalk, clearly very much in love.

"How cute," I thought. "That makes me happy." I made another mental note to add this to my list.

A bit farther, and it was time for another turn. There I was greeted by what appeared to be a grandfather pulling his little granddaughter in a red wagon. Seeing their expressions filled my heart with joy. I thought of carefree summer days when my grandpa would hook a garden cart behind his tractor and pull me around the yard. I watched the grandfather beam at his granddaughter and recalled the love my grandfather had shown me as a child. Again, I felt happy. I made another mental note to remember that moment for my list.

In that short drive, I had spotted three bits of happiness worthy of collecting. How many times had I made that same drive—dozens, perhaps hundreds? What joy had I robbed myself of because I was in the habit of rushing past the good that was happening around me on that journey?

Embracing this newfound philosophy of making a place in my life for the things I enjoy, I forced myself to make time to visit a local Lebanese deli. The most wonderful aromas greeted me at the door. The counter was lined with all different kinds of *baklava*, their tops beautifully golden, shimmering with syrup. Some were stuffed with chopped walnuts, some with pistachios, still others with homemade cheese. Behind a shield of glass sat bowls heaped with some of my favorite foods: *hummus*, *baba ganoosh*, *dolmeh*, *tabouleh*, *fatoosh*, *kibbe* (baked and fried), *eetch*, *sfeeha*, bread with *zataar*. And just when I thought it couldn't get any better, my eyes landed on the drink menu. They served Arabic coffee!

Instantly I thought of Vergine. She and Annie had always been full of lessons for me. Not only had Vergine taught me how to line my eyes when I was a child; she'd also taught me to make Arabic coffee in a long-handled copper pot called an *ibrik*. While she stirred the strong, finely ground coffee with water on the stove, I would line up tiny cups and saucers ready to be filled. The first cup would always be for Mom, who liked hers unsweetened. After hers was poured, we would add lots of sugar to the pot before filling our cups.

Like one of the grown-ups, I would take dainty nips at the hot, cardamom-infused potion until I reached the last swallows, which were always thick and gritty from the sludge that had settled to the bottom. Then I would reach inside and twist my thumb in a circle on the bottom of the cup. Placing the saucer upside down atop the vessel, I would carefully flip the cup and saucer over together in one fell swoop and hand them to Vergine. Everyone would gather around to watch as she waited for the dripping coffee grounds to write my fortune along the sides of the cup. From time to time she would tip the cup slightly and peer inside to see if it was ready. Deciding it was not yet time, she would return the cup to its resting place on the saucer.

Finally, with a great flourish, Vergine would turn the cup right side up and examine it with a raised eyebrow, offering oohs and ahs and a few "very interestings" to heighten the suspense. Then she'd proceed to tell me what a beautiful life I would have. My days would be filled with joy. I would marry a kind and loving man who'd treat me like a jewel. He would be handsome like Armenia's legendary Prince Ara, and we would be blissfully happy together.

Sometimes she would tell me that I'd encounter some challenges along life's road, but that God in his wisdom would turn them into blessings.

"See, here, Mahtob?" she'd say, pointing to the pattern the grounds had made in the cup. "See the steep mountains? These are obstacles you will have to overcome. Everyone has them. Life is not always rosy, you know. But look here." She would direct with the tip of her little finger. "Do you see the sun shining over the mountains? That's God smiling down on you. He loves you very much, and he will always take care of you. You must remember that when you come to life's mountains. They may seem bad at first, but God is going to use them to bless you. This is a very, very good fortune. God has beautiful plans for you."

Ceremoniously she would set my cup on the table, take my face in her hands and plant a big kiss on my cheek. Sometimes Annie would take the cup and examine it, nodding with an expression of intense study. She would confirm Vergine's reading with a smile, and then she, too, would nestle my cheeks in her hands and kiss me.

As far as Annie, Vergine, and their mom, Nana, were concerned, I was one of their children, the girl they longed to have. And so, as I grew, they had nurtured me with all the love and instruction they showered on their sons, sharing their heritage with me through their history, their food, and their unyielding optimism.

Smiling, I ordered a cup of Arabic coffee to go with my lunch. The man at the counter, taking me to be a naive American coed, refused to make it for me. "What do you mean no?" I asked in astonishment.

"Is too strong for you. You no like. For you, American coffee," he insisted in broken English.

"No, I don't want American coffee."

"For you, is better," he said, trying to be helpful.

"I know what it is," I countered. "I grew up on it." He clearly could not tell from my fair complexion that there is an Armenian branch on my family tree.

Against his better judgment he relented. But just to prove his point, he served up an entire ibrik-full in a grande to-go cup as if it were a mocha or a latte. To prove my point, I sat down and drank every last drop. I was tempted to ask him to read my cup, but I figured I wouldn't like what he had to say. He probably wouldn't have seen my handsome Prince Ara.

Back in class, our group discussion revealed that I wasn't the only one who had struggled to recognize the blessings that were all around. The consensus was that many of us shared a tendency to coast through life on autopilot.

The sad reality was that I was just too busy to be happy. I was a full-time student with a part-time job, and I worked on two psych research projects. On top of all that, I was dealing with the added stress of my father's intrusions, being stalked by a fellow student, and a lupus flare, not to mention that I had no idea what I would do with my life after graduation. I needed to find a job and a place to live. Happiness had not been my top priority.

That quickly began to change, however. My coursework demanded it. As the weeks wore on, my happiness lists grew longer—and my outlook on life improved. Without realizing it, I had internalized the collecting-happiness tool. I woke up each morning with a goal of savoring every bit of joy I could find in the course of the day. And I found a lot. Repeatedly I would find myself struck by the graciousness of God. I started to think of my happiness log as a gratitude journal. There was so much in my life to be thankful for that it became a challenge to choose just five items to write down.

Another surprising discovery from our group discussions was how uplifting it felt to share our happiness with others. Listening to others recount the highlights of their week, I experienced a bit of their joy and vice versa. I was particularly struck by the similarities and differences in our lists. There were so many reasons to be happy that I had overlooked.

We learned from and encouraged one another with unconditional positive regard. Within the bounds of our group, it was okay to be vulnerable and to share our most intimate thoughts and insecurities. There was an atmosphere of mutual respect and compassion that I had never dreamed could be possible among near strangers. I hadn't been prepared for the group environment to offer such a healing presence.

Several weeks into the semester, I had an appointment to see Dr. Beals. I knew she would be disappointed that I hadn't held up my end of our bargain, and the fear of being fired as a patient gnawed at me. How would I ever find another rheumatologist who shared our treatment philosophy?

Inside the exam room, I tried to still my nerves as I waited. I heard her footsteps approaching. She paused outside the closed exam room and lifted my chart from the plastic pocket on the door, then she turned the knob and entered with a smile.

Beneath her white lab coat, Dr. Beals wore beautifully tailored designer clothes, and despite her long hours, her hair and makeup were always impeccable. She greeted me with her typical cheeriness, full of enthusiasm and warmth. "It's always a pleasure to see you, dear," she said, wrapping her arms around me in a big hug. "Look at you. You look fantastic! What are you doing?"

That wasn't the reaction I had expected. "I feel great," I said, "better than I've felt in ages. I'm taking this fascinating class." I told her all about Dr. Kaufman's tools and especially about collecting happiness.

"Well, it sure seems to be agreeing with you," she said glancing down at my chart. "Oh, I see here that you've stopped your meds. How are your symptoms?" She eyed me with a suspicious look that told me red flags were going off for her.

"I really think I'm doing better without the meds than I was with them," I said, pleading my case, "I didn't get any worse after I started them, but I didn't really get much better either. I expected my symptoms to worsen after I stopped, but I don't feel like they did."

"How's your energy?"

"Not perfect, but much better than it was. I make it through the day much more easily. I'm tired, but it's normal exhaustion, not the crippling lupus fatigue. There's a difference."

"Hhhmm. Are you getting more sleep?"

"I wish. Who has time to sleep? Between classes and work and homework and my research projects, I'm still stretched pretty thin."

"So you're not under any less stress, I see."

"No."

"And things with your dad?"

"The same. I've been praying for him, though, and you're right, it helps. I don't know why I didn't think of it. That should have been the first thing I thought of. Guess I was just so caught up in being miserable that I needed someone to point it out to me."

"I'm glad it's helping, dear. How's your appetite?"

"Normal."

"Exercise?"

"None. The police gave me a key card to get in to the faculty parking lots, so now I don't walk nearly as much as I did. But it's nice that I get to park right outside the building when I go to class. It does make me feel a bit safer. So the drama with my dad has had at least one perk," I joked.

"Now there's the Mahtob I know, finding the silver lining to every cloud. Hop up on the exam table. Let's check you out."

As Dr. Beals examined me, I told her more about Dr. Kaufman's theories. "Dr. Kaufman says we carry our memories of life experiences almost like photographs in our minds and that we can choose which snapshots we take with us from the event. Like the whole parking situation thing. I could be upset that I'm afraid for my safety because my dad's hounding me or because some backstabbing fellow-Spartan is working for him or because there's not a whole lot the police can do to protect me. Those things are all true.

"Or I could focus my attention on the good that's coming from the bad. If my dad weren't causing these problems, then the police wouldn't have given me the special parking permit. If they hadn't given me the parking permit, I would have missed out on the great bumper sticker I saw the other day. I parked next to this old beater of a car that was completely covered in bumper stickers. It was *so* tacky. But I couldn't help but stop and read a few, and one of them said something like, 'It's not our differences that divide us. It's our inability to recognize, accept, and celebrate those differences.' I like that."

"Say, 'ah,' " Dr. Beals got in as I took a breath.

"Ah."

"Good."

"And there's this other car that's always parked outside of my philosophy class. All semester I've been trying to figure out what the license plate means. It says, 'B-U-G-U-Y.' I usually go in the side door because it's closer to my classroom, but the other day I used the front door of the building. It turns out the department of entomology is housed in that hall. All of a sudden, the lightbulb went on. The department of entomology—the study of insects. B-U-G-U-Y . . . bug guy. Isn't that clever? And guess what? The car is a Volkswagen Beetle."

Dr. Beals smiled appreciating a fellow scientist with a sense of humor.

"Anyway," I went on, "these are the photographs I'm choosing to carry with me. The good is no less real than the bad, so why not focus on it?"

Dr. Beals listened with genuine interest as she checked for swollen glands, examined the color of my nail beds, and noted the temperature and texture of my skin. She tested my reflexes, muscle strength, and range of motion. She listened to my heart and breathing, tapped on my stomach to measure my spleen, pressed on my abdomen to check for tenderness.

"Hmm, you certainly are looking and sounding great. Whatever it is you're doing, keep it up. You're on the right track. I want to run some labs to confirm that things really are improving as they appear to be." She helped me down from the table and pointed me toward the comfortable chair.

I braced myself. This was the point in our appointment when we usually played the bargaining game. She would propose different meds, and I would make the case for abstaining from them. In the end we would find a compromise we could both feel good about.

"I'm going to be honest with you," she said. "I'm encouraged to see you doing so well, but I still have some concerns. I don't think you're out of the woods yet." She looked over her shoulder at me as she washed her hands at the sink across the room. "You need to pay very close attention to the messages your body sends you. At the very first hint of an increase in symptoms, I want you to get back in here."

She turned and looked me in the eye. "This is serious stuff we're dealing with. We're not just talking about your health today; we've got to think about the future too. The decisions you make now could have consequences down the road."

"I know," I said.

"Good. I'll call you with the lab results as soon as I get them. Until then, keep doing what you're doing. It seems to be making a significant difference."

The labs confirmed that my health had indeed improved. Spurred on by the noticeable progress I had experienced by changing my attitude, I immersed myself in research on nutrition and wellness.

Early on, my father had planted in me the seeds of a holistic approach to health care. He was an osteopath who believed the body was designed to heal itself given the proper conditions. I was beginning to believe this could be true for me. I just had to figure out how to create the right conditions.

There was surprisingly little literature available about diet and lupus. The closest I could find was a small book, little more than an extended pamphlet, on nutrition and fibromyalgia. It was a place to start.

I carefully tracked how I felt after eating different foods. Noticing that meat seemed to take a toll on my body, I became a vegetarian. Milk made me bloat, and sometimes, after just one sip, I had shooting pains in my abdomen. After reading up on the subject, however, I decided that my problem was likely not the milk itself but perhaps the pesticides in animal feed and growth hormones and the antibiotics the cows were routinely given to boost milk production. I discovered I could drink organic milk by the gallon with no discomfort.

Pleased by my findings, I ate as much organic produce as possible. I tried yoga and explored deep-breathing exercises, visualization, and guided imagery. Above all, I wholeheartedly embraced Dr. Kaufman's tools. Within three months, for the first time since my diagnosis, my lupus was in full remission. Even DSG hadn't accomplished that.

William James, one of the founding fathers of psychology, has been credited with saying, "The greatest discovery of my generation is that a human being can alter his life by altering his attitude." Dr. Kaufman's class gave me that gift, teaching me to alter my attitude in ways that would forever alter my life.

One other class exercise in particular impacted me. Dr. Kaufman asked us to pair up with someone we didn't know and arrange our desks to face each other. Our instructions were simply to gaze into each other's eyes until he signaled us to stop—no talking, no making faces, no communicating in any way. This was not a staring contest. There would be no winner or loser. We were simply to gaze into each other's eyes and take in the experience.

Rising from our chairs and stepping from the comfort of our small groups, anxiety levels soared filling the room with nervous laughter. Even though MSU wasn't an unfriendly place, looking others in the eye was somehow outside of the norm. Week after week I passed the same people on my way to class. We rode the same buses. We sat beside each other in lectures. We almost never made eye contact.

I partnered with a girl from the other side of the room . She looked as uneasy as I felt. "Okay, I'm starting the timer," Dr. Kaufman announced. "Make eye contact and don't break it until I tell you to. You may feel the urge to giggle, blink repeatedly, stare at your partner's nose, or alternate your gaze from one eye to the other. Those are learned responses. Resist them. If your mind wanders, gently bring it back to the present. Focus on simply gazing into your partner's eyes. Let everything else pass away."

As he let his voice trail off I felt immensely uncomfortable. And apparently I wasn't alone;; the room was atwitter with anxious chuckles.

"Shh," Dr. Kaufman whispered gently. "Focus on your partner's eyes." I could feel my body tensing, my shoulders rising toward my ears and hunching forward. This was a feeling I knew well. It transported me back to high school. I was a freshman sitting in morning chapel. I felt intensely self-conscious, as if everyone in the room were staring at me. My nerves made my stomach growl, and I developed a twitch. I could feel it coming on but was powerless to stop it.

It had gotten better as I settled into high school life, but now sitting opposite my unknown classmate, it was back. I blinked to try to fight it off. My body felt jittery. I couldn't hold it back any longer. My head jerked awkwardly to the right. I bit my lip and returned my gaze to my partner's eyes.

"Focus," I told myself, echoing Dr. Kaufman's instructions. "Gently bring your attention back to the present." My classmate had striking eyes, a hypnotizing shade of crisp green. I focused on them and forced myself to breathe. Something about her eyes was soothing. I lost myself in them and, as I did, I had the sensation of everything else in the room literally floating off into the distance. We were engulfed in silence. I didn't even discern her face. The only thing I saw was the beautiful pair of green eyes gazing back at me. Somehow I felt wholly at ease.

Ever so gently, Dr. Kaufman's voice broke our trance. Time was up. We could look away. I felt energized and slightly disoriented. Having lost all sense of time during the experience, it was shocking to learn that five minutes had elapsed. I would have guessed it had been only thirty seconds, a minute at the most. Had I really maintained eye contact with someone for a full five minutes? It was unthinkable. It was baffling. It was exhilarating!

Our assignment for the next week was to practice our newly honed eye contact skills. Suddenly the thought of looking someone in the eye for a fraction of a second as we passed on the sidewalk didn't seem so intimidating. And it proved not to be.

That one experiment made a significant difference in my shyness. Being forced to face my fear, to literally stare it down, freed me from its power. Now, whenever I feel that old insecurity rising back to the surface, I am no longer stuck in the awkwardness of the early days of high school. Instead, I am reminded of the five minutes I shared with a beautiful green-eyed stranger—the five minutes that taught me it is okay to be seen.

A human being *can* "alter his life by altering his attitude." That is a lesson Dr. Kaufman taught me well. Yet I was still so introverted when I was in his class that I never once spoke to him. I never told him how much I appreciated his instruction or how invaluable I found his lessons to be. He changed my life and we never really met.

We aren't always aware of the ways we touch others. An act of silliness, a smile shared in passing, an unexpected compliment, a life lesson passed on to a nameless face—these seemingly insignificant events were life altering for me.

CHAPTER 29

The men with whom I have had relationships needed to grapple with my past, and their methods for doing so have varied widely. In my late twenties, I was introduced to a man by some mutual friends who joined us on our first date. We went bowling and then had a leisurely dinner. Conversation moved with ease, and when our meal ended he invited me to go for a walk along the water. As we strolled we made the usual first-date small talk—family, siblings, work, education and so on.

I can usually tell when someone knows about my past. They're a little nervous and uneasy, wanting to know more yet not knowing how to ask. But this time I got none of those signals. So when he casually asked if there was anything he should know about me, I smiled, looked him in the eye and said, "Nope, I'm just your typical girl next door."

On Monday morning the friend who arranged the date came to my office. "So, how'd it go?" she asked. "You seemed to really hit it off."

I told her about our walk along the shore and our conversation. "It's nice to meet someone who doesn't know about my past for a change," I said, which sent her into a roar of laughter.

"He didn't tell you?" she questioned. "When he found out who you were, he went straight to the bookstore, bought the book, and stayed up all night reading. He hadn't slept in two days. I don't know how he managed to stay awake through dinner, let alone a walk on the beach."

I felt like a fool. Here I'd fed this guy a line, and he'd graciously played along.

After our second date, I told him that for the next two weeks, I would be extremely busy. I was working a lot of hours and in the midst of a move. Mom would be coming to stay with me to help, and I would simply have no time left for a social life.

I thought that was the last I would hear from him, but two weeks and a day later, my cell rang while I was at the hardware store buying caulk for my new bathtub and shades for my living-room windows. He wanted to take me to dinner.

"No, sorry," I told him. "I still don't get to have a social life. This week-end the only thing on my agenda is unpacking and getting settled. Right now I'm at the store buying supplies. Tonight I caulk the tub and install blinds. That's all the excitement I can handle at the moment."

"Then I'll come help you," he offered. "It'll be easier with an extra pair of hands."

Being intensely independent, I immediately set him straight. "I don't need help. I am perfectly capable of doing these things on my own. Mom didn't have a man around the house to do this kind of stuff for her. She did it herself and she taught me while she was at it. When I was twelve, I changed a doorknob—"

"Okay, okay, I get it. You don't need my help. So I'll just come and watch."

I couldn't think of any more excuses, so I gave in. When he arrived I was standing in the bathtub spreading the caulk. I hopped out just long enough to answer the door. I was a mess, wearing grubby work clothes with white paste smeared all over my hands and arms. "Come on in," I said, heading right back to the task at hand. "I'm almost done in the bathroom. You can keep me company while I finish."

That was exactly what he did. He leaned against the sink chatting while I finished repairing the seal around the tub. He never once told me that I wasn't doing it right or that he could do it better.

I let him help with the blinds. "Not because I can't do it on my own,"

I reminded him. "You're here. I might as well put you to work." He just laughed and opened the box. When the tasks were completed, we made our way to the couch.

This time we did talk about my past—what I remembered about my time in Iran, what it was like to grow up with the fear of being kidnapped, how it felt for the world to have access to so many of the details of my youth. I told him about my dad's documentary and the student who had stalked me on his behalf. And then I explained how it was that I had come to live in his town.

After my dad's documentary, creatively titled *Without My Daughter*, was released in 2002, things seemed to quiet down a bit. My roommates and I graduated. Trish married Scott, and Brian moved to the west side of the state. I rented a small apartment and lived alone for the first time. I was twenty-five and had a job at Carson City Hospital where my parents had met. I felt quite grown-up. But unsettling things continued to happen.

One day I came home from work and discovered the toilet lid was down. Someone had been inside my apartment. At work everyone laughed it off, saying that I was just being paranoid, that spending my days on a locked inpatient psych unit was taking its toll on me. But a few days later, early on a Saturday morning, I woke to the sound of my front door slamming. Apparently the intruder had returned and, startled to find me home, had bolted.

I told myself it hadn't really happened, that I had dreamt it. Mom came over later that morning and we went to a graduation ceremony. We were gone for a little over two hours. When we returned, Mom went into the bathroom and came back out to ask me if I had been cleaning the toilet before we left.

"No, why?" I walked into the bathroom. This time the toilet seat was up.

I packed a bag and went to stay with Mom, whose house was more secure. But even though I felt safer there, I was furious. I felt as if I were setting a precedent; that if I ran I'd spend the rest of my life running. I was determined to fight back, to catch whoever was doing this. I was certain my dad was involved, though I didn't think he was the one break-ing in. My guess was that he had someone doing his bidding.

For six months I left the apartment set up as if I still lived there. I tried everything I could think of to catch the person in the act. I worked with the police and private investigators. I even set up motion-activated surveillance cameras. Whoever was breaking in was keeping a close eye on me. He saw through my every move. I installed sensors in the gar-den so that a camera hidden inside the apartment would start recording anytime someone passed by. He must have gone in, hit rewind, and re-recorded over the section of the tape that showed him entering. Then he left the TV on so I'd know that trying to catch him was a waste of time.

Twice I must have been close, though. The first time, you could see he'd been in a hurry to leave; there was a clear path of destruction from the TV to the door. In his haste to escape he had bumped into both the coffee table and the dining table and knocked over a plant. The second time he must have been too rushed to erase his image from the tape, so he took it with him when he left.

I don't know what it was with him and the bathroom, but there was definitely some sort of fixation. He kept leaving the toilet seat and lid in different positions. Once he defecated in the toilet and didn't bother to flush. He wanted me to know he'd been there.

This was a horrible time in my life. With every break-in I felt more frustrated and more vulnerable. To fight that feeling I took shooting les-sons, but I stopped short of getting a gun. I didn't want to live like that. I am a strong proponent of the right to bear arms, but I personally am not comfortable around guns. I didn't want to carry a weapon, although I found it empowering to shoot one.

After six months the police called to say they were closing the case. I hung up, called Mom, and asked her to help me move out of the apart-ment. The next morning we threw everything I owned into boxes as movers loaded them into a truck. Just like that I had walked away from my life.

I was absolutely miserable. I was an intensely independent twenty-five-year-old who was living back home with Mommy. I appreciated having a place to go, but I hated being there. I wanted my own life.

As he always does, God had put just the right people in my life at just the right time. Fearing for my safety, a friend offered me a job several hours away, in a town where I had never been and had no history. And that's how I ended up in my new community by the water. I moved there quietly, leaving my old life behind in the hope of beginning anew.

I told all this to my new friend sitting on the couch, and he asked if I'd had any problems since my move. I started to say no when I was cut short by a noise at the front door. We both froze, eyes darting nervously from each other to the door. The storm door creaked as it opened. It sounded like someone was turning the knob, trying to get in just feet from where we sat, hearts racing.

Silently we sprang to our feet and moved toward the other side of the house. I grabbed my cell phone. My new friend jumped into action, pushing me into the bathroom. "Stay in here and lock the door. I'm going out to see who it is."

"No, you're not," I protested, "I'm calling the police."

"They may not get here in time," he whispered. "I'm going out. Don't open the door until I tell you it's safe." Then he raced down the hall toward the garage.

I raised the blind and checked to be sure the bathroom window hadn't been painted shut. It would be my backup escape route.

The day after I had moved in, winter had hit with a vengeance, and several feet of snow already blanketed the ground. I trembled as I listened to it crunching under the weight of footsteps proceeding along the back of the house. The seconds felt like hours as I debated whether or not to call the police. Maybe it was nothing. Having only been in the house for a couple of days, I hadn't yet come to know its sounds. Maybe there was a reasonable explanation.

As I waited, my fear turned to anger. This was ridiculous. What more could I do to escape my father's grasp? This has to end, I thought as I raised the phone to dial 911. That's when I heard the back door open.

"It's me," the familiar voice shouted. His footsteps grew louder as he approached the locked bathroom door and I imagined the trail of snow he was leaving all down the hallway. "It's me," he repeated. I opened the door just a crack and saw him standing in the hall with his pants caked with snow to his knees and a screwdriver in his hand. His expression gave nothing away. "Come here. I want to show you something."

He led me to the front door and opened it. The storm door stood wide open. "Look outside. How many sets of footprints do you see?"

"Just one," I smiled, breathing a sigh of relief.

"Just one," he repeated with a laugh, glancing down at the screwdriver in his hand and shaking his head. "It must have been the wind. Had me fooled, though."

"Yeah, me too. The timing couldn't have been more perfect. We were definitely primed for a good scare." I pulled the storm door shut and locked it so it wouldn't blow open again. I closed the door and turned the knob to satisfy myself that it was secure. Then we collapsed onto the couch, laughing.

I nodded toward the screwdriver. "Really?" I teased.

"Yeah, tell me about it. Not sure what good a screwdriver would have done me if there really had been someone out there, but it's all I could find."

We went on joking about the incident and laughing at our reactions, but deep down I seethed. No matter how many times I moved or how far away from home I went, I still infected the lives of those near me with fear and danger. They didn't deserve that.

I looked at this guy sitting opposite me on the couch and knew that even though everything had worked out fine this time, it might not the next time. Was it ethical to expose another person to such risks? Was it selfish of me to ask someone to live that life for me?

I tried to push the questions from my mind. I knew the answers, and I didn't like them.

We dated for several months. After that night, when we had put his questions to rest, I really did become just the typical girl next door. That's the way it almost always went in my life, and that was the way I preferred it. With my friends and colleagues, I wasn't Mahtob, the *Not Without My Daughter* daughter. I was just Mahtob, a normal person with an interesting story.

I never asked why he'd felt he had to read the book before we met or why he hadn't told me right away that he had. I suppose he was excited about our date and wanted to learn everything he could about me. It wasn't that different from the start of any budding relationship—where each person is discovering who the other one is and whether the two of you are a good fit or not. He just got a head start on his research. Other men have gone about it differently, only wanting to know what I decided to tell them when I decided to share it.

Once when I was in my early thirties, a different coworker decided to play matchmaker. For almost a year she tried to arrange for me to meet her friend, and each time I'd made an excuse. I had just come out of a very serious relationship, and my heart was still on the mend. But one afternoon the coworker appeared at my desk while I was engrossed in my work. With my back to her, I issued a distracted greeting and continued to write.

"How's your day going?" she asked.

"Fine," I said, trying to finish my thought before I lost it.

"What do you have going on this weekend? Anything fun?"

Still distracted, I finished writing and put down my pen. "No, just a quiet weekend at home. I actually don't think I have any plans for a change."

It was just the response she'd hoped to elicit. "Great. Then you're free for dinner on Saturday. I'll let him know."

There was no graceful way out of it, so I said yes. We hit it off from the start. Months into our relationship, however, he told me what had happened when my coworker told him about me.

At the time, he'd known nothing of my story. But that very evening he'd turned on the TV to find *Not Without My Daughter* playing. He watched the movie. But then, when we met, he had felt guilty for having pried into my past without my permission. To him, it didn't feel fair that he had access to the intimate and traumatic details of my childhood before we came to know and trust each other enough to share such things. It was in some way an invasion of my privacy, a betrayal.

After we had known each other for quite some time, he once again turned on the TV to find the movie playing. This time, though, he was angered by what he saw and had to turn it off. Having developed a relationship with me, he found it hard to tolerate the idea that I had endured such violence.

He's not the only one to have had those feelings. Once the curiosity of the notoriety fades, what's typically left is the reality of my father's abuse. That's a much harder thing for people who care about me to accept. More often than not, they are left holding the anger that I so deliberately let go of in the years after our escape. Some feel a need to protect me, even if that means putting themselves in harm's way.

To me it's flattering, humbling, and sad, all at the same time. I pay my childhood very little thought now. It is a thing of the past, just one of the many threads in my tapestry, and I've had decades to develop an appreciation for the good that has come into my life because of it. It serves me well, however, to catch an occasional glimpse of my past through the eyes of those who care about me.

My family rarely talks about what happened. We've moved on with our lives. Recently, though, one of my cousins asked me about the abuse Mom and I experienced in Iran. Hearing of my father's extreme brutality infuriated her. Expounding about what a jerk my father was, she realized to her amazement that in all the years since our escape, she had never once heard Mom speak ill of the man. It was true. Mom spoke openly and matter-of-factly about our experiences, but she did not speak harshly about my father.

Others have been less kind. Most of the people in my family can't remember a single good thing about my father anymore. Given the magnitude of his betrayal, this is not surprising. My father earned their disdain. I don't pity him for that.

Growing up, I was especially close to my Uncle Pete, my mom's brother. He was my protector. A Vietnam veteran and a General Motors worker, he was invincible in my eyes. Uncle Pete hated my father not only for what he had done to us in Iran, but also for the threat he posed to our family even after our escape.

Shortly before my thirtieth birthday, Uncle Pete and Myrt, a long-time family friend, made the three-and-a-half-hour drive to visit me for the weekend. At a local steakhouse, we reminisced about how I had always had him wrapped around my little finger. "Mandy," he said, "you know there's nothing in the world I wouldn't do for you, right?"

Years had passed since I had thought of myself as Mandy, but I liked that he still called me by my assumed name. It would have felt strange coming from almost anyone else, but not from him. I reached across the table and patted his burly arm. "I love you, too, Uncle Pete," I told him with a smile. The way he grinned back at me, I couldn't help noticing how much he had grown to look like Grandpa.

"You know," he said, "you broke my heart when you were a little girl."

"I did, huh?" I said playfully, thinking he was teasing me as usual. He had Grandpa's good looks and his sense of humor too. "Now, how'd I do that?"

"When you were young, we all thought your dad would show up and do something stupid. And I was ready for him. I was going to do what-ever it took to keep my little Mandy Sue safe." His voice caught in his throat, and I realized his eyes were misty. For all his tough talk, my Uncle Pete was softhearted and sentimental when it came to me.

"One day you gave me a great big hug, and you looked up at me with those big brown eyes of yours and said, 'Uncle Pete, if my daddy comes back to take me, you won't shoot him, will you?' That just broke my heart. No little girl should have to worry about things like that."

I remembered well my fear that someone in my family would kill my father to protect me. Even in my youth, I had recognized the intensity of their conviction to keep me safe. I had been afraid of my father, but at the same time, I still cared about him. I didn't want him to be hurt because of his love for me, however warped his expression of that love may have been. My concern was also for my family members, who loved me enough to resort to violence on my behalf. Violence begets violence. As a child it seemed that no matter how resolutely I clung to peace, violence swirled all around me. I swallowed hard to choke back the lump that was rising in my throat.

"You *would* have shot him," I said in jest, trying to lighten the mood. "If it meant protecting me, you wouldn't have thought twice about it. I've always known you've got my back!"

"Absolutely!" he exclaimed with gusto, smacking his hand on the table. "I wasn't going to go looking for him, but if he showed up, I was going to take care of you. No one better think they can mess with my Mandy Sue and get away with it, not as long as I'm around!"

"Exactly. That's exactly why I worried about you. I didn't want you to pay the price for my safety. Plus, I didn't want to have to go visit you in prison. I don't think orange is your color," I teased.

I had the luxury of choosing a path of peace, in part, because I was protected by an army of loved ones who were willing to go to any extreme for my well-being. I could speak softly because they would carry a big stick on my behalf. I prayed unceasingly that my dad would never show up at my door, not only because I was afraid of him, but also because I was afraid of how far my loved ones would go to protect me from him.

CHAPTER 30

E ager to continue delving through the box, I set down the yellow
notebook in exchange for a manila envelope. As I begin to open it,
however, I realize the day has slipped away and I haven't eaten. So I head
for the freezer to see what's for dinner.

Mom speaks love through food. If she can't be here to heap my plate
with homemade delicacies steaming from the stove, she makes sure
I still get a good meal courtesy of a freezer stocked with single-serve
containers of her devotion. Whether we're together or not, she is forever providing for me. Scanning my options, I decide on a pasty. The
story goes that during the logging days, Finnish settlers in Michigan's
frigid Upper Peninsula used to take these pastries stuffed with meat and
veggies to work with them. In the morning they would place the warm
bundle on their heads beneath their hats to offer a little extra warmth
until lunchtime.

I toss the pasty in the oven and set the timer. Twenty minutes—
that's enough time to do a little more digging. The clutter grows in my
sunroom with each new round of excavation. I step over crumpled newspaper and grab the manila envelope as I sink into the recliner. The return
address says "Undergraduate Program, Department of Psychology." My
name is written across the front with a neon green highlighter. It clearly
belongs to me, but I don't recognize it.

Leafing through its contents, I recognize the paper records of my academic career. A certificate declaring me a lifetime member of Psi Chi, the national honor society in psychology. A letter congratulating me on graduating in the top 15 percent of my class and announcing my induction into the Golden Key International Honour Society. Another certificate announcing my membership in Phi Beta Kappa, which I'm told puts me in the company of presidents and Nobel Prize recipients.

That I, of all people, would be selected for such honors is a mystery to me. At that time, there was so much going on in my life that I was hardly able to register, let alone appreciate, the magnitude of these distinctions as they were bestowed upon me. Sliding the pages back into the envelope, I spot another paper, which I recognize as my transcript. Examining it, my eyes go first to the listing for fall semester 2000. That was the semester my dad found me. I was taking eighteen credits, well above the full-time student requirement of twelve credits per semester. And I got a 4.0 in every class. I don't know if I did it to spite my dad or if I did it in spite of him.

My grades became proof to me that I was surviving, that my dad was not defeating me. They were a tangible measure of my resilience. Four semesters in a row I got nothing but 4.0 GPA. At a time when I felt so utterly and completely helpless, academic achievement became my avenue of regaining a measure of control in my life. Perhaps I should thank my dad for the hand he had in pushing me to my books as an escape from reality. . . .

Refolding the transcript, I set it on the stand beside me, and reach for Grandma's afghan. The comforting aroma of the pasty baking in the oven swirls around me. I press back in the recliner and the footrest extends, inviting my eyes to close.

I wake to the chiming of the oven timer. Dinner is ready. Pasties are at the top of my list of ultimate comfort foods. In the fall, Mom and I make huge batches together, often two hundred or more at a time, to put in the freezer. That may seem like a lot, but once they're shared with family members, we usually end up having to ration our supplies by summer.

After dinner I debate taking the rest of the night off from the box, but my curiosity gets the best of me. *Just one more item,* I tell myself.

One item and no more. Kneeling beside the open box, I rifle through its contents until I spot a picture of me dancing with Pastor Mueller at a wedding. My heart catches in my throat. I love him so dearly.

I've kept in touch with many of my teachers from Salem over the years, and we still get emotional when we see each other. Pastor Mueller and I can't even look at each other without crying. I can scarcely think of him without tears welling in my eyes. The love and protective instincts of those who nurtured me at Salem has only grown with the years. Mr. Milbrath, my fourth grade teacher, freely admits that he still bristles at the sound of an airplane overhead when he's on playground duty. The danger is gone, yet the need to protect me is still deeply ingrained in him.

With the photo of Pastor Mueller is an old card from Mrs. Janetzke. She and Mrs. Norder had been my wonderful fifth grade teachers. Having heard that my lupus was once again active, Mrs. Janetzke reached out to me offering her prayers and encouragement. She fostered my love of music, science and art, but the most important lesson she taught me was to serve the Lord with joy. When my dad first found us, Mrs. Janetzke's immediate reaction was to invite Mom and me to seek refuge on her family's farm. She and her husband would gladly hide us as long as we needed. We didn't take her up on the offer, but knowing we had the option was a great comfort.

My heart overflowing with warmth and gratitude, I set aside the photo and the card and pull the next item from the box. But the instant I see the envelope with its flowery stamps, I stiffen with anger. Yet again I have come face-to-face with a part of my past that I've dedicated my life to putting behind me. *Why didn't I stop when this was still fun? Why did I have to keep digging?*

I have successfully avoided this envelope since Mom gave it to me about four years ago.

I was at the office that day when Mom arrived for one of her frequent visits. We lived several hours apart, but no distance was sufficient to separate us for long. While I worked, she let herself in and busied herself in my kitchen. That evening when I pulled into the garage, I knew I would find my stacks of papers tidied, the laundry well underway, and the house filled with the most wonderful aroma of onions sautéing in olive oil, meat braising, and rice steaming.

Mom always knew how to make a house—any house—feel like home. She whipped together gourmet meals with unparalleled efficiency, cleaning as she went so that no matter how many courses she prepared, she always worked in a neat and orderly kitchen.

Knowing my long work hours made it difficult for me to cook the Persian food I loved, she took every opportunity to prepare my favorite meals. Heritage is transferred through food, and she refused to let mine slip from my grasp. She was determined not to let the apathy of young adulthood rob me of the cultural richness that was my birthright.

When I came home that day, I intentionally made a lot of noise slamming the car door, stomping on the steps and knocking before I walked in. "Hello, I'm home," I shouted, peeking around the corner into the hallway, making sure Mom knew I was there. Her startle response had long been stuck in overdrive, and her hearing wasn't what it once was. Often she would look up to find someone standing in the room and jump, her hand grasping for her heart and her lungs gasping for air.

As predicted, she was standing at the stove. Stirring a big stockpot of *khoresh bademjan*, a mouthwatering stew of eggplant and braised beef, she shook her head and uttered her usual refrain: "I don't know how I ended up with so much. I was trying to make a small batch." It was what she always said when she stirred a pot of khoresh. I had never known her to actually succeed at making a small batch. If she did, what would she leave behind for me to eat when she went home?

Mom has never understood the idea of family members sharing a house, but not their meals—each person eating on his or her own timetable, parked separately in front of the TV or at the computer. In our home mealtime was family time. Even when I was a kid and it was just the two of us, proper etiquette was the order of the day. Food went in serving dishes studded with serving spoons. The place settings always included at least one knife, fork, and spoon, each neatly placed in its proper spot. And the napkin, whether paper or linen, always went on the lap. During meals the phone went unheeded and the television was turned off. The dinner table was where we spent quality time talking with each other, and conversation was more palatable when paired with Mom's cooking.

As we passed dishes back and forth, I asked about her drive. She asked about my day at the office. Pleasantries out of the way, she got to what was really on her mind.

"Has anything suspicious happened lately?" *Translation: Is your dad causing problems again?*

"No, everything's been quiet." *Translation: Argh, not again! What's he up to now? Why won't he just leave us alone?*

"Has your dad tried to contact you?"

"Not that I'm aware of. I stopped checking my MSU e-mail account a couple of years ago. I think he gave up on sending me e-mails for every Hallmark holiday once the account filled up with junk mail. "What's going on? Has something happened?"

"Mahtob, you know if you ever want to have contact with your dad, you can. It's always been your choice to make."

"I know. If I wanted to communicate with him I would have—with or without your permission. But I've never wanted to. I have no interest in hearing his lies. Where's all this coming from?"

"I got a package from Kombiz. He's been talking with your dad. Kombiz thinks it would be good for you to reconnect with him."

I was stunned. "Amoo Kombiz said that? I don't believe it. How could he? He can think whatever he wants. I am not opening the door of communication with my dad—end of story."

"Kombiz says your dad is sick and he may not be alive much longer. Maybe you should consider contacting him, if for no other reason than for his medical history. You don't know what kind of health challenges you'll face in the future. Maybe it would be good for you to know more about the medical history on his side of the family. Both of his parents died young. Ameh Bozorg had some health problems too. I don't know if she's still living. Kombiz says your dad has had kidney transplants. You know when your lupus first flared, it affected your kidneys."

I took a bite of Persian salad, not believing what I was hearing. First Amoo Kombiz was pushing me to communicate with my dad, and now Mom was pushing the idea. *What is happening here?*

"Mahtob, you should think about this. Don't just say no without really making sure that's what you want. Whatever you decide, I'll support your decision. Your dad and Kombiz have been talking on the phone and e-mailing. Kombiz sent me a letter asking me to give you their correspondence. He also wrote you a letter."

"This is just another of my dad's ploys. When one approach doesn't work, he changes his tactics. He is only interested in controlling me and perpetuating his lies. There's nothing he has to say that I need to hear." I paused. "And I can't believe Amoo Kombiz would fall for this. He of all people should be able to see through my dad and his manipulative schemes."

"Maybe you should talk with Kombiz then. Maybe he can find out more about your dad's health issues for you. Just read the packet and think about it before you make up your mind."

She handed me the envelope, and I tossed it aside. I burned with anger at the thought of my Amoo Kombiz, my cherished adopted uncle, betraying me by conspiring with my father.

Amoo Kombiz and my dad were close friends for much of their lives, but their friendship ended over my dad's treatment of Mom and me in Iran. Through the years, Kombiz had stepped in to support Mom's efforts to raise me to respect and appreciate my Persian roots. When I was younger, pomegranates, or *anar* as I knew them, were not readily available in Michigan. Kombiz lived in California, where they were plentiful, and once a year would send me an entire case to enjoy in celebration of No-ruz.

Eating pomegranates was one of my happiest memories of our time in Iran. There's an art to eating anar. You start by rolling the beautiful red Christmas-bulb-shaped fruit on the counter. The key is to press firmly enough to break the seeds on the inside, coaxing them to release their juice, but not to press so hard as to crack the pomegranate's leathery skin. This is a time-consuming process that calls for great patience. I remember watching with anticipation as my dad rolled a pomegranate for me, the sound of the seeds bursting within their protective membrane, the science of deducing at precisely what moment the pomegranate had been rolled as much as it could possibly endure without rupturing the skin, the delight of being handed the perfectly prepared anar, turning it over in my hands to find just the right spot to bite into, then bringing it to my lips and sinking my two front teeth into the peel to release a geyser of luscious crimson juice.

The pomegranate would deflate as I imbibed the bright, crisp juice, allowing me to squash some of the innermost seeds that couldn't be reached before. When I'd sucked the last drop of liquid from the anar, I would gleefully relinquish it to my dad. With his strong hands he would rip the casing asunder, revealing the treasure trove of seeds hiding in the inner sanctum of the fruit—the seeds no amount of rolling or squeezing could reach. These he would deftly scrape out with his thumbs into a bowl for me to eat like other American children would eat jellybeans or gumdrops.

Mom did her best to carry on the tradition, but having not grown up with pomegranates to roll, her mastery of the art fell short. At times, in her haste, she would press too firmly from the start and the skin would crack. Other times, unable to read the pomegranate's cues, she would juice it beyond its limit and the pomegranate would burst, emptying its precious juice into a pool on the counter. Then overcompensating, she would stop rolling too soon, before maximizing the available juice, and the pomegranate would be left with partially juiced seeds that weren't good to eat. More often than not, however, the stars would align and, beaming with joy, Mom would hand over the quintessential pomegranate.

I don't know which of us appreciated those moments more: her for being able to give me such a cherished gift or me for receiving it.

Handing down this tradition and others was a great source of delight for my Amoo Kombiz too. Sometimes he scheduled his visits during No-ruz in an effort to fill the void my dad had left behind. He loved to tell me the time-honored stories of the Persian New Year. My favorite was the tale of the ram.

"Mahtob Jon," he would start, "you see, we live in a vast universe on a planet held in place by a giant ram. All year long that ram balances the earth on one horn. As you would imagine, it is no easy task. The planet is quite heavy, and the ram's neck gets tired from carrying the weight of the world. Once a year, at the precise moment of the vernal equinox, the ram turns his head, shifting the earth from one horn to the other. This is the moment the No-ruz celebration begins. If you're still and watch very closely," he would add with a smile, "You'll see the eggs on the haft sin jiggle."

This wasn't news to me. I had seen it for myself. When we were in Iran, we had been bombed by Iraq at the very moment the ram shifted horns. The eggs had done more than jiggle that year.

I look now at my haft sin, and a sense of gratitude washes over me. I am so thankful that I no longer have to worry about the eggs jiggling for any reason other than the annual turning of the mythical ram's head. I shift my attention once more to the small envelope in my hands. The postage is fitting for the No-ruz season—three 41-cent stamps, each depicting a single flower: a red spiky flower, a yellow tulip with veins of red on each petal, and an iris. How like my adopted uncle to see to details like that.

Over the years, Amoo Kombiz was a steady influence in my life, a link to what was good about my Persian heritage and a buffer from its dangers. It was my Amoo Kombiz who sat me down to flip though the yellowed pages of his photo albums to show me pictures of the gregarious young man who would become my father. It was my Amoo Kombiz, the nuclear physicist, who gave me ideas for my elementary school science projects. It was the same Amoo Kombiz who videotaped my high school graduation and taught me how to connect the wires of the video recorder to the TV so we could watch our home movies.

By opening the door of communication with my dad, however, Amoo Kombiz crossed the line from trusted family member to double-crossing conspirator. I felt especially threatened because Kombiz knew so much about my life. I had gone to great lengths to prevent my dad from finding me. I didn't want to have to walk away from my life again.

Feeling betrayed and disappointed, I did not read the packet from Amoo Kombiz the night Mom gave it to me. The following morning, I grabbed the envelope and hastily threw it into my computer bag. Slowing just long enough to give Mom a kiss on the cheek, I shouted, "Have a good day," and headed to the office.

Work proved to be a good distraction, and before I knew it, I looked out my office window and saw that mine was the sole vehicle in the parking lot. Shutting down my laptop, I reached for my computer bag—and spotted the envelope again. No matter how preoccupied I kept myself, I had learned that no amount of busyness was sufficient to free me from dealing with my ever-resurfacing past.

With a heavy sigh, I turned the envelope over in my hands, admiring the cheerful blooms on the postage stamps. *It's just information*, I reminded myself just as I had been doing since my dad first resurfaced in my life.

It's a good thing he's changed his approach, I told myself. *It means he's realized how ineffective his previous methods were. He's now one attempt closer to giving up and leaving me alone.*

This is just information, I repeated to myself, leaning back in my office chair and retrieving a thick stack of typed pages from the envelope.

The first letter was from Amoo Kombiz and bore the date June 22, 2008. *It's just information*, I reminded myself yet again with a breath. Below the date was the greeting line. "Dear Betty Jon," the word *Jon*

261

indicating a close affection. *How could he stab us in the back and still have the nerve to call her Betty Jon? Who does he think he is?*

It's just information, I repeated, knowing my blood pressure was on the rise and my neck had already turned red and blotchy, a telltale sign that I was upset. *It's just information.*

Dear Betty Jon Greetings:

How are you and how is life treating you? I have not heard from you for such a long time. I hope all is well with you and Mahtob . . .

Surprise surprise, guess whom I talked [to] recently? That is the subject of this letter.

Here is the background. My cousin sent me the address of a site for Javad Maroofi. He is the foremost well-known pianist in Iran. He died several years ago. I was looking at his site and came across another Persian composer who lives in Vienna. His name is Sassan Mohebbi. He reminded me of Shardad Rohani, another well-known Persian musical conductor and soloist. Number of years ago. . . . I looked into his site, and he had a bunch of pictures. At the bottom of his pictures, there was a picture of Moody with him and Sassan's wife. At first I thought it was Moody's wife. Anyhow, I sent a response to Sassan that Moody was a friend of mine and if you get this message, please respond to me. He took my message to himself and forwarded it to Moody in Iran. A day later I got a call from Moody and we talked at length before our telephone call got cut off. He however, gave me his email address. I sent him my email address and the next day he called back. Then I called him and we talked at length. We have had several emails. I am enclosing our exchanges. . . . I would like to discuss this with you.

Please hear me out. I am still 100% on your side and you can trust me 100%. I know what he did was inexcusable. I also think that he dearly loves Mahtob and wants to establish relationship with her. I also believe that Mahtob is ultimately responsible if she wants to have anything to do with her father. I think for Mahtob's sake, not so much for Moody's sake, if Mahtob talks with her father, it will be good for her. Moody told me that he has lost both of his kidneys and bought a spare kidney and that one also has failed. He goes every two weeks and gets his blood filtered, the dialysis machine. How I found out was to ask him about the bandage on his arm in that picture. That is what he told me.

I know he has created a documentary called "Without My Daughter." He has dropped the "Not." He told me he is going to send it to me. I have not seen it. However, I have my own opinion about it. I think that is more propaganda than a documentary. I told him that this would create a more wedge between himself and Mahtob. Any defense on his part will become an offense on you and this is not something that Mahtob would appreciate. Putting all that aside, again, I am only thinking of Mahtob. Deep down I think there is a pleasure in forgiving that there is not in vengeance. Regardless of everything else, he deeply loves your daughter and is very proud of her. I know there is logistical problem and may offer a challenge in the public view and mind.

I would be more than happy to play the middleman. I can have a conference call connecting you/Mahtob and him. This way, Mahtob can talk with her father without any publicity or knowledge of anyone else. I don't think Moody would commercialize this.

I will leave it to your judgment and Mahtob. In no way do I wish to tell you or Mahtob what to do. It is her call.

Do read my exchanges with Moody. It is very interesting to hear him say yes he knows he made a mistake.

Anyway. I give you all the information and read them and please let me know.

Do take care.

Love, Kombiz

By this time it was dark outside, and I was irate. Hands trembling, I reached above my desk and closed the blinds. The hope that Mom had misjudged the intentions of the letter had vanished. Kombiz really was trying to facilitate a reunion, knowing full well what my dad had done to us in Iran and that Mom and I lived every day of our lives in fear of being found by him. *And then he had the nerve to talk to me about* forgiveness. *Give me a break! He knew I had forgiven my father. Did he think forgiving him meant I had to take more of his abuse?*

I turned the page to find a letter addressed to me, "Dearest Mahtob Jon." *Again with the term of endearment. What a traitor.*

Dearest Mahtob Jon:

Hope all is well with you and you have a great life. I am certain that you do. I just communicated with your mom and asked her to consider allowing you to establish communicating with your father.

Since when does she have to give me permission to communicate with my dad? It had always been my decision. What was it with people thinking she calls the shots where my dad was concerned? Even the night we left our house in Iran, it was my decision to keep going. I didn't want to go back to him when I was six, and I certainly don't want to at twenty-eight.

I have talked with him two times and we have exchanged emails. I have enclosed our exchanges for your use. He wants to establish communication with you. It is your decision and your call. I only consider what is best for you and how you would look at it 20–30 years from now.

Well, considering that my stance hasn't changed in the first twenty-two years since our escape, I seriously doubt it will change in the next.

I know he truly loves you and he regrets for what happened to you.

Really? He regrets what happened to me? What happened to me was his doing. Does that mean he regrets what he did to me? Does he take responsibility for his actions? Because all the information I have tells me he only regrets that he was outsmarted. He regrets that things didn't go his way. He regrets being exposed as a controlling and abusive fiend. Does he really regret the choices he made that destroyed our family? I seriously doubt it.

I also know that there was an attempt by a European news media to arrange a meeting between you and him several years ago and you turned it down.

Exactly! I want to be left alone. I want him to stop harassing me.

I am willing to play go between [for] you and your father and allow the two of you to talk on the phone. I will place a conference call between you and him. No one else other than your mom needs to know. If you decide you want to continue, that again is your call and your decision. If you don't want my meddling, I am sending you his contact number. And you can do it on your own.

I had broken my relationship with my sibling for several years over the issue of politics. We finally made up and there is a great feeling of establishing relationship rather than a broken relationship.

Again, this is my suggestion and you make the decision. Whatever you decide, I will support you.

Love, Uncle Kombiz

Sitting alone in my office, the hum of the overhead light competing with the throbbing of my heart in my ears, I turned the page and immediately lost myself in their e-mail exchanges. When I finished reading, the words of the two men echoed in my head. I was awash in a churning sea of competing emotions.

CHAPTER 31

"D ear God," I pray, alone in my sunroom. For the first time since that now long-distant night, I again gaze at the dreaded envelope in my hands. "Please give me eyes and a heart of compassion. Please help me remember that these words are merely information. There is no danger here, only information. Amen."

I was so upset by my initial reading of the packet from Kombiz that I stuffed the pages back into their envelope and buried the whole thing in this box. My strategy for dealing with my dad hadn't changed with time. I remained resolute to avoid all forms of communication with him.

What did change was my relationship with my beloved Amoo Kombiz. Since it seemed he was on a mission to reunite me with my father, I sadly made the decision to excise *him* from my life as well. I wasn't surprised by the fact that my dad had made use of an opportunity to manipulate yet another person into helping him in his quest to control me. The surprise for me was that Kombiz would betray me by falling for my dad's ploy.

For many years, I have been making a concerted effort to reframe my dad's attacks as "just information." I've had lots of practice and still, it requires a conscious effort. When I learned to control my thinking in this way, I really did find it empowering. It allowed me to take a step back and objectively examine my dad's methods independent from the emotions they conjured up in me. From that vantage point, I could more clearly recognize his desperation. It is this perspective that revealed to me the power I held over him. I may not have been able to stop him from hounding me, but my persistent avoidance was having an impact.

When I was sixteen, his message had been that I am *his* daughter; I have the blood of Fatimah and he *will not allow* me to be anything but Muslim. By the time I was twenty-two, he was invoking the name of my God, a God in whom he had forbidden me to believe, in an ineffectual attempt to sway me into correspondence with words like, "May our Lord and Savior, Jesus Christ, Keep you . . ." His incessant stream of e-mails had been incapacitating until I learned to change my viewpoint and began seeing them as "just information." Sometimes, though, despite my best efforts, I failed miserably. That had certainly been the case the evening I sat alone in my office and read the packet that I now hold in my hands. Even so, maybe I have ignored these pages long enough. Plus, it's No-ruz, and I miss my uncle. Maybe it's time to bury the hatchet, especially now that there is no reunion to be facilitated. Now there truly is only information.

My dad died on August 22, 2009. I learned of his passing on the day it happened. A friend from Germany saw it on the news and called. My dad's death had little impact on me. As far as I'm concerned, he died the day he told us we couldn't leave Iran.

Taking a deep breath, I revisit the words I first read four years ago.

From Kombiz to Moody

Dear Bozorg, as we always called you Moody Jon:
I was glad to get your call and sad to hear about your health status. First thing first, and that is about Mahtob. . . . I was always at awe as how great she was. It is most regrettable that you did not witness her growing up. . . . Considering what she went through, she came out really well. She excelled in her studies, she was a sociable child, highly responsible human being. One

thing she for sure inherited from you was her drive and independence. She was not someone whom someone could railroad her into something she did not want to do. She obeyed her mom and loved and respected her immensely. I know and witnessed that Betty dedicated her life to her and the result is quite notable. . . .

As I mentioned to you, several years ago, there was an attempt by a European media (TV or Newspapers) to sponsor getting you and Mahtob together in Europe. She was quite an adult and could travel with no restrictions. However, Mahtob turned that idea down. I think it is opportune time to revisit that issue and see if that idea can come to fruition. If I establish communication with Betty and Mahtob, I will pursue that option. . . .

I think Mahtob and you can establish relationship. Most assuredly, you must be confident that Betty is not, was not and would not oppose such a move. I am as confident on this issue as knowing my name. She would not at all interfere and she would leave it up to her. If she does not want and would not want, it would be her decision. The only thing you can do, is to put her under the knife and remove that gene of yours that you gave her. If you could remove that gene, then she would be willing to do anything anyone would say. . . .

To express the degree of Betty's absence of malice, it suffices to say that she would not object if she would select a Persian man to be her husband. In fact, for a while, Mahtob had a friend of Persian descent. . . .

I consider . . . religion to be the cause of Man's most miseries, regardless of the type of religion we are talking about. If we would abolish religion in its entirety and adhere to a single and simple principle of treating others the way we want to be treated, the need for all religions and the cause of human abuse goes away. It is fundamentally ludicrous that we kill and destroy others because the God that we have never seen is not the God described by the way others perceive. The reason I mention this is because once I noted that Mahtob does also have strong religious beliefs. We discussed the issue at length and I reached that conclusion. You should accept it as her choice as I accepted that as my children's choice. . . .

Anyhow, I have no idea if you value my judgment or not. However, if it still has any value with you, I must share with you that you simply have a fantastic daughter. As I conveyed to Sassan, your just punishment for that stunt you pulled was not to have witnessed the growth of this marvelous daughter of yours. I don't think any other punishment would have been appropriate. . . .

Past is past and I am not going to dwell on it. Your friends were all disappointed to a great deal, more than you can ever imagine. We were all at awe why you did what you did. The concern for humanitarian cause can be shared with others. However, those of us who knew you and considered you as our leader, our hero, the man with integrity, wisdom, leadership qualities second to none, were totally shocked. Anyway, someday I will share with you what went through our minds. . . .

Kombiz

From Moody to Kombiz

Kombiz Jon, Ghorbanat Gardam!

Thank you for your beautiful, long, and informative letter. I enjoyed reading it and I was hoping it would never end! It made me both happy and sad. . . .

Thank you so much for telling me so much about Mahtob. You made me feel more proud of her than before. I knew she was intelligent, and had leadership qualities. I wish her happiness and success. You know that my love for her is double fold: one as my daughter, and another, since the very first look at her face, I saw my mother's face in her. At that moment I thanked God to have given me a daughter and given me back the mother whom I had lost as a young boy. So, I loved and cherished her—and she knew that. I say that because when I would come home from the hospital she would run to me, circle her arms around me and would kiss me on the cheek, saying "Daddy loves me YE ALAME."

As far as my treating Betty while living in Iran is concerned, we had a loving three member family. Knowing the cultural differences with my Iranian relatives, we stayed away from them, instead we mixed with other mixed cultures (Iranian husbands with American wives). We had such a warm and friendly home (I should say LOVING HOME). Our family relation was envied by many of our American and British friends. Unfortunately, Betty's co-writer in her book and the movie "Not without My Daughter" had ignored this, instead I was presented as a cruel abusive beating man, who separated a child from her mother (or vice versa) And Betty was introduced as an abused woman. On the contrary, I loved and cherished my wife and daughter.

Generally speaking, I sympathize with Betty (as is described in the BOOK and the MOVIE Not Without my Daughter). Who in a sound mind and with a kind heart and an HONEST judgment would NOT do so?! a lady with her beloved daughter been KIDNAPPED, and taken to a foreign country as uncivilized as I-RAN; beaten up regularly; taken hostage and imprisoned with no food (the little food they had was full of WORMS and ROACHES) or freedom to talk or to leave house; who had no water to take a bath with (except one and a half times during her 18 months spent in IRAN—you know "Iranians take one shower A YEAR"; who had been threatened to death; who had to ESCAPE to FREEDOM (to the United States!) In freezing rain and blizzard with tiny little girl (Her BLOVED DAUGHTER) against watching eyes of her husband's CRUELL family and the BRUTAL Pasdaran police, as well as other uncountable ODDS and DANGERS and NATURAL DISASTERS and BOMBS and EXPLOSIONS. . . .".

Not only I SYPATHIZE with THAT Betty and her DAUGHTER, All powers to her who could take her DAUGHTER across the frozen Mount Zagros to FREEDOM (she should not be a heroine in the eyes of abused wives but ALL the HONORABLE people regardless of their gender and marital experiences), but I also sympathize with her SYPATHIZERS throughout the world, especially with the women who like THAT Betty, have been abused and mistreated by anyone, let alone their HUSBANDS!. . . . More so I am glad to see there are so many freedom lovers and those who are against human abuse and oppression. But more than that, I am SURPRIZED that how few are the number of her readers who love JUSTICE and have respect for rights of women!! (let's be honest, they are at least more than the occupants of the so called WHITE HOUSE—BLACK house fits better). God knows, my heart bleeds for SUCH Betty, and her DAUGHTER!

BUT, SUCH BETTY NEVER EXISTED!!

It only was Mr. William Hoffer's brain child—NOT the daughter of Mr. Harold and Mrs. Fern Lover whom I married on June 6th 1977 at the mosque on Richmond Avenue in Houston, Texas U.S.A. Neither was she the one mothered my child. And nor was the REAL Betty who became Mrs. MAHMOODY! The REAL Betty L. Lover, Smith who later became the REAL Mrs. MAHMOODY, was the lady who was being treated like a queen. She received a set of diammond rings at the wedding as her dowry. Three days later on her birthday, I gave her a surprise birthday party, along with punch and cake a big meal, a diamond watch. Soon after I started my medical practice in Texas, we sent round trip tickets for her children and parents to fly south to Texas to spend summer holidays with us. While in Corpus Christi, we took them first class gourmet restaurants with food of different nations including Mexican, Irish, Japanese and of course, to sea food buffets. As with other relatives, siblings and friends of Betty, we took them for three hour ride to the Mexican boarder towns for sight seeing and shopping. And on vacation to summer resorts in Texas. Don't mention the trips to Padre Island sandy beaches, to swim in the warm waters of Gulf of Mexico.

Catching my breath, I remind myself yet again that this is only information. *This is only information. This is only information.*

In just a few months my private practice in Texas flourished and my income was raised to around $30,000 a month. Soon after that we bought the biggest and most attractive two-story marble house on the block in an affluent neighborhood of the city. The house was surrounded by velvety St. Augustine grass, resembling a green Persian hand-made carpet. It had lots of flowers with a unique cactus garden, as well as olive, palm, orange and grapefruit trees. . . .

It was not a coincident that the REAL Betty in Iran too, was enjoying SIMILAR conveniences. Here too, we had a large villa-type house in Pasdaran (an affluent part of North Tehran), with a nice lawn, lots of flowers, several trees, including a cherry tree (Mahtob and our neighbor girls of her age would pick cherries for us) . . . In addition, this house in Tehran had a swimming pool. This, was an advantage over our Texas house. The house was fully furnished with Italian furniture, and American appliances, as well as Persian hand made carpets, a color T.V. and an electric organ. She was free to go shopping or visiting with her friends any time she pleased (she always had bundles of ESKENAS to spend shopping) On several occasions she bought some Persian hand made gifts and sent to her folks in the States. Mr. William Hoffer, her co-writer had politicized a nice family relation to attack not only me, but The Islamic Republic of Iran.

Kombize AZZI ZAM, my coming to Iran was not to carry signs in support of the POLITICAL system in Iran, (not at all) but instead, to help the war victims, the injured, who were mostly my relatives, my fellow town's men and women, if nothing else, my fellow country men and women. And even if not that, they were HUMAN BEINGS. As an Iranian well trained physician (Anesthesiologist) I had a duty toward my people to serve them during an unwanted imposed war! Honest to God, If I, as an Iranian physician would NOT come to help, would doctors from say Canada, Holland, or France would go to a war torn foreign land and help the many war victims? And now if offering such services at such a critical time and era has annoyed some Iranians overseas, let it be so. They are annoyed because they were not correctly informed. I really think what I did, when I did it deserves a HUMANITERIAN RECOGNITION AWARD. I am proud of what I did. I think teaching at the university and training generations of young doctors for my country in addition to offering my medical services, is some thing to make all IRAN LOVERS if not proud, but at least happy. Because I DID what so many of them longed to do but did NOT get the opportunity to do so. You know A friend in need is a friend indeed. I think I accomplished my mission.

Now HONESTLY you judge, I separated Mahtob from a parent, or that was Betty who separated Mahtob from her NATURAL FATHER? She took her AWAY from a kind loving and warm home! . . .

You may forward a copy of this letter to [our mutual friends] to inform them of the truth may be reconsider their thinking about my actions. I hereby apologize if I had caused them hard feeling.

> Please stay in touch.
> My love to all,
> Ghobanat, Moody.

P.S. convey my love to Mahtob, if you ever get in touch with her . . .

What nerve! He apologized to his friends, but not to me! And what an empty apology at that. He's not really saying he's sorry. He just wants them to buy into his delusional version of the truth.

Breathe, I remind myself. *This is only information.*

From Kombiz to Moody

Moody Jon Salaam,

Your English is still excellent. Let me ask a personal question. Deep down, do you not think that you made a big mistake? It blows my mind when I think of what you were, what you could have and what you did not have. How dare you left me? You even left Faryar. You did not even say good bye. Please do not tell me it was a two-week vacation. If you did not have a BS and a MS in math, I would have said, you are poor in arithmetic. You did not know that the math degrees would someday come to haunt you. If you had not pursued the math major, now you could have a way out. . . .

Well, dear friend. Do take care of yourself. You are still a lucky man. You have a daughter who is safe, happy and has a great life. . . .

Pleasant dreams.
Kombiz

From Moody to Kombiz

Kombize Azziz,

It is about 1:30 pm your time. I hope you enjoyed you lunch, but b/4 you take your little cat nap read the answers to YR Q's. . . .

"How dare you left me? You even left Faryar."

Never left you guys! I had not taken your phone numbers with me. So I had no access to all of you. You should excuse me for that.

"Please do not tell me it was a two-week vacation"

It was not a two-weeks-vacation! It was not supposed to! We had plan to stay awhile. It was open enden stay. . . . So it was by no means a 2wks.vac. and if the war had ended, we would all together have returned to the States. There was no need for Betty to Kidnap Mahtob and make a big deal about it! It would have been enough for Betty to tell me she wanted to return to America.

"Let me ask a personal question. Deep down, do you not think that you made a big mistake?"

Yes, I do. I never thought:

1) Betty would destroy our family. She had a comfortable life here in Iran that was envied by most of her foreign friends! . . .

2) That the Iranian Government official would so mistreat me. I had to work and teach six months almost free for them to accept my American Medical Diploma. Besides, my colleagues were jealous of my American training and high skills. They caused all kinds of problems for me. Despite all of that, I persevered and was able to train generations of young doctors for MY PEOPLE, the job few others would do! I did such a good job and for such a long time that they finally name me the PHISICIAN OF THE YEAR in 2003. Disregarding this accomplishment, a few months later they made a coup against me and retired me OVER NIGHT, in favor of a young doctor of their Mafia group. Of course on the other side of the coin, I am glad that I was—and still am—useful for my country and the people I love! Let us be honest about it, it has cost me my comfortable family life, if not much more.

"Your English is still excellent."

. . . My gosh, I lived I life time in Eglish speaking world. Besides I am from ABADAN! . . .

Fadayat, Moody.

From Kombiz to Moody

Dear Moody:

Hope all is well with you and you are in great spirits enjoying your health and your life.

I am going to write to you in detail and share with you what is in my heart and soul. What I am going to share with you is my thoughts, ideas, and beliefs, rightly or wrongly. If I don't share with you what I think and what I believe, then our friendship is worthless.

1) On the subject of your relationship with Mahtob, I hope and pray to God that you establish a relationship, if for nothing else, for her sake.

I fundamentally believe in the value of blood attracting blood. I think you attract Mahtob and Mahtob attracts you. Father-daughter relationship is as holy as son-mother relationship. I firmly and truly believe that any man on Earth is extremely lucky to be her father. She is that good. I don't think you can detect how good of a person Mahtob is. You must truly understand and accept that she went through a major trauma in life and in spite of all the love and respect I have for you, it is my firm belief that you were the cause of that induced trauma.

I give you the benefit of the doubt and accept that you had no desire, intention or wish for her to be traumatized. I have known you and accepted you to be a highly compassionate man. You were compassionate with your patients, friends, and associates. I fully remember that everyone respected you and everyone spoke so highly of you.

In spite of all of these facts and figures, you made a colossal error in judgment. You took an American spouse to Iran with full knowledge that you would want to raise your daughter in Iran in spite of the fact that you knew full well her Mom would do everything possible not to allow that to happen. Mahtob had to go through a trauma of escaping from Tehran under extremely risky and poor conditions. Then you caused her to grow up without the presence, the guidance and the love of a loving father.

In spite of everything that her mom did for her, there was always the element of risk of being abducted. This being a tug of war by default and the nature of the beast. Putting alarm in the house, in the car, being constantly cognizant of the environment provided a very precarious situation. In spite of all of that, she grew up to be a very healthy woman without anger or damning the male species. I fundamentally believe that if she does not wish to have a relationship with you, it is 100% her decision. . . .

Never did I hear Betty say anything unkind about you, at least in my presence. It must be totally clear that if she had fabricated a story in the book, Mahtob is sufficiently strong that she would have challenged that. Mahtob is anything but a patsy. She holds her ground and fights for her beliefs. Such persons do not become valedictorian. Anytime I saw her, I thought of you and how sorry I was for you to miss her growing up.

2) There is zero doubt in my mind that she adores her mom and she should. She has been her total support and her closest friend in all of these years. You may create a documentary to challenge Betty's book, film or her claims. These will undoubtedly drive a bigger wedge between you and Mahtob. Any defense on your part will be construed as an offense toward Mahtob. You win support by other people and may gain sympathy from others. However, tell me frankly, what would that do to Mahtob? Would Mahtob think better of you if you challenge her Mom? Her mom has been in Mahtob's eyes and mind, her salvation. Then comes her father and after all these years, creates a book, creates a documentary, and challenges her mother. Unless Mahtob has totally forgotten what she went through, then there may be a chance. If what Betty wrote in the book is 80% true, you have zero chance in heck to get Mahtob's love.

3) The only possible avenue . . . with Mahtob (forget about everyone else in the world) ought to be in my humble opinion that you were wrong and you made a colossal mistake.

It is perfectly plausible for you to defend yourself in the eyes and the minds of the people of the world. However, with Mahtob, she was there. She remembers if she was taken away from her mother. She remembers if you slapped her mom. She remembers if you imprisoned her mom. If these were not true, she would have hated her mom for such fabrication and she would have jumped on the plane to come to Iran the minute she turned 18.

There are certain things that Betty could not have lied or exaggerated. If you don't agree with me, do talk to a child psychologist in Iran. Be absolutely honest and frank with him. That will be in a closed door room between you and a psychologist. Tell him that these things and events occurred in front of Mahtob. She witnessed these events. She is now a grown woman. Ask him how could you establish a relationship? Let a psychologist tell you what your approach ought to be. Ask if your documentary will help or hurt your relationship with Mahtob. . . .

4) Moody Jon, let me be very frank with you. It is absolutely OK with me for you to defend yourself and try to justify what you did. This you could do with all the people in the world except me. I was there, witnessed it and know everything about this case. Here is my recollection and why I am not buying your story.

a. . . . Once the revolution took place, you changed overnight. You argued strongly in favor of Khomeini and the fact that Iran must follow Islamic doctrine. Do you remember the long telephone conversations we had? . . . You can try to convince others that you wanted to go to Iran for humanitarian reasons. But please don't try it with me. Do you know why? This would tell me you are telling me that "you are so stupid that I can pull this one over your eyes."

b. In my last trip to Michigan, I visited you and Betty. She
was hiding your passport with full fear of you taking
Mahtob out of the country. I did tell her that under no
conditions she should go to Iran. I never understood why
she did. When we had dinner in a restaurant, I asked you
if you were contemplating to go to Iran to practice. Do
you remember your answer? Please let me refresh your
memory. I knew you were not telling me the truth. You
said "how could I as I don't know the medical terms and
the procedures in Iran."

c. As I said before to you on the telephone. I was in Athens
being a tourist. I noticed that my passport had expired.
I went to the US Embassy and while I was waiting,
I heard an American woman talking with the staff
requesting them to take her American Passport to the
Swiss Embassy and send it to the Swiss Embassy in Iran
where she would go and get her passport. She had done
it in Tehran and when she arrived in Athens she got
her US passport. We got to talk while we were waiting
and then she shared how life was so tough on American
women married to Iranian men. She then said there
was this American lady in Tehran pleading with the
Swiss Embassy to let her escape with her daughter out
of Iran. Her husband was American educated doctor.
In the USA, I had tried to contact you and had called
you several times. I got a response that your telephone
number in Alpena was cut off and there was no number.
I became convinced that you all had left for Iran. When
this woman who was also married to an Iranian man in
Tehran, in Athens told me about an American woman
in Tehran being captive, I made the connection. I asked
the woman the name of the woman. She was not sure
but said something that sounded like Mohammady. I

said was it Mahmoody, she said, oh yes, that is what it was. . . . Thus, when I read in her book about going to the Swiss Embassy, I knew that was 100% true.

d. The next news I heard was from a Persian man. An Iranian guy who had left Iran and was amongst the circle of your friends, called me in California and said I have a message for you from Betty Mahmoody. She is in Iran and has been kept in captivity and she is extremely unhappy. He said she just wants you to know but has asked me for you not to get in touch with Moody. He would beat her up and make life miserable for her. . . . First, I did not know where you were and secondly, I could not do anything as that would have put Betty's life more in danger. I was very saddened and disappointed. . . .

e. When Betty was finally out of Iran and back in Michigan, she contacted me. . . . My first question to her was that why you went to Iran when I told you not to. She had remembered my caution. However, she told me that she was afraid that if you take Mahtob to Iran alone, she would never be able to see her daughter. Can I share with you something? I would put that probability at 95%. In other words, if you had taken Mahtob to Iran, you would have raised her as an Islamic daughter and to hell with the mother. Do you know how many Middle Eastern men have done this? I therefore, do not blame Betty a bit for going to Iran with you. . . . She did tell me that you would have returned to USA after some times. However, you knew that if you returned with her to the USA, she would surely divorce you, and she said she would have. For this reason, you had no intention of returning to the USA or allowing Mahtob to come to USA. Betty could have but without Mahtob. In fact the reason you wanted

Betty to come to USA was to liquidate your assets in Michigan. It was for this reason that even when you realized that you had no permit to work as a doctor, you did not want to come to USA. You left your properties and belongings in the USA to convince her that your trip to Iran was a short term. What also convinced her that there might be a chance for you all to return was that you swore on the Koran to return.

When you said that you became a victim of politics between Iran and USA, I totally disagree. You became a victim of your own prejudice and fanaticism. You put your own political ideology above the welfare of your family. I never forget the cusses you used to make against the News media when we were watching TV in your Alpena House. You cussed at America. I told myself "how . . . he does this when his wife is American?" I asked myself what your reaction would have been if she had said "God Damn Iran?" You said as clear as I remember "God Damn America" . . .

You can't mix religion with politics and most certainly cannot mix religion with the principle of maintaining a family. Your first and foremost responsibility was to your precious daughter and her mother.

What you did became the greatest disaster for the image of Iranian Man and an Islamic Man in the minds of the people of the world. . . . I once participated in a huge Iranian Conference in Berkeley, California. The attendees consisted of so many Iranian PhDs from USA and abroad. . . . One afternoon, the agenda was on the subject of *Not Without My Daughter* . . . Even those who disliked Betty's book had no sympathy for your actions . . .

I don't think there were any winners in this entire scenario. Betty was not at all a winner. She has had a miserable life. A life always under the threat of losing her child is no life. Mahtob for sure did not win, and you were the biggest loser. . . .

It was not your job to stop the war or help the patients. You helped the patients here and they are also God's creatures. What difference does it make where a person is born and what they kind of religious ideologies does he have. At the end of the day, he/she is a creature of God. You made a choice to live in this country. Your license to practice medicine did not state that you only save Persian patients. . . . With that much money you had, you could have sponsored several kids in Iran or Tibet for that matter.

Don't think back for I should have, would have, could have. That is gone and over with. Playing the blaming game is never fruitful. It is a waste of time. You must have one notable goal. And that is to establish relationship with your daughter.

You can't do that by attacking her mother. By challenging her mother, you will have zero, no more than zero, chance of establishing relationship with Mahtob. Is there any other way? Would you be my friend if I chastise your mom? Why should Mahtob be any different?

What you did for Betty and Mahtob, you get no brownie point from me. . . .

I hope you did not get upset with me as I shared with you what was in my heart,

Ghorbanat, Kombiz

I drop the letters in my lap and lean back in my chair. Every inch of my body aches with tension. Reading my dad's words, I still hear the familiar snarl of the fox who hunted me as a child. How I detested his rants. With seemingly no provocation, he would launch into tirades—lengthy diatribes filled with lies and exaggerations, grandiose denunciations that often made little or no sense and had no grounding in reality. The more he shouted, the more worked up he became, and before long things were sure to erupt into physical violence. I can see his voice on the page, each bolded word a fist flying through the air.

I shake with fury. I want to scream at him and tell him he forgot that we didn't just have one pool; we had two pools. Baba Haji and Ameh Bozorg's pool had a shallow layer of stagnant green water in it the entire time I was there, and the pool in the courtyard of our last apartment was an empty cement hole in the ground. Even if it hadn't been, the feral Persian cats would have rendered it useless.

So much of what he claimed, virtually every aspect of what he claimed, is blatant deceit. If he were going to lie, he should at least have made his lies plausible. But even if what he said had been true, would that justify his brutality? So he bought his wife a diamond watch. Does that afford him the right to hold her hostage or to beat her or to threaten to kill her? So we had a pool. Does that make it okay for him to beat my mom in front of me or to tell me I'll never see her again?

I pick up the pages and angrily flip through them once more. The word valedictorian jumps out at me. Had my dad really asked Kombiz if I had been the valedictorian? If so, perhaps it had been in one of their phone conversations. Whatever the case, Kombiz was telling him what a miracle it was that in spite of everything he put us through, I grew into a well-adjusted adult, and my dad's concern seems to be whether or not I was the top of my class. *That's just like him—obsessed with status, prestige and perfection.*

Was that the root of the debilitating self-consciousness I battled for so long? I never would have lived up to his expectations. If I had grown up with him playing an active role in my life, I always would have felt like my best, if it wasn't better than everyone else's best, wasn't good enough. His concern wasn't for me. His concern was for how I impacted his status. He wanted to be able to brag that he was the father of the valedictorian. I remember that air of self-importance well. I always wanted to believe my dad loved me, but now I wonder if he knew what love was. Was he even capable of love? His love for me existed in relation to himself. He didn't love me for who I was—for my personality, my character, my convictions, not even for my accomplishments. He loved me because I was *his*.

In my dad's eyes, none of this was about me. He was using me as a pawn in his attempt to save face and to attack Mom for what he saw as a personal slight. If he truly believed the story he was portraying to the rest of the world, and if his concern were truly for me, he would have been petitioning courts within days, if not hours, of my supposed kidnapping. He would have worked tirelessly and utilized any means necessary to recover me, just as Mom had worked tirelessly to protect me from him.

And Kombiz got it! He understood that I remembered for myself what had happened. He understood that I wouldn't let myself be manipulated by my dad's fabrications. After all those years, my dad remained arrogant enough to think he could lie to me and I would accept his word as truth, completely disregarding my own memories and Mom's memories and even the documentation of the government agencies in Iran, Turkey, Switzerland, and the United States—as if his saying it made it so.

That was the ultimate in grandiosity—textbook magical thinking. He exhibited no regard for reality. My dad created his own reality, and in his eyes anyone who said otherwise was simply wrong.

My eyes continue to dart about the pages. "Humaniterian recognition award"? Once again, he was the victim. The world had done him wrong. It was all about him.

The saddest part of reading this now is having to acknowledge that my dad really had no empathy for me. I can understand his not having empathy for Mom. It's reasonable—well, as reasonable as any of this is— that she would be the target of his contempt. But no empathy for me? He knew the truth. He knew what he did to us. How could he not feel empathy for me, his daughter—the one he claimed to be so heartbroken over losing?

Was he that callous, or was he simply delusional? Did he know he was lying, or had he told the lies so many times that they had actually become real to him? I suppose it doesn't really matter.

The emotional strain of confronting my past has drained me, and I am overcome with exhaustion, but I make a purposeful effort to shift my focus to the positive. The good in my life far outweighs the bad or the difficult. Yet the dangers from my past, real or perceived, keep resurfacing. Each time they do, I find myself stuck in this same dance. I feel threatened, which leads to feeling angry. Then I have to work through the whole cycle of coming to terms with it all over again.

Feeling older than my years, I lumber to the kitchen for a midnight snack. I visited Annie and Vergine last week, and they sent me home with stuffed grape leaves and hummus. I've rationed the treats diligently, not wanting them to run out. I pull them from the fridge and put the kettle on to make a cup of tea. Leaning against the counter, I eat the last few bites of dolmeh and hummus, savoring the blend of olive oil and spices.

While I wait for the water to boil, I head back to the letters. Most confusing to me is how it could be that Kombiz was the one to propose the idea of a reunion. I think back to when I first read these words sitting in my office. I felt so betrayed that my beloved Amoo Kombiz would suggest to my father that he should "establish a relationship" with me. A familiar wave of sadness washes over me. *How could he do that to me?* Reminding myself once more that this is "only information," I revisit Kombiz's words, genuinely hoping for an answer.

> On the subject of your relationship with Mahtob. I hope and
> pray to God that you establish a relationship, if for nothing else,
> for her sake.

"For her sake." There it is. I didn't hear those words before. In my rage, I stopped listening after "I hope and pray to God that you establish a relationship." I resolve to give Kombiz the benefit of the doubt and choose to cast his motives in the best possible light. He was proposing a reunion for my sake. I don't have to agree with him in order to entertain his perspective.

Outside the moon is shining bright in the clear night sky. The wheatgrass on my haft sin has really taken off. It is nearly time to throw it away. Looking at it, I wonder if Amoo Kombiz also planted wheat grass this year. I had considered contacting him after I learned of my dad's death, but I hadn't.

I glance down once more at his words. "For her sake." Was he calling my dad out for my sake? Was he trying to get my dad to take responsibility for his actions, to acknowledge that he had been the cause of the trauma in my life? Was Amoo Kombiz really attempting to elicit an apology from my dad? Was that it? Did he think an apology would in some way benefit me?

The kettle whistles and I head back to the kitchen to fix my tea. I lean over the mug and let the steam warm my face. Closing my eyes, I inhale slowly and deeply. Then I exhale, willing the tension to drain from my body.

"For her sake." The words echo through my mind. *What else did I miss?*

Determined to read the pages once more strictly for informational purposes, setting aside all emotion, I curl up in my chair and start from the beginning. Forcing myself to see with new eyes, I find myself once more engrossed in their conversation.

> Moody Jon, let me be very frank with you. It is absolutely OK with me for you to defend yourself and try to justify what you did. This you could do with all the people in the world except me. I was there, witnessed it and know everything about this case. . . .
>
> You became a victim of your own prejudice and fanaticism. . . .

How had I previously missed all these valid points that Kombiz was making? He said all the things I would have said to my dad had I felt it worth the risk. How fascinating that Kombiz, of all people, had said these things to my father. They had so much in common—both Iranian, both well-educated men of science, both lovers of the arts, both intensely proud of their heritage. Where had their paths diverged?

There is much about Iranian politics—and American politics for that matter—that I do not understand. But Mom and Kombiz each described my father's ideological and behavioral shift the same way. One day he was a happy-go-lucky, gregarious, gentle man, and the next he was a fanatic militant who was prone to violent outbursts. Why did my dad stop seeing people as people and start seeing them as Iranian or American, good or evil?

I continue to read, and another image begins to solidify in my mind—one of two old friends rekindling their long-dormant kinship. I see each of the men sitting at their computer on opposite sides of the globe, thoroughly enjoying this reconnection—laughing and joking, exchanging small talk and sharing fond memories, their smiles only fading when the calls for accountability rang out.

"Let me ask a personal question. Deep down, do you not think that you made a big mistake?"

"Yes, I do. I never thought . . . Betty would destroy our family."

There, that was it. My dad had the opportunity to acknowledge the truth, to admit his mistake, and what did he do? He pointed the finger of blame at Mom. It makes me sad to read that, yet at the same time it's validating. It's the answer I expected from him.

That is a big part of the reason I decided as a child not to engage him in conversation. I didn't feel the need to open myself up to any more of his lies or manipulation. Yet a part of me, even to the end, held out hope that when confronted with the truth he would be honest, at least with himself and with me. I guess I can be thankful that by not communicating with him for all those years I was spared a lifetime of such deceit.

I firmly believe that even to the day he died, my dad thought Mom and not his own behavior was to blame for his misery. He thought Mom gave Iranians a bad name by telling our story, rather than seeing that *his* actions reflected poorly on his nation, on his culture, and on his religion. Mom has always gone out of her way to draw a distinction between the actions of one man and the character of an entire nation. She's the one who raised me to celebrate my Iranian heritage. What a sad and twisted irony that my dad didn't recognize that.

Folding the letters, I slip them back into their envelope and walk into my study to turn on my computer. The walnut desk feels refreshingly cool and solid beneath my fingers. Lights flicker across the screen, and my mind struggles to come to terms with everything I have just read.

The last time I tried to make sense of the contents of these pages, I was completely overwrought with emotion. I felt angry, betrayed, and threatened. Now I just feel sad. I feel sad for my dad and the poor choices he made, sad that he squandered his life in such a way, sad that so many people were negatively affected.

When I found out he had died, I was momentarily relieved. I thought that at last this whole saga was over. That relief gave way to fear of reprisal by the people who had taken up his cause. And then, almost in that same instant, the sadness hit. It wasn't sadness for my father, whose life had just ended. I was sad that this man had let his dysfunction rule his life.

I google the words, "DSM-IV criteria Narcissistic Personality Disorder." A description pops up on the screen, and instantly my eyes meet with the truth my heart already knows: "grandiosity . . . need for admiration . . . lack of empathy . . . sense of self-importance . . . fantasies of unlimited success, power, brilliance, beauty, or ideal love . . . interpersonally exploitative." And so on.

It doesn't excuse him. It doesn't justify him. It doesn't in any way make what he did okay, but it does help me make sense of it. It does help me understand my dad's level of dysfunction and the implications it had in our family.

I feel a strange sense of relief. I spent years obsessed with understanding the workings of the human mind so I could keep myself from falling apart. And yet I spent so little time truly exploring what prompted my dad to do the things he did. Now, after taking in his conversation with Kombiz, I realize I owe my resilience, in a large part, to his absence from my life. I got to have the best of both worlds. Mom and Kombiz and a whole host of others along the way helped make sure I was given the good my dad had to offer while insulating me, for most of my life, from the bulk of his destructive devices.

These letters in so many ways validate my decision to exclude my father from my life. They're also a gift in that they present me, as an adult, with a glimpse into the man he was. He was just as I remembered, and now I don't have to wonder if my memories have been distorted by my opinions or the opinions of others.

It wasn't the gift Kombiz intended to give me, but it was the gift I needed. What Kombiz didn't understand was that I didn't need to talk to my dad to make peace with his place in my life. I did that years earlier, and I laboriously repeated the process each time he resurfaced. This was no exception.

CHAPTER 32

Light surrounds me. It pours in through my bedroom window and warms me in its glow. I open my eyes to a new day and know what I must do. Wrapping my dad's old sweater around me, I stop in the kitchen just long enough to start a pot of coffee before I make my way back to my desk. The comforting aroma of Berres Brothers' Highlander Grog fills the room as I begin to type.

> Hi, Amoo Kombiz,
>
> I think about you so much, but especially this time of year. I pray you are happy and healthy and that our new year brings you much joy.
>
> Mom brought me boxes of old pictures. Some belonged to my dad before my parents met. I thought you might enjoy this photo of two handsome men.
>
> Oh, I threw in a pic of my haft sin too. The only thing missing is anar and my favorite Persian uncle.
>
> Love, Mahtob

I scan a black-and-white photo of Kombiz and my dad and attach it to the message. Before I hit Send, I add the words, "A belated Eid Eshoma Mobarak!" to the subject line. A belated Happy New Year.

The e-mail is generic, to be sure, but it's been years since we have spoken. I want to feel him out before I say what I have to say.

He doesn't make me wait long for his response. The following morning I awake to his reply.

Hello Precious Mahtob Jon:

Eide Shoma Mobarak as well. No, it is still not too late for Eid Mobaraki. The New Year celebration continues until Sunday which is the thirteenth day of the first month. We call that Sizdeh Bedar. Sizdeh is 13th in Farsi.

This No-ruz is entirely Persian tradition and has nothing to do with religion. It starts with the last Tuesday of the year when people create bon fire and jump over it. As they jump over it, they recite my yellowness to you, and your redness to me. This tradition is left from Zoroastrian days where Persians worshiped fire. They would set fire and would signify exchanging their yellowness (weaknesses and bad parts to the fire to burn away) and would take the redness, purity, heat and warmth from the fire.

We just did that couple or weeks ago where a restaurant owner set four sets of containers on the asphalt of a parking lot and several hundred Persians came over and jumped over the fire. Kids had the most fun. What was interesting, they had put several layers of metal containers and bricks on the asphalt and after everything was cleaned up, there were no sign of damage to the asphalt.

Many years ago, the Persian community in the San Jose area decided to do the same, but in a public park. They went to the police department to get a permit for such an event. As they explained to the officers that they were going to put several bonfires in the park so the kids and adults would jump over them.

The officers asked "you are going to do what?!!!!!!, setting bon fire and have kids jump over them. When was the last time you had your head examined."

They said but this is a Persian tradition going 4000 years old.

They said we don't care, you are just not going to do it.

So, finally, police said, we will have a fire truck in hand and you will pay for the cost and we will monitor the process. So, they did and the next year, things got a bit easier. However, there are still idiots on this planet. Two ladies were there with long skirts made with nylons. All it would take is one of their skirts would catch on fire. I can just see the headline in the paper the next day.

I was very impressed with your Haft Sin and also greatly appreciated sharing the picture with your dad. First, there was only your dad and I did not see another guy in the picture justifying "two handsome" guys. Who was the other one?

The other point I would like to share is the use of the word "dad" by you. I would have thought you would refer to him as your father and not dad. I am very happy that this is the word you selected. I don't know if you ever forgave him or not. I hope for your sake that you did.

Ihad several frank exchanges with him once we established email communication and couple of times telephone conversation. One time I asked him if he was every sorry for what he did. He said "of course." I shared those exchanges with your mom. I don't know if she shared them with you. He once told me that he was making $30,000 a month in Corpus Christi and had the most affluent house in that city. He blew it all over his religious ideology. It is so regrettable for him to be that dedicated to a cause which was worthless, in my view. He learned of his grave error in judgment that was already too late. If you want me to, I will forward those exchanges with him.

Tell me something about yourself. A) where you are with respect to your education (finished University and became a child psychologist) single or are in a relationship? Where you are in your religious beliefs? I vividly remember where once in a car we discussed religion and you were very emphatic with your belief. Please forgive me, but I don't follow any religion, especially Islam. It is my belief that Religion as a belief has afflicted more damage to mankind that all other causes combined. Having said that, I respect everyone's right to his or her religious ideology. Do take care and be absolutely certain that I have always loved you and will do so for always.

Love, Uncle K.

I feel the weight being lifted off my shoulders as I read those gracious words. Kombiz was right when he wrote to Mom, "Deep down I think there is a pleasure in forgiving that there is not in vengeance." I breathe a prayer of gratitude, then open my eyes and begin typing.

My dear Amoo Kombiz,

It is so great to talk with you! You are exactly as I remembered and that makes me so happy. I laughed aloud when I started reading your email and saw that your first priority was to teach me about my Persian heritage. I so appreciate your lessons. I don't remember the jumping over fire tradition. The only fires I remember in Iran were the result of Iraq's bombs. It sounds like a fun tradition, and it's interesting to see how the color references permeate even western culture today. Calling someone yellow-bellied is calling them weak or cowardly. How fun to celebrate No-ruz with so many Persians. . . .

Last year for No-ruz, I hosted a big dinner. My pastor and his family came and so did my college roommate and her family. Mom and I made all kinds of Persian food. I was living in a small apartment and the only way all twelve of us could eat together was to serve the meal on the floor so we had a traditional Persian meal seated on my living room floor.

There were several small children there and when they found out we were eating on the floor, they must have assumed we were having a pretend meal with imaginary food like a pretend tea party. You should have seen their faces when we started placing huge platters of rice and Khoreshes and Kebabs before them. It was such fun! We planted wheatgrass and colored eggs and they helped me set up the haft sin. I told them the story you used to tell me as a little girl about the ram who holds the world on one horn all year long.

This year Mom and Vergine were visiting me. . . . Anyway, Vergine came that day because she wanted to make Armenian food with Mom and me. We've been cooking together since I was a little girl. So we set up the haft sin together and before we started cooking the Armenian food, we ate Shish Kebab with sumac and rice (you should have seen the Tahdeeg. It was beautiful. I can't take any credit, Mom made it) with Ghormeh Sabzi and Mom's delicious Torshi. She still makes a year's worth every summer.

We've found a restaurant that has authentic Persian food. The Torshi's not good though. Mom teased the waiter so much about it that he told us to bring our own the next time and to bring some for him too. Haha! We did. On our freedom day, we went for lunch and left him a jar of Torshi. He wasn't working that day, and I haven't been back since to hear if he tasted it.

As for the picture, don't sell yourself short. I'm sure you're still a very handsome man. Mom brought me boxes and boxes of loose photos. I haven't gone through them all yet but I've already come across several fun pictures of you and your family. Someday, I'll scan the others for you.

My dad is my dad. I had to come to grips with that. It was a waste of energy to burn with anger every time someone called him that. . . . Whenever he was mentioned, he was mentioned in relation to me. For a while I tried calling him Moody, but that made people uncomfortable, so I learned to deal with dad.

Yes, I did forgive my dad. I forgave him for what he did to

us in Iran probably within the first year of our escape. I know how you feel about religion, but it was religion that taught me to forgive and for that I am grateful. Where I really struggled was forgiving him for his repeated intrusions in my life. I was terrified of him. Even when he was silent, I was afraid. When he reappeared, especially when I was at university and he was filming his documentary, my hatred reappeared as well. That intrusion, more than any of his previous intrusions, paralyzed me. I became very, very depressed and it took a heavy toll on my physical health. He really made my life difficult for many years. It took a lot of soul searching for me to learn to forgive him once more.

Your evaluation of Mom was correct. She is a kind and integrity filled woman. She gave me your letters along with her encouragement to communicate with my dad. She thought it would be especially good for me to learn more about his medical history given the health issues I've faced over the years. I was the one who was adamant about not having anything to do with him. I had forgiven him, but I didn't trust him and I was still afraid of him. I refused to endure any more of his abuse or his lies.

Reading your correspondence just bolstered my stance. So much of what he said was just blatant lies. You said he was sorry. I've read his words over and over hoping to see that sorrow and I don't think it is there to be found. He was sorry that he didn't get what he wanted. He wasn't sorry for his actions. He wasn't sorry for the pain he caused Mom and me. He wasn't sorry that we lived in fear because of him. He wasn't sorry for his physical and emotional brutality. He was only sorry that Mom and I got away and that we told the world what he did.

As for loving me, I believe he did love me, but he didn't love me for who I was. He loved me because I belonged to him and because I reminded him of his mother. He really showed very little concern for me or my well-being. He was concerned with saving face and with bashing my mom. I had become an obsession to him, not an object of his selfless love, rather a symbol of a slight he had experienced.

Reuniting with me would have served as a means of victory for him. It would have been his chance to bombard me with his lies in an attempt to convince me that what I remember never happened. He said as much in a message he left on the answering machine at Mom's house when he was filming his documentary. . . .

Your evaluation of me was also correct. I had not forgotten. In fact, my initial response to hearing his message was to turn to Mom and ask, "Did he forget I was there!?"

When Mom gave me the packet you sent, I burned with anger. I was furious with YOU for falling prey to his manipulative powers. I thought you of all people would be able to see through his charm and his lies. I put the envelope away and didn't pull it back out for a couple of years.

Only recently have I reread those pages, and I owe you an apology. You knew the truth and you boldly confronted him with it. I shouldn't have doubted your love and the honesty of your intentions. Never have you betrayed me. You weren't his puppet, you were acting out of genuine concern for my well-being. I know now that you wanted only what was best for me and I respect you for doing what you thought was for my good. Thank you. It must have been an uncomfortable position for you to be in.

My dad's actions left a wide wake of destruction. He didn't only hurt Mom and me, it must have been painful for you to lose a friendship you held so dear. It really means a lot to me that in spite of the way he treated you, you continued to treat Mom and me as family.

To answer your questions, I got my degree in Psychology,

only a bachelor's, and have worked in the field since graduating in 2002. I guess I'm like my dad. I have many interests. I could never pick one to pursue on a graduate level though, maybe someday . . .

As for love . . . I avoided relationships all through my adolescence, mostly out of fear that I would end up with an abusive spouse. Still I seemed to usually have a very close platonic male friend. There were several such close friendships over the years and even today, I continue to be blessed with dear male friends. It wasn't until I was in my twenties that I started to let down my guard enough to have more serious relationships . . .

As for religion, I believe this life is brief and relatively insignificant. Our death leads to a life that will last for eternity. In my view, that is the life that counts. Religion for me ensures that thanks to Jesus' death and resurrection, I will be spending eternity in heaven instead of hell—simply by believing, not because of my own value or works or money or for any other reason. Simply by faith, through the grace of God, I am saved for all eternity.

What's there to lose in believing? If I'm wrong and death is the end, then what have I lost? Nothing. If the Bible is true and I don't believe, when I die I go to hell. You're the mathematician, you tell me—is that not a worthwhile wager?

I agree with you that people throughout history have done and continue to do abhorrent things in the name of religion. No religion is exempt from those who hijack the cause and use it for their evil purposes. When that happens, the devil rejoices for to him that is a victory.

Just because my dad was Persian and did horrible things does not mean that all Persians are horrible people. The same with religion. And like I don't condone my father for the things he did, I don't condone religious zealots, regardless of their religious orientation, for the evil they do.

Like you, I hold dear the values of freedom of religion and the separation of church and state. Far be it from me to tell anyone what they must think or believe. I think we should all be free to make our own decisions—good, bad or indifferent.

In sharing my beliefs with you, I'm not saying you must believe as I do. If you did, would I rejoice? Absolutely! Just as you, my dear uncle, would rejoice if I denounced religion. On this, I'm afraid, we will have to continue to agree to disagree.

I am happy and healthy and living a good life. I have endured my fair share of challenges, but life continues to be filled with immeasurable blessings. The Bible says to give thanks in all circumstances and that's what I try to do. I've seen firsthand how the bad leads to a generous abundance of good.

Have you heard of The Weaver's Poem? I've attached it for you. I remember that you're a lover of the arts. Perhaps you'll appreciate it's imagery, even if you don't subscribe to its meaning. Reading it, I can't help but think of the beauty of the colorful Persian carpets that are such a part of our heritage. I hope it puts your mind at ease to know that I have forgiven my dad. I am not a bitter prisoner to hatred.

I hope you are well and I send you all my love and my deepest respect,

Mahtob

EPILOGUE

This book has given me a beautiful gift. The memory of the pain and anguish of my past that I have carried with me all these years, I no longer have to carry. As I lay down my pen, so to speak, I set aside those details. I relinquish my mind and my heart from the duty of remembering.

Tamoom . . . it is finished. I am hunted no more.

Now I am free.

ACKNOWLEDGMENTS

First and foremost I give thanks to God for the opportunity to embark on this literary adventure. Some people are beset with a burning desire to tell their stories, to be heard and understood. From deep within their core emanates a need, a compulsion even, to write about their experiences. I've never felt that urge. And yet, since childhood, others have been asking me to tell my story—strangers who have come to know bits of me through books or films, journalists, documentarians . . . and publishers. I found the interest flattering and more than a bit bewildering. And so it is with sincere humility and genuine appreciation for the remarkable opportunities that God has placed before me that I accepted this invitation.

This project would likely not have come to fruition without the efforts of Anja Kleinlein. Anja was a legend in the publishing world and a very dear family friend. For many years it had been her dream for me to write a book sharing my experiences from my perspective and shedding light on the good that has so graciously come from the bad in my life. In the last year of her life, Anja worked tirelessly as my agent to negotiate the terms of my contract. For her it was a labor of love. I wish I could have finished writing in time for her to see this book take shape before she was called to her heavenly home.

The writing process was challenging on many levels, and I am extremely grateful for the support of my family and friends. As they always do, they rallied around me, bending over backward to do anything and everything in their power to encourage and sustain me during this prolonged and often painful period of self-reflection. I am especially indebted to my two new agents, Michael Carlisle, who after many years rode back into my life on a very white horse, and Sebastian Ritscher, who took a chance on a stranger. Together they set me free from what had become a toxic situation.

Last and certainly not least, I thank my mom for her unconditional love and her wisdom. Maybe now that I'm done writing, she'll finally tell me which events we remember differently.

ABOUT THE AUTHOR

A Phi Beta Kappa graduate of Michigan State University, Mahtob Mahmoody has worked in the field of mental health and is an advocate for public awareness of health and welfare initiatives. She is represented by AEI Speakers Bureau and lives in Michigan.